THE AUSTRALIAN
Women's Weekly

Everyday
STUDENT
COOKING

acp
books

Project editor Stephanie Kistner
Editor Monique Gill
Designer Corey Butler
Food director Pamela Clark
Food editor Cathie Lonnie

ACP Books
Editorial director Susan Tomnay
Creative director Hieu Chi Nguyen
Director of sales Brian Cearnes
Marketing director Matt Dominello
Brand manager Renée Crea
Production manager Cedric Taylor

Chief executive officer John Alexander
Group publisher Pat Ingram
Publisher Sue Wannan
General manager Christine Whiston
Editorial director (AWW) Deborah Thomas

Produced by ACP Books, Sydney.

Printed by Everbest Printing Co. Ltd., China.

Published by ACP Magazines Ltd,
54 Park St, Sydney, NSW 2000 Australia;
GPO Box 4088, Sydney, NSW 2001.
Ph: +61 2 9282 8618 Fax: +61 2 9267 9438
www.acpbooks.com.au
acpbooks@acpmagazines.com.au
To order books phone 136 116.
Send recipe enquiries to
reccipeenquiries@acpmagazines.com.au

RIGHTS ENQUIRIES
Laura Bamford, Director ACP Books.
lbamford@acpmedia.com

UNITED KINGDOM: Distributed by
Australian Consolidated Press (UK),
Moulton Park Business Centre, Red House Rd,
Moulton Park, Northampton, NN3 6AQ
 Ph: (01604) 497 531 Fax: (01604) 497 533
books@acpmedia.com

AUSTRALIA: Distributed by Network
Services,GPO Box 4088, Sydney, NSW 2001.
Ph: +61 2 9282 8777 Fax: +61 2 9264 3278
networkweb@networkservicescompany.com.au

CANADA: Distributed by Whitecap Books Ltd,
351 Lynn Ave, North Vancouver, BC, V7J 2C4
Ph: (604) 980 9852 Fax: (604) 980 8197
customerservice@whitecap.ca www.whitecap.ca

NEW ZEALAND: Southern Publishers Group,
44 New North Rd, Eden Terrace, Auckland.
Ph: (64 9) 309 6930 Fax: (64 9) 309 6170
hub@spg.co.nz

SOUTH AFRICA: Distributed by PSD
Promotions (Pty) Ltd, PO Box 1175, Isando,
1600, Gauteng, Johannesburg, SA.
Ph: (011) 392 6065 Fax (011) 392 6079
orders@psdprom.co.za

Clark, Pamela.
The Australian women's weekly
everyday student cooking.

Includes index.
ISBN 1 86396 537 8.
1. Quick and easy cookery.
I. Title. II Title: Australian women's weekly
641.512

Cover
Photographer: Chris Jones
Stylist: Wendy Berecry

Back cover
Photographer: Ian Wallace
Stylist: Sarah O'Brien

CONTENTS

NO EXPERIENCE, NO CASH? NO WORRIES

This could well be your first go at organising a kitchen on your own or planning and shopping for a week's worth of menus. Who knows – it could be the first time you've actually cooked a meal, for yourself, by yourself, full stop. Well, none of these endeavours is exactly rocket science but at the same time none is genetically programmed into your psyche either, so this little book is meant to gently guide you around the kitchen while simultaneously, hopefully, inspire you to experiment with other foods and different ideas. You'll soon feel confident enough to develop individual recipes and even make these personal favourites for your flatmates and friends. Here are just a few tips to get you started.

Equipment You'll probably move in with a cardboard box full of family seconds or find that your kitchen already contains a "batterie de cuisine" of miscellany. You can also frequent garage sales for a month or so to selectively pick up other people's various rejects. Just don't waste a lot of money purchasing designer utensils or specialised equipment until you realise the need. You will need a couple of good sharp knives (one serrated for bread and tomatoes and the like); two cutting boards (one for meat, poultry, et al and the other for fresh food that's not to be cooked, like fruit and vegetables); a kettle and a toaster; a frying pan, baking dish, oven tray and deep casserole; three gradated-in-size saucepans and a couple of mixing bowls and spoons; a can opener, grater and peeler; measuring cups and spoons; a colander and a smaller sieve; a potato masher, tongs, whisk, spatula and egg turner; and maybe a pepper mill, rice cooker and salad spinner. A microwave oven and a food processor or blender will also do nicely, thank you very much, but you will survive without them.

The Larder Just for starters – plain flour; cornflour and bicarbonate of soda; granulated and brown sugars; honey; salt and black pepper; vegetable and olive oils; a few different varieties of pasta, grains, dried pulses and rice; biscuits and crackers; tomato sauce, mayonnaise and mustard; vinegar, balsamic and otherwise; worcestershire, soy and Tabasco sauces; canned tomatoes, soups, beans and other vegetables; canned fruits; canned salmon, tuna and anchovies; tetra paks of stocks; an assortment of dried herbs and spices; jars of curry pastes (Thai and Indian); various teas and instant coffee; an assortment of nuts and dried fruits; and a few jams, chutneys and marmalades. As far as perishables go, keep garlic,onions and potatoes on hand, as well as margarine or butter, cream, cheese and milk, and bacon and eggs.

Your Freezer Hopefully, your new digs will house a fridge with a decent-size, working freezer – a kitchen "tool" that can become a student's best friend. Buy big pieces of meat when on supermarket special; package them in meal-size portions and pop them in the freezer for those nights when the kitty is empty. Cook a curry, pasta sauce, soup or casserole in quantity and freeze in individual portions. When preparing slow-to-soften legumes and pulses, boil two or three times what you want on the day then freeze the remainder in one-cup portions. Freeze leftovers. Buy seasonal fruit and veg in large amounts; prepare them as per their particular requirements then freeze in small portions in snap-lock plastic bags. Freeze bread for toast rather than have it go mouldy before you can finish the loaf. Two important freezer tips: potatoes and foods containing dairy products don't freeze well; and move food from freezer to fridge before you leave the house in the morning – don't leave food out to defrost on the kitchen bench.

Pamela Clark

Food Director

Low in fat

Cooked in less than 30 minutes

Suitable to freeze

Cheap

BREAKFAST

French toast with berry compôte

preparation time **15 minutes** cooking time **10 minutes** serves **4**

4 eggs
½ cup (125ml) cream
¼ cup (60ml) milk
1 teaspoon finely grated orange rind
1 teaspoon ground cinnamon
¼ cup (85g) honey
100g butter, melted
8 thick slices (320g) sourdough bread
¼ cup (40g) icing sugar

Berry compôte
1 teaspoon arrowroot
⅓ cup (80ml) water
2 cups (300g) frozen mixed berries
2 tablespoons caster sugar
1 tablespoon finely grated orange rind

1 Whisk eggs lightly in medium bowl; whisk in cream, milk, rind, cinnamon and honey.
2 Heat a quarter of the butter in medium frying pan. Dip two bread slices into egg mixture, one at a time; cook, uncovered, until browned both sides. Remove both slices of french toast from pan; cover to keep warm. Repeat with remaining butter, bread slices and egg mixture.
3 Make berry compôte.
3 Dust french toast with icing sugar and serve with warm berry compôte.

Berry compôte Blend arrowroot with the water in small saucepan until smooth; add remaining ingredients. Cook until mixture almost boils and thickens slightly.

serving suggestion Serve french toast with freshly whipped cream.

Eggs benedict

preparation time **20 minutes** cooking time **30 minutes** serves **8**

8 eggs
8 english muffins
200g shaved ham

Hollandaise sauce
¼ cup (60ml) white wine vinegar
3 black peppercorns
1 bay leaf
2 egg yolks
125g butter, melted
1 teaspoon lemon juice

1 Make hollandaise sauce.
2 Half-fill a large frying pan with water; bring to a boil. Break eggs into cup, one at a time, then slide into pan. When all eggs are in pan, allow water to return to a boil. Cover pan, turn off heat; stand about 4 minutes or until a light film of egg white sets over yolks. Remove eggs, one at a time, using slotted spoon; briefly place spoon on saucer lined with absorbent paper to blot up any liquid.
3 Meanwhile, split muffins in half; toast until just crisp and browned lightly.
4 Place two muffin halves on each serving plate; layer ham on one muffin half. Top with an egg, hollandaise sauce and other muffin half.

Hollandaise sauce Combine vinegar, peppercorns and bay leaf in small saucepan. Bring to a boil then reduce heat; simmer, uncovered, until reduced by half. Strain into small jug; cool. Blend or process yolks until smooth. With motor operating, gradually add 1 teaspoon of the melted butter (it must be bubbling hot) to yolks; blend or process until mixture starts to thicken. Then, with motor operating, add 2 teaspoons of vinegar mixture at a time, alternating with 2 teaspoons of remaining melted butter, processing until sauce thickens and all butter and vinegar have been incorporated; stir in juice.

Denver omelette

preparation time **10 minutes** cooking time **15 minutes** serves **4**

10 eggs
⅓ cup (80g) sour cream
2 fresh red thai chillies, chopped finely
2 teaspoons vegetable oil
3 green onions, sliced thinly
1 medium green capsicum (200g), chopped finely
100g leg ham, chopped finely
2 small tomatoes (260g), seeded, chopped finely
½ cup (60g) coarsely grated cheddar

1 Break eggs into large bowl, whisk lightly; whisk in sour cream and chilli.

2 Heat oil in large non-stick frying pan; cook onion and capsicum, stirring, until onion softens. Place onion mixture in medium bowl with ham, tomato and cheese; toss to combine.

3 Pour ½ cup of the egg mixture into same lightly oiled frying pan; cook, tilting pan, over low heat until almost set. Sprinkle ⅓ cup of the filling over half of the omelette; using spatula, fold omelette over to cover filling.

4 Pour ¼ cup of the egg mixture into empty half of pan; cook over low heat until almost set. Sprinkle ⅓ cup of the filling over folded omelette, fold omelette over top of first omelette to cover filling. Repeat twice more, using ¼ cup of the egg mixture each time, to form one large layered omelette. Carefully slide omelette onto plate; cover to keep warm.

5 Repeat steps 3 and 4 to make second omelette, using remaining egg mixture and filling. Cut each denver omelette in half.

Egg-white omelette

preparation time **25 minutes** cooking time **20 minutes** serves **4**

12 egg whites
4 green onions, chopped finely
¼ cup finely chopped fresh chives
¼ cup finely chopped fresh chervil
½ cup finely chopped fresh flat-leaf parsley
½ cup (60g) coarsely grated cheddar
½ cup (50g) coarsely grated mozzarella

1 Preheat grill.

2 Beat a quarter of the egg white in small bowl with electric mixer until soft peaks form; fold in a quarter of the combined onion and herbs.

3 Pour mixture into medium heated lightly oiled non-stick frying pan; cook, uncovered, over low heat until omelette is browned lightly on the bottom.

4 Sprinkle a quarter of the combined cheeses over half of the omelette. Place pan under grill until cheese begins to melt and omelette sets; fold omelette over to completely cover cheese. Carefully slide onto serving plate; cover to keep warm.

5 Repeat process three times with remaining egg white, onion and herb mixture, and combined cheeses.

Eggs ranchero-style

preparation time **10 minutes** cooking time **30 minutes** serves **4**

1 small red onion (100g), chopped finely
4 medium tomatoes (600g), chopped coarsely
2 tablespoons water
1 tablespoon balsamic vinegar
1 medium red capsicum (200g), chopped finely
4 eggs
4 corn tortillas

1 Cook onion in lightly oiled large non-stick frying pan, stirring, until softened. Add tomato, the water and vinegar. Bring to a boil then reduce heat; simmer, uncovered, 15 minutes, stirring occasionally. Add capsicum; cook, uncovered, 5 minutes.

2 Using large shallow mixing spoon, press four shallow depressions into tomato mixture. Working quickly, break eggs, one at a time, into cup, sliding each egg into one of the hollows in tomato mixture. Cover pan; cook over low heat, about 5 minutes or until eggs are just set.

3 Divide warmed tortillas among plates. Use egg slide to carefully lift egg and tomato mixture onto each tortilla.

Buttermilk pancakes with glazed strawberries

preparation time **15 minutes** cooking time **15 minutes** serves **4**

4 eggs
2 tablespoons caster sugar
1½ cups (375ml) buttermilk
100g butter, melted
1½ cups (225g) self-raising flour

Glazed strawberries
⅓ cup (80ml) water
½ cup (170g) marmalade
1 tablespoon caster sugar
2 tablespoons lemon juice
250g strawberries, quartered

1 Beat eggs and sugar in small bowl with electric mixer until thick; stir in buttermilk and half of the butter.

2 Sift flour into large bowl; whisk egg mixture gradually into flour until batter is smooth.

3 Heat heavy-base medium frying pan; brush pan with a little of the remaining butter. Pour ¼ cup of the batter into pan; cook, uncovered, until bubbles appear on surface of pancake. Turn pancake; cook until browned. Remove from pan; cover to keep warm. Repeat with remaining butter and batter.

4 Serve pancakes with glazed strawberries.

Glazed strawberries Place the water, marmalade, sugar and juice in small saucepan; bring to a boil. Add strawberries, reduce heat; simmer, uncovered, about 2 minutes or until strawberries are hot.

Rösti with ham and cherry tomatoes

preparation time **15 minutes** cooking time **25 minutes** serves **4**

200g shaved ham
200g cherry tomatoes
4 large potatoes (1.2kg), grated coarsely
1 egg white, beaten lightly
Vegetable oil, for shallow-frying
2 green onions, chopped coarsely

1 Cook ham and tomatoes in lightly oiled large frying pan until browned lightly. Remove from pan; cover to keep warm.

2 Combine potato and egg white in large bowl; divide into eight portions. Heat oil in same cleaned pan; cook potato portions, in batches, forming into flat pancake shapes while cooking, until browned on both sides and cooked through. Drain on absorbent paper.

3 Serve rösti topped with ham and tomato; sprinkle with chopped onion.

Porridge with three toppings

preparation time **5 minutes** cooking time **5 minutes** serves **4**

3½ cups (875ml) hot water
1½ cups (135g) rolled oats
½ cup (125ml) milk

1 Combine the water and oats in large microwave-safe bowl, cover; cook
on HIGH (100%) 2 minutes, pause and stir. Cook, covered, on HIGH (100%)
3½ minutes, pause and stir. Cover; stand 5 minutes, stir in milk.
2 Serve with the topping of your choice.

Toppings
Apple and pear compôte

Peel, core and coarsely chop one large apple and one medium pear. Place fruit
in medium saucepan, combine with ⅓ cup (80ml) apple juice and 1 tablespoon
lemon juice over medium heat. Bring to a boil then reduce heat; simmer, covered,
stirring occasionally, about 15 minutes or until fruit softens and liquid is
absorbed. Makes enough compôte to accompany four servings of porridge.

Cinnamon sugar

Combine 1 teaspoon ground cinnamon with 2 tablespoons caster sugar in
small bowl. Sprinkle over bowls of porridge. Any remaining cinnamon sugar
can be sprinkled over hot buttered toast for a quick snack.

Honey and yogurt

Divide ⅓ cup (95g) low-fat vanilla yogurt and 1 tablespoon honey among
bowls of porridge.

tip Porridge can also be made in a saucepan. Combine the water and
oats in medium saucepan; cook, uncovered, about 10 minutes or until soft.
Stir in milk.

Cheese, corn and bacon muffins

preparation time **20 minutes** (plus standing time) cooking time **25 minutes**
makes **12**

½ cup (85g) polenta
½ cup (125ml) milk
3 bacon rashers (210g), rind removed, chopped finely
4 green onions, chopped finely
1 ½ cups (225g) self-raising flour
1 tablespoon caster sugar
310g can corn kernels, drained
125g can creamed corn
100g butter, melted
2 eggs, beaten lightly
50g piece cheddar
¼ cup (30g) coarsely grated cheddar

1 Preheat oven to moderately hot. Oil 12-hole (⅓-cup/80ml) muffin pan.
2 Mix polenta and milk in small bowl, cover; stand 20 minutes.
3 Meanwhile, cook bacon, stirring, in heated small non-stick frying pan for
2 minutes. Add onion to pan; cook, stirring, for another 2 minutes. Remove
pan from heat; cool bacon mixture about 5 minutes.
4 Sift flour and sugar into large bowl; stir in corn kernels, creamed corn and
bacon mixture. Add melted butter, eggs and polenta mixture; mix muffin
batter until just combined.
5 Spoon 1 tablespoon of the batter into each hole of prepared muffin pan.
Cut piece of cheese into 12 equal pieces; place one piece in the centre of
each muffin pan hole. Divide remaining batter among muffin pan holes;
sprinkle grated cheese over each. Bake, uncovered, in moderately hot oven
about 20 minutes or until muffins are well risen. Turn muffins onto wire rack.
Serve muffins warm.

tip Leftover muffins can be stored, covered, in freezer for up to three months.

Breakfast on a muffin

You can use either four english muffins split into halves or, if you prefer, eight crumpets with any one of the following topping recipes:

Tomato, spinach and cheese

preparation time **10 minutes** cooking time **5 minutes** serves **4**

Preheat grill. Layer 60g baby spinach leaves, 2 thinly sliced medium tomatoes and ²/₃ cup (80g) shredded cheddar on muffins or crumpets. Place on oven tray under grill until cheese melts.

Banana, peanut butter and honey

preparation time **5 minutes** cooking time **5 minutes** serves **4**

Preheat grill. Spread ⅓ cup (95g) peanut butter then ⅓ cup (120g) honey on muffins or crumpets; top with 2 thinly sliced medium bananas. Place on oven tray under grill until honey starts to sizzle.

Mixed berry

preparation time **5 minutes** cooking time **5 minutes** serves **4**

Combine ½ cup (160g) raspberry jam with 1 ½ cups (225g) thawed mixed frozen berries. Spoon berry mixture onto toasted muffins or crumpets; serve with 1 cup (280g) yogurt.

Tuna and avocado

preparation time **10 minutes** cooking time **5 minutes** serves **4**

Preheat grill. Using back of fork, mash one medium avocado, one drained 95g can tuna in springwater and 1 tablespoon lemon juice in small bowl. Spread over muffins or crumpets; sprinkle with ²/₃ cup (80g) shredded cheddar. Place on oven tray under grill until cheese melts.

Breakfast fry-up

preparation time **10 minutes** cooking time **20 minutes** serves **4**

4 medium egg tomatoes (300g), quartered
2 tablespoons balsamic vinegar
Cooking-oil spray
300g mushrooms, sliced thickly
½ cup loosely packed fresh basil leaves, torn
¼ cup loosely packed fresh coriander leaves
¼ cup loosely packed fresh flat-leaf parsley leaves
200g shaved ham

1 Preheat oven to moderately hot.
2 Combine tomato and half of the vinegar in medium shallow oiled baking dish; spray with oil. Roast, uncovered, in moderately hot oven 20 minutes.
3 Meanwhile, cook mushrooms and remaining vinegar in medium oiled frying pan until tender; stir in herbs. Transfer to serving dishes; cover to keep warm.
4 Heat ham in same pan. Serve with mushroom and tomato mixtures.

Caramelised banana and hazelnut waffles

preparation time **10 minutes** cooking time **15 minutes** serves **4**

4 packaged belgian-style waffles
40g butter
4 medium ripe bananas (800g), sliced thickly
2 tablespoons brown sugar
½ cup (75g) toasted hazelnuts, chopped coarsely
⅓ cup (80ml) pure maple syrup

1 Preheat oven to moderately slow.
2 Place waffles, in single layer, on oven tray; heat, uncovered, in moderately slow oven about 8 minutes.
3 Meanwhile, melt butter in medium frying pan; cook banana, stirring, about 2 minutes or until hot. Add sugar; cook, uncovered, over low heat, 2 minutes or until banana is caramelised lightly.
4 Divide waffles among serving plates; top with banana mixture, nuts and syrup.

Chocolate banana bread

preparation time **15 minutes** cooking time **1 hour** serves **12**

You need about 2 large overripe bananas (460g) for this recipe.

1 cup mashed banana
¾ cup (165g) caster sugar
2 eggs, beaten lightly
¼ cup (60ml) extra light olive oil
¼ cup (60ml) milk
⅔ cup (100g) self-raising flour
⅔ cup (100g) wholemeal self-raising flour
¾ cup (90g) coarsely chopped toasted walnuts
¼ cup (45g) finely chopped dark eating chocolate

1 Preheat oven to moderate. Grease 14cm x 21cm loaf pan; line base and long sides with baking paper.
2 Combine banana and sugar in large bowl; stir in egg, oil and milk. Add remaining ingredients; stir until combined.
3 Spread mixture into prepared pan; bake, uncovered, in moderate oven about 1 hour. Stand bread in pan 5 minutes; turn onto wire rack to cool. Serve bread warm with butter.

tip Leftover banana bread can be toasted, if desired.

Banana pancakes

preparation time **10 minutes** cooking time **10 minutes** serves **4**

1 cup (150g) self-raising flour
2 tablespoons caster sugar
1¼ cups (310ml) buttermilk
1 egg, beaten lightly
2 teaspoons pure maple syrup
20g butter, melted
1 medium banana (200g), sliced
½ cup (40g) toasted pecans, chopped

1 Sift flour into a large bowl, stir in sugar. Whisk in combined buttermilk, egg, maple syrup and butter until batter is smooth. Stir in banana.
2 Heat large non-stick frying pan. Pour ¼ cup of the batter into pan, allowing room for spreading. Cook, uncovered, until bubbles appear on surface of pancake. Turn pancake; cook until browned. Remove from pan; cover to keep warm. Repeat with remaining batter.
3 Serve pancakes with pecans and extra maple syrup, if desired.

Blueberry bircher muesli

preparation time **15 minutes** (plus standing time) serves **4**

2 cups (180g) rolled oats
1 cup (250ml) fresh orange juice
250g natural yogurt
¼ cup (90g) honey
½ cup (125ml) soy milk
1 large green apple (200g), grated coarsely
120g fresh blueberries
¾ cup (75g) toasted walnuts, chopped coarsely

1 Combine oats, juice, yogurt, honey and soy milk in a large bowl; stand, covered, 30 minutes or overnight.
2 Stir in apple.
3 Just before serving, top muesli with blueberries and walnuts.

Chocolate croissant with mocha

preparation time **10 minutes** cooking time **10 minutes** serves **4**

⅓ cup (25g) ground espresso coffee
1 cup (250ml) boiling water
2 cups (500ml) milk
50g grated dark eating chocolate
4 large or 8 small croissants
50g dark eating chocolate, chopped coarsely, extra
Small marshmallows

1 Preheat oven to moderately slow.
2 Place coffee and the boiling water in coffee plunger; stand 5 minutes before plunging.
3 Plunge coffee or line a sieve with a piece of absorbent paper; place over a jug. Strain coffee mixture through paper – you will need ⅔ cup (160ml) strained coffee.
4 Combine milk and grated chocolate in a small saucepan; add coffee mixture, stir over low heat until chocolate is melted. Do not boil.
5 Meanwhile, split the croissants in half horizontally. Place extra chocolate on cut surface of base of croissants. Place croissant tops on tray beside bases.
6 Bake in moderately slow oven about 5 minutes or until chocolate is melted. Sandwich croissant tops and bases together.
7 Divide milk mixture among four heatproof serving glasses, top with marshmallows. Serve with chocolate croissants.

Bacon and eggs

preparation time **5 minutes** cooking time **10 minutes** serves **2**

4 bacon rashers (280g)
1 tablespoon vegetable oil
4 eggs
1 medium tomato (190g), halved

1 Preheat grill.
2 Cook bacon in medium frying pan, uncovered, until browned and cooked as desired. Remove from pan; keep warm.
3 Heat oil in same pan; cook eggs, uncovered, until cooked as desired.

4 Meanwhile, place tomato, cut-side up, onto baking tray; season with salt and freshly ground black pepper, if desired. Place under grill; cook tomato until browned lightly and just tender.

5 Serve bacon with fried eggs and tomato.

Baked beans with fried eggs

preparation time **10 minutes**   cooking time **2 hours 10 minutes**   serves **4**

1 cup (200g) dried borlotti beans
3 bacon rashers (210g), rind removed, chopped coarsely
1 medium brown onion (150g), chopped finely
1 clove garlic, crushed
1 tablespoon tomato paste
400g can crushed tomatoes
1½ cups (375ml) water
1 tablespoon worcestershire sauce
2 teaspoons dijon mustard
1 tablespoon maple syrup
4 eggs

1 Place beans in medium bowl, cover with cold water; soak overnight, drain.

2 Cook bacon, onion and garlic in large saucepan, stirring, until onion softens. Add drained beans, paste, undrained tomato, the water, sauce and mustard. Bring to a boil then reduce heat; simmer, covered, about 1½ hours. Uncover; simmer about 15 minutes or until beans soften. Stir in syrup.

3 Cook eggs, uncovered, in heated oiled medium frying pan until cooked as desired. Serve beans with eggs.

tip Store leftover beans in an airtight container; refrigerate up to 5 days.

Poached eggs, pancetta and asparagus

preparation time **5 minutes** cooking time **10 minutes** serves **4**

4 eggs
4 slices pancetta
400g fresh asparagus
30g butter, melted
¼ cup (20g) parmesan flakes

1 Half-fill a large frying pan with water; bring to a boil. Break eggs into cup, one at a time, then slide into pan. When all eggs are in pan, allow water to return to a boil. Cover pan, turn off heat; stand about 4 minutes or until a light film of egg white sets over yolks. Remove eggs, one at a time, using slotted spoon; briefly place spoon on saucer lined with absorbent paper to blot up any liquid. Grill pancetta until crisp.
2 Meanwhile, boil, steam or microwave asparagus until just tender; drain.
3 Divide asparagus spears among four serving plates. Top with poached eggs and crumbled pancetta. Drizzle with butter and top with parmesan flakes. Season with freshly ground black pepper.

Boiled eggs

preparation time **5 minutes** cooking time **5 minutes**

1 Choose saucepan to suit the number of eggs you are boiling; one egg in small saucepan, up to four eggs in medium saucepan, more eggs in large saucepan (there should be enough room to move eggs around). Add enough cold water to cover eggs. Stir constantly using wooden spoon over high heat until water boils; this will centralise each yolk. Boil, uncovered, until yolks are as soft or as firm as you like. As a guide, 3 minutes will give you set egg white and soft yolk. After 5 minutes, the yolk will be set.
2 Place saucepan of eggs under cold running water about 1 minute or until eggs are cool. This will stop a dark ring forming around yolk. Serve.

serving suggestion Serve eggs with toast soldiers.

Spinach scrambled eggs

preparation time **5 minutes** cooking time **10 minutes** serves **4**

20g butter
75g spinach leaves
8 slices pancetta
8 eggs
½ cup (125ml) light cream
4 slices crusty bread

1 Heat half the butter in large non-stick frying pan. Add spinach; cook, uncovered, until spinach is just wilted. Remove from pan and drain on absorbent paper; cover to keep warm.
2 Grill pancetta until crisp; cover to keep warm.
3 Combine eggs and cream in a bowl; whisk until combined. Season with salt and freshly ground black pepper. Heat remaining butter in pan. Add egg mixture; cook over low heat, stirring gently with wide spatula, until creamy and almost set.
4 Meanwhile, toast bread. Top with pancetta, scrambled eggs and spinach.

Maple rice pudding with pecans and dates

preparation time **10 minutes** cooking time **40 minutes** serves **8**

1½ litres (6 cups) milk
2 cups (500ml) cream
⅔ cup (160ml) maple syrup
¼ teaspoon ground cinnamon
⅔ cup (130g) white medium-grain rice
½ cup (85g) coarsely chopped seeded dates
½ cup (70g) toasted pecans, chopped coarsely

1 Combine milk, cream, syrup and cinnamon in large saucepan; bring to a boil, stirring occasionally.
2 Gradually stir in rice; cook, uncovered, over low heat, stirring occasionally, about 40 minutes or until rice is tender.
3 Serve rice pudding with combined dates and nuts.

Cinnamon toast with caramelised apples

preparation time **10 minutes** cooking time **10 minutes** serves **4**

4 large apples (720g)
60g butter
½ cup (100g) firmly packed brown sugar
¼ cup (60ml) water
¼ teaspoon ground cinnamon
300ml double cream
4-8 slices cinnamon and fruit bread
30g soft butter, extra
1 tablespoon cinnamon sugar

1 Peel apples and remove cores. Cut apples crossways into thin slices.
2 Heat butter in large frying pan. Add brown sugar, the water and apples; cook, stirring occasionally, until apples are just tender. Stir in cinnamon and ½ cup (125ml) of the cream.
3 Toast bread and spread one side with the extra butter; sprinkle with cinnamon sugar.
4 Serve toast with apple mixture and remaining cream.

Baked eggs with pancetta

preparation time **15 minutes** cooking time **20 minutes** serves **4**

2 teaspoons olive oil
1 small red capsicum (150g), chopped finely
6 slices pancetta, chopped finely
100g mushrooms, chopped finely
4 green onions, chopped finely
⅔ cup (50g) finely grated parmesan
8 eggs
2 teaspoons coarsely chopped fresh flat-leaf parsley

1 Preheat oven to moderately hot. Oil four ¾-cup (180ml) ovenproof dishes.
2 Heat oil in medium frying pan; cook capsicum and pancetta, stirring, until capsicum is just tender. Add mushroom and onion; cook, stirring, until onion just softens. Remove from heat; stir in half the cheese.

3 Divide capsicum mixture among dishes; break two eggs into each dish. Bake, uncovered, in moderately hot oven 5 minutes. Sprinkle remaining cheese over eggs; bake further 5 minutes or until eggs are just set. Sprinkle with parsley just before serving.

Spanish tortilla

preparation time **15 minutes** cooking time **30 minutes** serves **4**

800g potatoes, peeled, sliced thinly
1 tablespoon olive oil
1 large brown onion (200g), sliced thinly
200g chorizo sausage, sliced thinly
6 eggs, beaten lightly
300ml cream
4 green onions, sliced thickly
¼ cup (25g) coarsely grated mozzarella
¼ cup (30g) coarsely grated cheddar

1 Boil, steam or microwave potato until just tender; drain.
2 Meanwhile, heat oil in medium frying pan; cook brown onion, stirring, until softened. Add chorizo; cook, stirring, until crisp. Drain chorizo mixture on absorbent paper.
3 Whisk eggs in large bowl with cream, green onion and cheeses; stir in potato and chorizo mixture.
4 Pour mixture into heated lightly oiled medium non-stick frying pan; cook, covered, over low heat about 10 minutes or until tortilla is just set. Carefully invert tortilla onto plate, then slide back into pan; cook, uncovered, about 5 minutes or until cooked through.

Hangover cures

Classic bloody mary
Beetroot, carrot and spinach juice
Corned beef hash with poached eggs
Waffles with maple syrup and strawberries

Classic bloody mary

preparation time **5 minutes** serves **1**

1 cup ice cubes
60ml vodka
10ml lemon juice
¼ teaspoon tabasco
½ teaspoon horseradish
Dash worcestershire sauce
Pinch celery salt
150ml vegetable juice

1 Place ingredients in 340ml highball glass; stir to combine.

serving suggestion Serve with a trimmed celery stalk and season
with freshly ground black pepper.

Beetroot, carrot and spinach juice

preparation time **10 minutes** serves **1**

6 medium beetroots (1kg), peeled, chopped coarsely
5 large carrots (1kg), chopped coarsely
600g spinach, trimmed, chopped coarsely

1 Push ingredients through juice extractor. Stir to combine.

Corned beef hash with poached eggs

preparation time **10 minutes** cooking time **10 minutes** serves **2**

1 medium brown onion (150g), chopped finely
3 medium potatoes (600g), shredded
500g cooked corned beef, shredded
2 tablespoons finely chopped fresh flat-leaf parsley
2 tablespoons plain flour
2 eggs, beaten lightly
1 tablespoon vegetable oil
4 eggs, extra

1 Combine onion, potato, beef, parsley, flour and egg in large bowl; mix well.
2 Divide hash mixture into four portions; flatten to form patties.
3 Heat oil in large heavy-base frying pan; cook patties, uncovered, until browned both sides and potato is tender.
4 Meanwhile, poach extra eggs. Half-fill large shallow frying pan with water; bring to a boil. Break eggs into cup, one at a time, then slide into pan. Allow water to return to a boil, cover pan, turn off heat; stand about 4 minutes. Remove eggs with slotted spoon. Drain on saucer lined with absorbent paper.
5 Serve hash patties topped with poached eggs.

Waffles with maple syrup and strawberries

preparation time **15 minutes** cooking time **10 minutes** serves **2**

4 packaged belgian-style waffles
10g butter
250g strawberries, sliced thickly
¼ cup (60ml) pure maple syrup

1 Preheat oven to moderately slow.
2 Place waffles, in single layer, on oven tray; heat, uncovered, in moderately slow oven about 8 minutes.
3 Meanwhile, melt butter in medium frying pan; cook strawberries, stirring gently, about 2 minutes or until just hot. Add maple syrup; cook, stirring gently, until hot.
4 Divide waffles among serving plates; top with strawberry-maple mixture.

Romantic brunch for two
Pineapple, ginger and mint juice
Roasted muesli with dried fruit and honey
Scrambled eggs on corn cakes
Fruit salad with honey yogurt

Pineapple, ginger and mint juice

preparation time **5 minutes** serves **2**

1 small pineapple, peeled, chopped coarsely
2 cups firmly packed fresh mint leaves
2cm piece fresh ginger (10g)

1 Push ingredients through juice extractor into glass; stir to combine.

Roasted muesli with dried fruit and honey

preparation time **15 minutes** cooking time **15 minutes** makes **6 cups**

2 cups (180g) rolled oats
1 cup (110g) rolled rice
¼ cup (15g) unprocessed wheat bran
¼ cup (40g) pepitas
1 teaspoon ground cinnamon
⅓ cup (120g) honey
1 tablespoon vegetable oil
¾ cup (35g) flaked coconut
⅓ cup (50g) coarsely chopped dried apricots
⅓ cup (30g) coarsely chopped dried apples
⅓ cup (55g) sultanas

1 Preheat oven to moderate.
2 Combine oats and rice in large bowl, spread evenly on two oven trays. Roast, uncovered, in moderate oven 5 minutes.
3 Stir bran, pepitas and cinnamon into oats and rice on trays, drizzle evenly with combined honey and oil; stir to combine. Roast, uncovered, 5 minutes. Add coconut to mixture; stir to combine. Roast, uncovered, 5 minutes.

4 Remove trays from oven; place muesli mixture in same large bowl, stir in remaining ingredients.

tip Refrigerate leftover muesli in airtight container for up to three months.

Scrambled eggs on corn cakes

preparation time **10 minutes** cooking time **10 minutes** serves **2**

½ cup (80g) frozen corn kernels, thawed
½ cup (75g) plain flour
½ teaspoon sweet paprika
1 tablespoon finely chopped fresh coriander
2 tablespoons milk
2 egg whites
1 egg
1 egg white, extra

1 Combine corn, flour, paprika and coriander in medium bowl; stir in milk, mix until combined.
2 Beat egg whites in small bowl with electric mixer until soft peaks form; fold into corn mixture. Cook ¼-cup measures of corn mixture in heated oiled large non-stick frying pan until browned both sides and cooked through.
3 Combine egg and extra egg white in medium bowl; beat lightly with fork. Cook egg mixture in lightly oiled non-stick medium frying pan, stirring gently, until creamy and just set. Serve scrambled eggs with corn cakes.

Fruit salad with honey yogurt

preparation time **15 minutes** serves **2**

½ cup (130g) yogurt
1 tablespoon honey
100g peeled, coarsely chopped pineapple
100g seeded, peeled, coarsely chopped rockmelon
125g strawberries, halved
1 large banana (230g), sliced thinly
1 teaspoon lime juice
6 fresh mint leaves

1 Combine yogurt and honey in small bowl.
2 Combine remaining ingredients in large bowl; serve with honey yogurt.

Buffet brunch for friends
Fresh berry frappé
Sweet potato hash browns with chicken sausages
Fruit scrolls with spiced yogurt
Red fruit salad

Fresh berry frappé

preparation time **10 minutes** makes **4 cups**

You can also use frozen berries for this recipe.

300g blueberries
250g raspberries
40 ice cubes, crushed
¾ cup (180ml) fresh orange juice

1 Blend or process berries until just smooth. Push berry puree through fine sieve into large bowl; discard solids in sieve.
2 Stir in ice and juice; spoon into serving glasses.

Sweet potato hash browns with chicken sausages

preparation time **15 minutes** cooking time **25 minutes** serves **6**

6 bacon rashers, chopped
600g sweet potato, peeled
1 large potato (300g), peeled
4 eggs, beaten lightly
⅓ cup (50g) plain flour
¼ cup (60ml) vegetable oil
12 thin chicken sausages
2 small avocados (400g), sliced
100g watercress, trimmed

1 Cook bacon in non-stick frying pan, stirring, until browned; drain.
2 Coarsely grate potatoes into large bowl. Stir in bacon, eggs and flour; mix well.
3 Divide into 12 even portions. Heat a little of the oil in non-stick frying pan; add the portions to pan, press firmly with an egg slice to flatten. Cook over low heat until browned on both sides and cooked through; drain on absorbent paper. Cover to keep warm. Repeat with remaining oil and potato mixture.

4 Meanwhile, cook sausages under preheated grill until cooked through.
5 Serve hash browns with sausages, avocado and watercress.

Fruit scrolls

preparation time **10 minutes** cooking time **25 minutes** serves **6**

40g butter
¼ teaspoon ground nutmeg
1½ tablespoons brown sugar
2 teaspoons ground cinnamon
1 small apple (130g), peeled, cored, grated coarsely
⅓ cup (50g) finely chopped dried apricots
½ cup (125ml) orange juice
1 sheet ready-rolled puff pastry

1 Preheat oven to moderately hot. Lightly grease oven tray.
2 Melt half the butter in small saucepan; add nutmeg, sugar and cinnamon. Cook, stirring, over low heat, until sugar dissolves. Stir in apple, apricot and half the juice. Bring to a boil then reduce heat; simmer, uncovered, 2 minutes. Remove from heat; stir in remaining juice.
3 Spread fruit mixture over pastry sheet; roll into log. Cut log into six; place on prepared tray, 5cm apart, brush with remaining melted butter.
4 Bake, uncovered, in moderately hot oven about 20 minutes or until scrolls are cooked through.

serving suggestion Dust with icing sugar and serve with yogurt, if desired.

Red fruit salad

preparation time **10 minutes** serves **6**

1kg seedless watermelon
250g strawberries, quartered
150g raspberries
2 medium plums, sliced thinly
1 tablespoon caster sugar
⅓ cup (80ml) kirsch

1 Using melon baller, scoop watermelon into balls. Place watermelon in large serving bowl with strawberries, raspberries, plums, sugar and liqueur; toss gently to combine. Cover; refrigerate until ready to serve.

LUNCH

Pumpkin soup

preparation time **25 minutes** cooking time **25 minutes** serves **4**

2½ cups (625ml) water
1kg piece pumpkin, seeded, chopped coarsely
1 large brown onion (200g), chopped coarsely
2 medium tomatoes (300g), seeded, chopped coarsely
4cm piece fresh ginger (20g), grated
1 cup (250ml) chicken stock
150ml can light evaporated milk

1 Place the water, pumpkin, onion, tomato, ginger and stock in large saucepan. Bring to a boil then reduce heat; simmer, covered, about 20 minutes or until pumpkin is tender.
2 Cool soup mixture 5 minutes before blending or processing, in batches, until smooth. Pour each batch of processed soup into large jug while processing the remainder. Return all of the soup mixture to same pan. Stir in milk; stir over heat, without boiling, until soup is heated through.

tip Store leftover soup in well-sealed container; freeze up to three months.

Fresh tomato soup

preparation time **20 minutes** cooking time **35 minutes** serves **4**

700g medium tomatoes, seeded, chopped coarsely
1 large brown onion (200g), chopped coarsely
2 trimmed celery stalks (200g), chopped coarsely
1 clove garlic, crushed
1 litre (4 cups) chicken stock
400g can tomato puree

1 Place tomato, onion, celery, garlic and half of the stock in large saucepan. Bring to a boil then reduce heat; simmer, covered, about 15 minutes or until vegetables soften.

2 Cool mixture 5 minutes before blending or processing, in batches, until smooth. Pour each batch of processed soup into large jug while processing remainder. Return all of the soup to same pan. Stir in remaining stock and tomato puree. Bring to a boil then reduce heat; simmer, uncovered, 10 minutes.

tip Store leftover soup in well-sealed container; freeze up to three months.

Vietnamese beef, chicken and tofu soup

preparation time **20 minutes** cooking time **1 hour 5 minutes** serves **4**

3 litres (12 cups) water
500g gravy beef
1 star anise
2.5cm piece fresh ginger (15g), halved
¼ cup (60ml) soy sauce
2 tablespoons fish sauce
340g chicken breast fillets
1½ cups (120g) bean sprouts
1 cup loosely packed fresh coriander leaves
4 green onions, sliced thinly
2 small fresh red thai chillies, sliced thinly
⅓ cup (80ml) lime juice
300g firm tofu, diced into 2cm pieces

1 Combine the water, beef, star anise, ginger and sauces in large saucepan. Bring to a boil then reduce heat; simmer, covered, 30 minutes. Uncover; simmer, 20 minutes. Add chicken; simmer, uncovered, 10 minutes.

2 Combine sprouts, coriander, onion, chilli and juice in medium bowl.

3 Remove beef and chicken from pan; reserve stock. Discard fat and sinew from beef; slice thinly. Slice chicken thinly. Return meat to pan; reheat soup.

4 Divide tofu among serving bowls; ladle over soup, sprinkle with sprout mixture.

tip This soup is best served on day of making.

Smoked cod chowder

preparation time **25 minutes** cooking time **45 minutes** serves **4**

600g smoked cod fillets
1 litre (4 cups) milk
2 bay leaves
8 black peppercorns
2 bacon rashers (140g), rind removed, chopped finely
40g butter
1 medium leek (350g), sliced thinly
1 tablespoon plain flour
1 cup (250ml) dry white wine
4 medium potatoes (800g), cut into 2cm cubes
300ml cream
2 tablespoons coarsely chopped fresh flat-leaf parsley

1 Place fish in large heavy-base frying pan. Pour half of the milk over fish; heat almost to a boil. Drain fish; discard milk. Return fish to pan with remaining milk, bay leaves and peppercorns; heat almost to a boil. Drain over large bowl; reserve milk and fish, discard bay leaves and peppercorns.
2 Cook bacon in same cleaned heated pan, stirring, until browned and crisp; drain on absorbent paper.
3 Melt butter in same cleaned pan; cook leek, stirring, until softened. Add flour; cook, stirring, until mixture thickens and bubbles. Gradually add wine; stir until mixture boils and thickens. Add potato and reserved milk, reduce heat; simmer, uncovered, stirring occasionally, about 20 minutes or until potato is tender.
4 Meanwhile, discard skin and bones from fish. Flake fish into large pieces, add to chowder with cream; cook, stirring gently, until heated through. Remove from heat; stir in parsley.

serving suggestion Serve chowder sprinkled with bacon and accompanied with warm sourdough rolls.

tip Store leftover soup in well-sealed container; freeze up to three months.

Lamb shank soup

preparation time **30 minutes** cooking time **2 hours 30 minutes**
(plus refrigeration time) serves **4**

8 frenched lamb shanks (1.6kg)
1 medium brown onion (150g), chopped finely
2 trimmed celery stalks (200g), sliced thinly
2 medium red capsicums (400g), chopped coarsely
2 cloves garlic, crushed
2 litres (8 cups) water
400g silverbeet, trimmed, chopped finely
⅓ cup (80ml) lemon juice

1 Heat large lightly oiled saucepan; cook lamb, in batches, until browned.
Cook onion, celery, capsicum and garlic in same pan, stirring, about
5 minutes or until onion softens. Return lamb to pan with the water. Bring
to a boil then reduce heat; simmer, covered, 1¾ hours.
2 Remove soup mixture from heat; when lamb is cool enough to handle,
remove meat from bones then chop coarsely. Refrigerate cooled soup and
meat, covered separately, overnight.
3 Discard fat from surface of soup mixture. Place soup mixture and meat
in large saucepan. Bring to a boil then reduce heat; simmer, covered,
30 minutes. Add silverbeet and juice; simmer, uncovered, until silverbeet
is just wilted.

tip Store leftover soup in well-sealed container; freeze up to three months.

Greek lentil, spinach and dill soup

preparation time **20 minutes** cooking time **35 minutes** serves **6**

2 tablespoons olive oil
3 medium brown onions (450g), chopped finely
1 trimmed celery stalk (100g), chopped finely
1 medium carrot (120g), chopped finely
2 cloves garlic, crushed
1 fresh long red chilli, sliced thinly
1½ cups (300g) brown lentils
3 litres (12 cups) water
150g baby spinach leaves
1 tablespoon red wine vinegar
½ cup lightly packed fresh dill sprigs

1 Heat oil in large saucepan; cook onion, celery and carrot, stirring, about 5 minutes or until softened. Add garlic and chilli; cook, stirring, until fragrant.
2 Add lentils, stir to coat; add the water. Bring to the boil then reduce heat, simmer, uncovered, about 20 minutes or until lentils are tender.
3 Add spinach, stir until wilted. Stir in vinegar and sprinkle with dill.

tip Store leftover soup in well-sealed container; freeze up to three months.

Pea and ham soup

preparation time **15 minutes** cooking time **2 hours** serves **6**

Blue boilers – or field peas – are a special variety of pea grown specifically for being dried and used whole; when dried and halved, they're called split peas.

2 cups (375g) dried peas (blue boilers)
1 medium brown onion (150g), chopped coarsely
2 trimmed celery stalks (200g), chopped coarsely
2 bay leaves
1.5kg ham bone
2.5 litres (10 cups) water
1 teaspoon cracked black pepper

1 Combine ingredients in large saucepan. Bring to a boil then reduce heat; simmer, covered, about 2 hours or until peas are tender.
2 Remove ham bone; when cool enough to handle, remove ham from bone, shred finely. Discard bone and fat; remove and discard bay leaves.
3 Blend or process half of the pea mixture, in batches, until pureed; return to pan with remaining unprocessed pea mixture and ham. Reheat soup, stirring over heat until hot.

tip Store leftover soup in a well-sealed container; freeze up to three months.

Vichyssoise

preparation time **20 minutes** (plus refrigeration time)
cooking time **50 minutes** serves **6**

50g butter
2 medium leeks (700g), trimmed, sliced thinly
750g coliban potatoes, peeled, chopped coarsely
2 cups (500ml) chicken stock
2 cups (500ml) water
300ml cream
2 tablespoons coarsely chopped fresh chives

1 Melt butter in large saucepan; cook leek, covered, about 20 minutes or until softened, stirring occasionally (do not let leek brown).
2 Add potato, stock and the water. Bring to a boil then reduce heat; simmer, covered, until potato is tender. Cool 10 minutes.
3 Blend or process soup, in batches, until smooth; place soup in large bowl. Stir in cream, cover; refrigerate 3 hours or overnight. Divide among serving bowls; sprinkle with chives just before serving.

tip Store leftover soup in well-sealed container; freeze up to three months.

Gazpacho

preparation time **25 minutes** (plus refrigeration time) serves **4**

3 cups (750ml) tomato juice
8 medium egg tomatoes (600g), chopped coarsely
1 medium red onion (170g), chopped coarsely
1 clove garlic, quartered
1 lebanese cucumber (130g), chopped coarsely
1 small red capsicum (150g), chopped coarsely
2 teaspoons tabasco
4 green onions, chopped finely
½ lebanese cucumber (65g), seeded, chopped finely
½ small yellow capsicum (75g), chopped finely
2 teaspoons olive oil
1 tablespoon vodka (optional)
2 tablespoons finely chopped fresh coriander

1 Blend or process juice, tomato, onion, garlic, coarsely chopped cucumber and red capsicum, in batches, until pureed. Strain through sieve into large bowl, cover; refrigerate 3 hours.
2 Combine remaining ingredients in small bowl. Divide soup among serving bowls; top with vegetable mixture.

Spring vegetable soup

preparation time **15 minutes** cooking time **15 minutes** serves **4**

1 tablespoon olive oil
1 small brown onion (80g), chopped finely
1 clove garlic, crushed
350g baby carrots, sliced thickly
3 cups (750ml) chicken stock
2 cups (500ml) water
¼ cup (55g) farfalline, risoni or any small soup pasta
200g fresh asparagus, sliced thickly
1 cup (125g) frozen peas
⅓ cup (25g) grated parmesan
1 tablespoon finely chopped chives

1 Heat oil in large saucepan, add onion and garlic; cook, stirring, until onion softens. Add carrot; cook, stirring, 2 minutes.

2 Add stock and the water; bring to a boil. Stir in pasta; reduce heat then simmer, uncovered, about 8 minutes or until tender. Return to a boil, add asparagus and peas; simmer, uncovered, until tender.

3 Serve sprinkled with cheese and chives.

tip This soup is best served on day of making.

Easy beef and barley soup

preparation time **20 minutes** cooking time **3 hours** serves **6**

1kg gravy beef
1 tablespoon olive oil
2 medium brown onions (300g), chopped
2 cloves garlic, chopped
¾ cup (150g) pearl barley
2 teaspoons cracked black pepper
2 cups (500ml) beef stock
1.5 litres (6 cups) water
½ cup coarsely chopped fresh flat-leaf parsley

1 Trim fat from beef, cut into 1cm pieces.

2 Heat oil in large pan; cook onion and garlic, stirring ,until onion is soft.

3 Add beef, barley, pepper, stock and water. Bring to the boil then reduce heat; simmer, covered, for 3 hours, stirring occasionally. Stir in parsley.

tip Store leftover soup in well-sealed container; freeze up to three months.

Tuscan bean soup

preparation time **15 minutes** cooking time **2 hours 30 minutes** serves **6**

2 tablespoons olive oil
3 medium brown onions (450g), chopped coarsely
2 cloves garlic, crushed
200g piece speck, chopped
2 medium carrots (240g), chopped coarsely
2 trimmed celery stalks (200g), chopped
2 x 400g cans tomatoes
¼ medium savoy cabbage (500g), shredded
1 medium zucchini (120g), chopped coarsely
2 sprigs fresh thyme
2 cups (500ml) beef consomme or stock
2 litres (8 cups) water
400g can borlotti beans, rinsed, drained
6 thick slices italian bread

1 Heat oil in large saucepan or stock pot. Add onion, garlic and speck; cook, stirring, about 5 minutes or until onion is soft.
2 Add carrot, celery, undrained crushed tomatoes, cabbage, zucchini, thyme, consomme and the water. Bring to the boil then reduce heat; simmer, uncovered, 2 hours. Add beans and simmer, uncovered, a further 20 minutes. Season with salt and freshly ground black pepper.
3 Meanwhile, toast bread. Place toast in base of serving bowls; top with soup.

tip Store leftover soup in well-sealed container; freeze up to three months.

Chicken soup with choy sum

preparation time **5 minutes** cooking time **15 minutes** serves **4**

1.5 litres (6 cups) chicken stock
2 tablespoons soy sauce
680g chicken breast fillets, sliced thickly
100g dried rice stick noodles
300g baby choy sum, chopped coarsely

1 Bring stock to a boil in large saucepan, add chicken. Reduce heat then simmer, uncovered, about 5 minutes or until chicken is just cooked through.
2 Add sauce and noodles; simmer, uncovered, about 5 minutes or until noodles are just tender. Add choy sum; simmer, uncovered, until choy sum is just tender.

tip This soup is best served on day of making.

Chicken laksa

preparation time **15 minutes** cooking time **10 minutes** serves **4**

250g fresh egg noodles
1 teaspoon peanut oil
¼ cup (75g) laksa paste
3¼ cups (800ml) light coconut milk
1 litre (4 cups) chicken stock
2 tablespoons lime juice
1 tablespoon white sugar
1 tablespoon fish sauce
2½ cups (425g) coarsely chopped cooked chicken
1 cup (80g) bean sprouts
½ cup loosely packed fresh mint leaves

1 Rinse noodles in strainer under hot running water. Separate noodles with fork; drain.
2 Heat oil in large saucepan; cook paste, stirring, until fragrant. Stir in coconut milk, stock, juice, sugar and sauce. Bring to a boil then reduce heat; simmer, covered, 3 minutes. Add chicken; stir until laksa is heated through.
3 Divide noodles among serving bowls. Ladle laksa over noodles; top with sprouts and mint.

tip This soup is best served on day of making.

Chicken noodle soup

preparation time **10 minutes** cooking time **25 minutes** serves **6**

2 teaspoons olive oil
1 medium leek (350g), chopped coarsely
1 large carrot (180g), chopped coarsely
2 trimmed celery stalks (200g), chopped coarsely
1 clove garlic, crushed
1.5 litres (6 cups) chicken stock
2 cups (340g) shredded cooked chicken
50g rice noodles
2 tablespoons coarsely chopped fresh flat-leaf parsley

1 Heat oil in large saucepan; cook leek, carrot, celery and garlic, stirring, until leek is soft.
2 Stir in stock. Bring to a boil then reduce heat; simmer, covered, about 20 minutes or until vegetables are tender.
3 Stir in chicken and noodles; simmer, uncovered, stirring, until noodles are tender. Stir in parsley.

tip Store leftover soup in well-sealed container; freeze up to three months.

Asian mushroom broth

preparation time **10 minutes** cooking time **10 minutes** serves **4**

Cooking-oil spray
4 green onions, chopped finely
1 trimmed celery stalk (100g), chopped finely
1.5 litres (6 cups) chicken stock
1½ cups (375ml) water
¼ cup (60ml) light soy sauce
500g mixed mushrooms, sliced thinly
½ teaspoon five-spice powder
2 tablespoons finely chopped fresh garlic chives

1 Cook onion and celery in lightly oiled large saucepan, stirring, until vegetables soften.

2 Add stock, the water and sauce; bring to a boil. Add mushrooms and five-spice. Return to a boil then reduce heat; simmer 2 minutes or until mushrooms soften.
3 Just before serving, sprinkle with chives.

tip Store leftover soup in a well-sealed container; freeze up to three months.

Mussels in fragrant thai broth

preparation time **20 minutes** cooking time **15 minutes** serves **4**

½ cup (100g) jasmine rice
1kg small black mussels
1 tablespoon vegetable oil
2 tablespoons green curry paste
1½ cups (375ml) water
1½ cups (375ml) fish stock
2 teaspoons fish sauce
2 teaspoons brown sugar
1⅔ cups (400ml) coconut milk
¼ cup coarsely chopped fresh coriander
4 green onions, chopped finely
1 tablespoon lime juice

1 Cook rice in large saucepan of boiling water, uncovered, until just tender; drain. Cover to keep warm.
2 Meanwhile, scrub mussels; remove beards. Heat oil in large saucepan; cook paste, stirring, until fragrant. Add the water, stock, sauce and sugar; bring to a boil. Add coconut milk. Return to a boil then reduce heat; simmer, stirring, 1 minute. Add mussels; cook, covered, about 5 minutes or until mussels open (discard any that do not). Remove from heat; stir in coriander, onion and juice.
3 Divide rice among serving bowls; top with mussels and broth.

tip This broth is best served on day of making.

Easy chicken caesar salad

preparation time **15 minutes** serves **4**

1 large cos lettuce, torn
50g bagel crisps, broken
1 large avocado (320g), sliced thickly
2 cups (320g) shredded cooked chicken
½ cup (40g) parmesan flakes

Dressing
1 large anchovy fillet, chopped finely
1 tablespoon lemon juice
¾ cup (170g) mayonnaise
1 tablespoon finely grated parmesan
1 tablespoon warm water
½ clove garlic, crushed

1 Combine lettuce, crisps, avocado and chicken in large bowl.
2 Combine ingredients for dressing in medium bowl.
3 Serve salad, drizzled with dressing and sprinkled with cheese flakes.

tip The dressing can be made up to four days ahead.

Baby rocket and parmesan salad

preparation time **25 minutes** serves **4**

30g parmesan
100g baby rocket leaves
40g semi-dried tomatoes, halved lengthways
2 tablespoons toasted pine nuts
2 tablespoons balsamic vinegar
2 tablespoons extra virgin olive oil

1 Using vegetable peeler, shave cheese into wide, long pieces.
2 Combine rocket with tomato and nuts in large bowl; add cheese, drizzle with combined vinegar and oil, toss gently.

Three-bean salad

preparation time **35 minutes** serves **6**

215g can butter beans, rinsed, drained
215g can red kidney beans, rinsed, drained
500g frozen broad beans, thawed, peeled
1 medium tomato (190g), peeled, seeded, chopped coarsely
1 small red onion (100g), chopped coarsely
¼ cup coarsely chopped fresh flat-leaf parsley

Dressing
¼ cup (60ml) olive oil
¼ cup (60ml) lemon juice
1 clove garlic, crushed

1 Combine beans with tomato, onion and parsley in large bowl.
2 Place ingredients for dressing in screw-top jar; shake well.
3 Pour dressing over bean mixture; mix well.

Bruschetta caprese

preparation time **10 minutes** serves **4**

½ long loaf turkish bread
50g baby rocket leaves
250g cherry tomatoes, sliced thickly
100g bocconcini, sliced thickly
2 tablespoons finely shredded fresh basil
2 tablespoons olive oil

1 Cut turkish bread crossways into four even pieces. Split each piece in half horizontally; toast both sides.
2 Top each piece of toast with equal amounts of rocket, tomato, cheese and basil; drizzle with oil to serve.

Gado gado

preparation time **1 hour** cooking time **35 minutes** serves **4**

2 medium potatoes (400g), sliced thickly
2 medium carrots (240g), sliced thickly
150g green beans, chopped
½ small green cabbage (600g)
Vegetable oil, for deep-frying
300g firm tofu, cut into 2cm cubes
2 medium tomatoes (380g), cut into wedges
2 lebanese cucumbers (260g), sliced thickly
2 cups (160g) bean sprouts
4 hard-boiled eggs, quartered

Peanut sauce
1 cup (150g) toasted unsalted peanuts
1 tablespoon peanut oil
1 small brown onion (80g), chopped finely
1 clove garlic, crushed
3 fresh red thai chillies, chopped finely
1 tablespoon lime juice
1 tablespoon brown sugar
½ teaspoon shrimp paste
1 cup (250ml) coconut milk
1 tablespoon kecap manis

1 Make peanut sauce.
2 Boil, steam or microwave potato, carrot and beans, separately, until potato is cooked through, and carrot and beans are just tender.
3 Meanwhile, drop cabbage leaves into large pan of boiling water; remove leaves and quickly plunge into cold water. Drain cabbage; slice finely.
4 Heat oil in small pan; deep-fry tofu, in batches, until browned. Drain on absorbent paper.
5 Place potato, carrot, beans, cabbage, tofu, tomato, cucumber, sprouts and egg in sections on serving plate; serve with peanut sauce.

Peanut sauce Process nuts in a food processor until chopped coarsely. Heat oil in small pan; cook onion, garlic and chilli, stirring, until onion is golden brown. Add peanuts and remaining ingredients. Bring to a boil, reduce heat; simmer, uncovered, 5 minutes or until mixture thickens. Cool 10 minutes.

Salade niçoise

preparation time **20 minutes** cooking time **10 minutes** serves **4**

200g green beans, trimmed, chopped coarsely
250g cherry tomatoes, halved
½ cup (80g) seeded black olives
2 lebanese cucumbers (260g), sliced thickly
1 medium red onion (170g), sliced thinly
150g mesclun
6 hard-boiled eggs, quartered
400g can tuna in springwater, drained

Vinaigrette
1 teaspoon olive oil
¼ cup (60ml) lemon juice
1 clove garlic, crushed
2 teaspoons dijon mustard

1 Boil, steam or microwave beans until just tender; drain. Rinse under cold running water; drain.
2 Meanwhile, place ingredients for vinaigrette in screw-top jar; shake well.
3 Place tomatoes, olives, cucumber, onion, mesclun and egg in large bowl with vinaigrette; toss gently to combine.
4 Divide salad among serving plates; flake fish over salad in large chunks.

Tuna pasta salad

preparation time **20 minutes** cooking **10 minutes** serves **4**

500g spiral pasta
2 x 400g cans tuna in oil
440g can corn kernels, drained
1 small red onion (100g), sliced thinly
1 medium red capsicum (200g), sliced thinly
2 trimmed celery stalks (150g), sliced thinly
¼ cup chopped fresh flat-leaf parsley
¼ cup (75g) mayonnaise
1 tablespoon plain yogurt
1 clove garlic, crushed
2 tablespoons finely grated lemon rind
2 tablespoons lemon juice
2 tablespoons wholegrain mustard

1 Cook pasta in large saucepan of boiling, salted water until just tender; drain.
2 Meanwhile, drain tuna; reserve 2 tablespoons of oil.
3 Combine pasta, tuna, corn, onion, capsicum, celery and parsley in large bowl.
4 Combine mayonnaise, yogurt, garlic, rind, juice, mustard and reserved oil in small bowl or jug. Add to pasta mixture, toss gently. Season with salt and freshly ground black pepper.

German hot potato salad

preparation time **10 minutes** cooking time **15 minutes** serves **2**

2 eggs
2 bacon rashers (140g), chopped
350g baby new potatoes
2 pickled gherkins, chopped finely
1 tablespoon finely chopped fresh flat-leaf parsley
⅓ cup (100g) mayonnaise
2 tablespoons sour cream
1 teaspoon lemon juice

1 Cover eggs with water in medium pan. Bring to boil then reduce heat; simmer, uncovered, 10 minutes. Drain and cool eggs under cold running water; shell and halve.

2 Meanwhile, fry bacon, uncovered, in dry heated pan until browned and crisp; drain on absorbent paper.

3 Boil, steam or microwave potatoes until tender; drain and halve.

4 Combine remaining ingredients in large pan; stir over low heat until just hot. Place mayonnaise mixture in large bowl with potato, bacon and egg; toss gently to combine.

Old-fashioned chicken salad

preparation time **40 minutes** cooking time **15 minutes** serves **4**

1 litre (4 cups) boiling water
1 litre (4 cups) chicken stock
350g chicken breast fillets
½ long french bread stick, sliced thinly
1 tablespoon olive oil
¼ cup (75g) mayonnaise
¼ cup (60g) sour cream
1 tablespoon lemon juice
2 trimmed celery stalks (200g), sliced thinly
3 large dill pickles, sliced thinly
1 tablespoon finely chopped fresh tarragon
1 large butter lettuce, leaves separated

1 Bring the water and stock to a boil in large frying pan; poach chicken, covered, about 10 minutes or until cooked through. Cool chicken in liquid 10 minutes; slice thinly. Discard liquid.

2 Meanwhile, preheat grill. Brush both sides of bread slices with oil; toast under grill until browned lightly both sides.

3 Whisk mayonnaise, sour cream and juice in small bowl. Combine chicken, celery, pickle and tarragon in large bowl; toss to combine. Place lettuce leaves on serving platter; top with salad and bread, drizzle with mayonnaise mixture.

tip Cooling chicken in liquid prevents it from drying out.

Greek salad

preparation time **25 minutes** serves **4**

4 medium egg tomatoes (300g)
2 lebanese cucumbers (260g)
2 medium green capsicums (400g)
1 medium red onion (170g)
1 cup (160g) kalamata olives, seeded
150g fetta
1 teaspoon crushed dried oregano
½ cup (125ml) extra virgin olive oil

1 Quarter tomatoes and cucumbers lengthways; cut into chunks. Slice capsicum into rings; remove and discard seeds and membranes. Cut onion into wedges.
2 Combine tomato, cucumber, capsicum, onion and olives in large serving bowl.
3 Break cheese into large pieces and place on top of salad, sprinkle with oregano; drizzle with oil.

Sang choy bow

preparation time **15 minutes** cooking time **15 minutes** serves **4**

1 tablespoon peanut oil
750g pork mince
2 cloves garlic, crushed
225g can water chestnuts, drained, chopped finely
1 teaspoon sambal oelek
1 tablespoon lime juice
1 medium red capsicum (200g), chopped finely
1 trimmed celery stalk (75g), chopped finely
2 tablespoons light soy sauce
2 tablespoons rice vinegar
8 large iceberg lettuce leaves
2 green onions, sliced thinly

1 Heat oil in wok; stir-fry pork and garlic about 5 minutes or until pork changes colour and is cooked through.

2 Stir in water chestnuts, sambal, juice, capsicum, celery, sauce and vinegar; cook, stirring, until vegetables are just tender.

3 Place two lettuce leaves on each serving plate. Divide pork mixture among leaves; sprinkle each with onion.

Fattoush

preparation time **30 minutes** cooking time **5 minutes** serves **4**

6 pocket pitta
Olive oil, for shallow-frying
3 medium tomatoes (450g), chopped coarsely
1 large green capsicum (350g), chopped coarsely
2 lebanese cucumbers (260g), seeded, sliced thinly
4 spring onions (100g), sliced thinly
1 ½ cups firmly packed fresh flat-leaf parsley leaves
½ cup coarsely chopped fresh mint

Lemon garlic dressing
2 cloves garlic, crushed
¼ cup (60ml) olive oil
¼ cup (60ml) lemon juice

1 Place ingredients for lemon garlic dressing in screw-top jar; shake well.

2 Halve pitta horizontally; cut into 2.5cm pieces. Heat oil in wok or large frying pan; shallow-fry pitta, in batches, until browned lightly and crisp. Drain on absorbent paper.

3 Just before serving, place about three-quarters of pitta in large bowl with dressing and remaining ingredients; toss gently to combine. Sprinkle remaining pitta over fattoush.

Warm chicken tabbouleh

preparation time **15 minutes** (plus standing time) cooking time **10 minutes**
serves **4**

1 cup (160g) burghul
600g chicken tenderloins, sliced thinly
2 cloves garlic, crushed
²/₃ cup (160ml) lemon juice
¼ cup (60ml) olive oil
250g cherry tomatoes, halved
4 green onions, chopped coarsely
1 cup coarsely chopped fresh flat-leaf parsley
1 cup coarsely chopped fresh mint

1 Place burghul in small bowl; cover with boiling water. Stand 15 minutes; drain. Squeeze burghul with hands to remove excess water.
2 Meanwhile, combine chicken, garlic and 1 tablespoon each of juice and oil in medium bowl; stand 5 minutes.
3 Heat 1 tablespoon of oil in wok; stir-fry chicken mixture, in batches, until chicken is browned and cooked through. Cover to keep warm.
4 Place burghul with tomato and onion in wok; stir-fry until onion softens, remove from heat. Add chicken mixture, parsley, mint, remaining juice and oil; toss gently to combine.

Skewered lemon prawns

preparation time **15 minutes** (plus refrigeration time)
cooking time **5 minutes** serves **4**

You will need to soak 12 bamboo skewers in water for at least an hour before use, to prevent them from splintering and scorching.

12 large uncooked king prawns (750g)
2 tablespoons olive oil
2 teaspoons grated lemon rind
Lemon wedges

1 Remove head and devein prawns; remove legs, leaving shell intact. Cut along the underside length of prawn, without cutting all the way through. Thread prawns onto skewers.

2 Place prawns in large dish; pour over oil and add lemon rind. Cover; refrigerate 3 hours.

3 Cook prawns, flesh-side down, on preheated oiled grill plate (or grill or barbecue) until browned lightly; turn. Cook until just cooked through; serve with lemon wedges.

Lamb and tabbouleh wrap

preparation time **20 minutes** (plus standing time) cooking time **10 minutes** makes **8**

1 cup (250ml) water
½ cup (80g) burghul
3 green onions, sliced thinly
2 medium tomatoes (380g), seeded, chopped finely
1 lebanese cucumber (130g), seeded, chopped finely
1 cup coarsely chopped fresh flat-leaf parsley
½ cup coarsely chopped fresh mint
1 tablespoon lemon juice
250g lean lamb strips
¾ cup (180g) prepared hummus
8 slices lavash bread

1 Combine the water and burghul in small bowl; stand 30 minutes. Drain; squeeze burghul with hands to remove excess water.

2 Combine burghul, onion, tomato, cucumber, herbs and juice in large bowl; toss gently until tabbouleh is combined.

3 Cook lamb, in batches, on preheated lightly oiled grill plate (or grill or barbecue) until cooked as desired.

4 Just before serving, spread hummus equally over half of each slice of bread, top with equal amounts of lamb and tabbouleh; roll to enclose filling. Cut into pieces, if desired, to serve.

tip Ready-made tabbouleh can be used in this recipe; you will need 2 cups.

Turkish herbed lamb pizza

preparation time **20 minutes** cooking time **35 minutes** serves **6**

600g lamb mince
1 tablespoon olive oil
1 small brown onion (80g), chopped finely
1 clove garlic, crushed
½ teaspoon ground cinnamon
1½ teaspoons ground allspice
¼ cup (40g) pine nuts, chopped coarsely
¼ cup (70g) tomato paste
2 medium tomatoes (300g), seeded, chopped finely
1 cup (250ml) chicken stock
2 tablespoons lemon juice
¼ cup finely chopped fresh flat-leaf parsley
¼ cup finely chopped fresh mint
2 x 430g turkish bread
½ cup (140g) greek-style yogurt
2 tablespoons cold water

1 Preheat oven to very hot.
2 Cook mince in heated large non-stick frying pan, stirring, until cooked through; place in medium bowl.
3 Heat oil in same pan; cook onion and garlic, stirring, until onion softens. Add spices and nuts; cook, stirring, about 5 minutes or until nuts are just toasted. Return mince to pan with tomato paste, tomato, stock and juice; cook, stirring, about 5 minutes or until liquid is almost evaporated. Remove pan from heat; stir in herbs.
4 Place bread on lightly oiled oven trays; spoon mince mixture over bread, leaving a 2cm border. Cook, uncovered, in very hot oven about 15 minutes or until browned lightly. Serve drizzled with combined yogurt and cold water.

Italian blt

preparation time **15 minutes** cooking time **15 minutes** serves **4**

4 medium egg tomatoes (300g), quartered
1 tablespoon balsamic vinegar
1 tablespoon finely chopped fresh basil
¼ cup (60ml) olive oil
8 slices pancetta (120g)
1 loaf ciabatta (350g)
1 clove garlic, crushed
100g bocconcini, sliced thickly
25g baby rocket leaves

1 Place tomato in medium bowl with vinegar, basil and 1 tablespoon of the oil; toss to coat tomato.
2 Cook tomato and pancetta on heated oiled flat plate, uncovered, until tomato is browned and pancetta crisp.
3 Cut bread into quarters, split quarters in half horizontally; brush cut sides with combined garlic and remaining oil. Toast bread, cut-side down, on heated flat plate.
4 Sandwich tomato, pancetta, bocconcini and rocket between bread pieces.

Chicken wraps

preparation time **10 minutes** cooking time **1 minute** serves **4**

1 large tomato (220g), chopped coarsely
1 medium avocado (320g), chopped coarsely
1 small red onion (100g), chopped coarsely
2 tablespoons coarsely chopped fresh coriander
½ cup (130g) bottled medium chunky salsa
3 cups (480g) shredded cooked chicken
8 large flour tortillas

1 Combine tomato, avocado, onion, coriander, salsa and chicken in large bowl.
2 Heat one tortilla in microwave on HIGH (100%) about 20 seconds or until tortilla is just flexible. Top with an eighth of chicken filling; roll to enclose filling.
3 Repeat with remaining tortillas and chicken filling.

Potato and rosemary pizza

preparation time **20 minutes**   cooking time **40 minutes**   serves **8**

3 medium potatoes (630g), unpeeled
1 teaspoon fresh rosemary leaves
2 tablespoons olive oil
1 cup (150g) self-raising flour
1 cup (150g) plain flour
30g butter
1 egg, beaten lightly
1/3 cup (80ml) milk
1/2 cup (40g) finely grated parmesan
2 cloves garlic, crushed

1 Preheat oven to moderately hot. Lightly oil 25cm x 30cm swiss roll pan.

2 Peel and coarsely chop one of the potatoes; boil, steam or microwave until tender, drain. Mash in small bowl; reserve 1/2 cup (110g) mashed potato. Using sharp knife, mandoline or v-slicer, cut remaining potatoes into 1mm slices. Pat dry with absorbent paper. Combine sliced potato in medium bowl with rosemary and oil.

3 Combine flours in large bowl; using fingertips, rub butter into flour until mixture resembles fine breadcrumbs. Add mashed potato, egg and milk; stir until combined. Turn dough onto floured surface; knead until smooth.

4 Roll dough into 25cm x 30cm rectangle; carefully lift onto prepared pan. Using palm of hand, press dough into corners of pan to ensure base is covered evenly. Top pizza base with cheese and garlic; layer potato slices, overlapping slightly, over base. Bake, uncovered, in moderately hot oven about 30 minutes or until potato is tender and pizza is browned lightly.

Tuna and fetta turnovers

preparation time **20 minutes** cooking time **15 minutes** makes **16**

400g can tuna in oil
100g ricotta
100g fetta, crumbled
50g sun-dried tomatoes, sliced thinly
2 teaspoons drained baby capers
2 tablespoons finely chopped fresh flat-leaf parsley
2 tablespoons toasted pine nuts
1 tablespoon lime juice
4 sheets ready-rolled puff pastry, thawed
2 tablespoons milk

1 Preheat the oven to moderately hot.
2 Drain tuna over a bowl, reserve 2 tablespoons of the oil. Flake tuna into medium bowl, add cheeses, tomatoes, capers, parsley, nuts, lemon juice and reserved tuna oil; mix well.
3 Cut four 12cm rounds from each pastry sheet. Place one heaped tablespoon of tuna mixture on each round; brush edges with a little milk, fold over to enclose filling. Press edges to seal; repeat with remaining tuna mixture and pastry.
4 Place turnovers on lightly oiled oven trays; brush with milk. Bake, uncovered, in moderately hot oven about 15 minutes or until browned lightly.

Cheese and spinach pastries

preparation time **15 minutes** cooking time **20 minutes** makes **20**

10 sheets fillo pastry
30g butter
3 green onions, chopped finely
250g spinach, chopped finely
2 teaspoons finely chopped fresh dill
2 eggs
125g fetta, crumbled
125g ricotta
¼ teaspoon ground nutmeg
½ cup (50g) packaged breadcrumbs
75g butter, melted, extra

1 Preheat oven to moderately hot. To prevent fillo drying out, cover with baking paper then damp tea-towel until ready to use.
2 Melt butter in medium frying pan; cook onion, stirring, until soft. Add spinach and dill. Cook, stirring, about 3 minutes or until spinach is wilted; cool.
3 Squeeze excess moisture from spinach mixture, place in medium bowl. Add eggs, cheeses, nutmeg and breadcrumbs.
4 Layer two sheets of fillo together, brushing each with some of the extra butter. Cut layered pastry crossways into four strips. Place 1 level tablespoon of spinach mixture at one end of each strip.
5 Fold opposite corner of fillo diagonally across the filling to form a triangle. Continue folding to end of fillo, retaining triangular shape. Repeat with remaining pastry, extra butter and spinach mixture.
6 Brush triangles with extra melted butter; bake on lightly oiled oven trays in moderately hot oven about 15 minutes or until browned lightly.

Tandoori chicken wraps

preparation time **10 minutes** cooking time **10 minutes** serves **6**

⅓ cup (100g) tandoori paste
200g plain yogurt
600g chicken tenderloins
6 roti or chapati
Cooking-oil spray
2 medium egg tomatoes (150g), sliced thickly
2 lebanese cucumbers (260g), seeded, sliced thinly
50g baby spinach leaves
½ cup firmly packed fresh mint leaves

1 Combine tandoori paste with 2 tablespoons of yogurt in medium bowl; add chicken, toss to coat with tandoori mixture.
2 Lightly spray roti (or chapati) on both sides with oil spray; cook on a preheated grill plate (or grill or barbecue) on both sides until browned lightly. Cover to keep warm.
3 Cook chicken on same heated, oiled grill plate (or grill or barbecue) until browned and cooked through; slice thinly.
4 Divide chicken among roti, top with tomato, cucumber, spinach, remaining yogurt and mint; roll to enclose filling. Cut wraps in half diagonally; serve warm.

Avocado caprese salad

preparation time **10 minutes** serves **4**

2 large vine-ripened tomatoes (240g)
125g cherry bocconcini
1 medium avocado (250g), halved
¼ cup loosely packed fresh basil leaves
1 tablespoon olive oil
1 tablespoon balsamic vinegar

1 Slice tomato, cheese and avocado thickly.
2 Arrange slices on serving platter; top with basil, drizzle with combined oil and vinegar. Season with freshly ground black pepper.

Chicken pitta pockets

preparation time **10 minutes** cooking time **10 minutes** serves **4**

600g chicken tenderloins
2 teaspoons seasoned salt
2 teaspoons olive oil
1 medium brown onion (150g), sliced thinly
¼ cup (75g) mayonnaise
2 teaspoons water
2 teaspoons wholegrain mustard
4 pitta pockets
4 green oak leaf lettuce leaves
8 pieces pickled sliced cucumber, drained
2 small egg tomatoes (120g), sliced thinly

1 Combine chicken and salt in medium bowl; mix well.
2 Heat oil in large non-stick frying pan; cook onion, stirring, until soft.
Remove from pan and keep warm.
3 Cook chicken in same pan, until browned on both sides.
4 Combine mayonnaise, the water and mustard in small bowl.
5 Trim each pitta to open. Fill with lettuce, cucumber, tomato, chicken, onion
and mayonnaise mixture.

Pissaladière

50g butter
1 tablespoon olive oil
3 large brown onions (600g), sliced thinly
2 cloves garlic, crushed
1 tablespoon drained baby capers
¾ cup (110g) self-raising flour
¾ cup (110g) plain flour
30g butter, chopped, extra
¾ cup (180ml) buttermilk
20 drained anchovy fillets, halved lengthways
½ cup (90g) small black olives

1 Preheat oven to moderately hot.
2 Heat butter and oil in large saucepan; cook onion and garlic, covered, stirring occasionally, over low heat about 30 minutes or until onion is soft but not browned. Cook, uncovered, 10 minutes; stir in capers.
3 Meanwhile, sift flours into large bowl. Rub in extra butter; stir in buttermilk to form soft dough. Turn dough onto lightly floured surface; knead until smooth.
4 Roll out dough to form a rough rectangular shape, about 25cm x 35cm. Place on an oiled oven tray.
5 Spread onion mixture over dough, spreading it to edges. Top with anchovy and olives in a diamond pattern. Bake, uncovered, in moderately hot oven about 30 minutes or until base is browned and crisp.

Sensational sandwiches

Each of these recipes takes 10 minutes to prepare and makes one sandwich.

Hummus and cucumber

Spread one slice of bread with 1 tablespoon prepared hummus; top with a quarter of a thinly sliced lebanese cucumber and another slice of bread.

Fruit and nut

Spread one slice of bread with 3 teaspoons chocolate hazelnut spread; top with 1 tablespoon sultanas and half of a thinly sliced small banana. Top with another slice of bread.

Chicken, avocado and cream cheese

Combine ¼ cup (40g) coarsely chopped barbecued chicken meat, a quarter of a coarsely chopped small avocado, and 1 teaspoon lemon juice in small bowl. Spread 1 tablespoon spreadable cream cheese on one slice of bread; top with chicken mixture, ¼ cup loosely packed mixed lettuce leaves and another slice of bread.

Tuna and sweet corn

Combine half of a drained 200g can tuna in springwater, 2 tablespoons drained and rinsed canned sweet corn kernels, and 1 tablespoon mayonnaise in small bowl. Spread mixture on 1 slice of bread. Top with a quarter of a thinly sliced lebanese cucumber and another slice of bread.

Peanut butter and vegies

Spread 1 tablespoon peanut butter over two slices of bread; top one slice with 1 tablespoon coarsely grated carrot and 1 tablespoon coarsely grated celery. Top with remaining bread slice.

Cheese, sausage and pickle

Spread 1 tablespoon of sweet mustard pickle over two slices of bread; top one slice of bread with one slice of cheddar and one cold cooked thickly sliced beef sausage. Top with remaining slice of bread.

Egg, tomato and mayonnaise

Combine half of a seeded, finely chopped small tomato, 1 tablespoon coarsely grated cheddar, one coarsely chopped hard-boiled egg and 1 tablespoon mayonnaise in small bowl. Spread mixture on one slice of bread; top with ¼ cup loosely packed mixed lettuce leaves and another slice of bread.

Cheese and vegies

Combine 2 tablespoons coarsely grated cheddar, 2 tablespoons coarsely grated carrot, 2 tablespoons coarsely grated celery, and 1 tablespoon sour cream in small bowl. Spread mixture over one slice of bread; top with another slice of bread.

Chicken tikka drumettes

preparation time **5 minutes** cooking time **20 minutes** serves **4**

12 chicken drumettes (960g)
⅓ cup (100g) tikka masala paste
½ cup (140g) plain yogurt
¼ cup coarsely chopped fresh coriander

1 Preheat oven to moderately hot.
2 Place chicken in large bowl with combined paste and 2 tablespoons of yogurt; toss to coat chicken. Place chicken, in single layer, on wire rack in large baking dish. Roast, uncovered, in moderately hot oven about 20 minutes or until chicken is browned and cooked through.
3 Meanwhile, combine coriander and remaining yogurt in small bowl.
4 Serve chicken drizzled with yogurt mixture.

serving suggestion Serve with steamed rice, lime pickle and pappadums.

Picnic for two
Quick beetroot dip
Pesto-grilled chicken drumsticks
Chef's salad
Baked ricotta rolls

Quick beetroot dip
preparation time **10 minutes** makes **1 cup**

200g can sliced beetroot, drained well
¼ cup (70g) low-fat plain yogurt
1 teaspoon ground coriander
2 teaspoons ground cumin

1 Blend or process ingredients until well combined.

Pesto-grilled chicken drumsticks
preparation time **10 minutes** cooking time **20 minutes** serves **2**

4 chicken drumsticks (600g)
2 teaspoons olive oil
1 tablespoon lemon juice
1 clove garlic, crushed
60g butter, softened
1 tablespoon bottled sun-dried tomato pesto

1 Preheat grill.
2 Make deep diagonal cuts across each chicken drumstick. Combine oil, juice and garlic in large bowl; add chicken, coat with oil mixture.
3 Combine butter and pesto in small bowl; press two-thirds of pesto mixture into cuts and all over chicken.
4 Place chicken under grill; cook, brushing with remaining pesto mixture occasionally, until cooked through.

Chef's salad

preparation time **20 minutes** (plus cooling time) cooking time **25 minutes**
serves **2**

1 small cos lettuce
2 medium egg tomatoes (150g), cut into wedges
100g finely sliced leg ham
50g finely sliced jarlsberg
2 hard-boiled eggs, quartered

Vinaigrette
¼ cup (60ml) olive oil
2 tablespoons white wine vinegar
1 teaspoon wholegrain mustard

1 Wash and separate lettuce leaves; tear into small pieces.
2 Place ingredients for vinaigrette in screw-top jar; shake well.
3 Combine lettuce tomato, ham, cheese and egg. Drizzle with vinaigrette.

Baked ricotta rolls

preparation time **10 minutes** cooking time **20 minutes** serves **2**

2 bread rolls
100g ricotta
2 tablespoons finely grated parmesan
1 clove garlic, crushed
1 egg white
2 tablespoons drained chopped sun-dried tomatoes in oil
2 tablespoons seeded black olives, chopped
50g drained bottled char-grilled eggplant
4 large fresh basil leaves

1 Preheat oven to very hot.
2 Cut lids from top of rolls, remove bread inside rolls, leaving 1cm shell.
3 Combine cheeses, garlic, egg white, tomato and olives in bowl. Place eggplant in bread rolls; top with basil then ricotta mixture. Replace lids, wrap rolls in foil; place on oven tray. Bake in very hot oven about 20 minutes or until hot.
4 Wrap in tea towel to keep warm during transportation.

BBQ lunch for friends

Sangria
Chicken, lemon and artichoke skewers
Panzanella
Char-grilled fruit with rum

Sangria

preparation time **10 minutes** serves **4-6**

750ml bottle dry red wine
30ml cointreau
30ml bacardi
30ml brandy
½ cup (110g) white sugar
2 cinnamon sticks
½ medium orange, peeled, chopped coarsely
½ medium lemon, peeled, chopped coarsely
6 medium strawberries, chopped coarsely

1 Place ingredients in a large jug; stir until well combined, serve with ice.

Chicken, lemon and artichoke skewers

preparation time **15 minutes** cooking time **15 minutes** serves **4**

3 medium lemons (420g)
¼ cup (60ml) olive oil
600g chicken breast fillets, chopped
2 x 400g cans artichoke hearts, drained, halved
24 button mushrooms

1 Squeeze juice from 1 lemon. Combine juice and oil in jar and shake well.
2 Cut remaining lemons into 24 wedges. Thread chicken pieces, artichoke, mushrooms and lemon onto 12 skewers.
3 Cook skewers on preheated oiled grill plate (or grill or barbecue) until cooked through. Brush with oil mixture during cooking.

Panzanella

preparation time **25 minutes** serves **4**

1 long loaf stale ciabatta, cut into 2cm pieces
6 medium tomatoes (1.1kg), chopped coarsely
2 trimmed celery stalks (150g), chopped coarsely
1 lebanese cucumber (130g), sliced thickly
1 medium red onion (170g), chopped coarsely

Vinaigrette
¼ cup (60ml) red wine vinegar
½ cup (125ml) olive oil
1 clove garlic, crushed
¼ cup finely shredded fresh basil

1 Combine bread cubes, tomato, celery, cucumber and onion in large bowl.
2 Place ingredients for vinaigrette in screw-top jar; shake well. Pour over salad; toss gently.

Char-grilled fruit with rum

preparation time **20 minutes** cooking time **20 minutes** serves **4**

You will need about three passionfruit for this recipe.

2 medium mangoes (860g)
½ cup (125ml) malibu
¼ cup (60ml) passionfruit pulp
1 tablespoon brown sugar
½ medium pineapple (600g), sliced thickly
300ml cream, whipped
2 tablespoons flaked coconut, toasted

1 Cut mangoes down each side of stone; cut a criss-cross pattern into flesh.
2 Combine malibu, passionfruit pulp and sugar in medium saucepan. Stir over low heat, without boiling, until sugar dissolves. Simmer, uncovered, 5 minutes. Combine mango and pineapple with passionfruit syrup in bowl.
3 Cook fruit on heated oiled grill plate (or grill or barbecue) until browned both sides and tender; brush occasionally with a little syrup during cooking.
4 Drizzle warm fruit with remaining passionfruit syrup. Serve with cream; sprinkle with coconut.

Sunday roast formal lunch
Roasted parsnip and garlic soup
Roast beef with yorkshire puddings
Middle-Eastern roasted pumpkin, carrot and potato
Chocolate self-saucing pudding

Roasted parsnip and garlic soup

preparation time **30 minutes** cooking time **1 hour 20 minutes** serves **8**

2 garlic bulbs
¼ cup (60ml) olive oil
2kg parsnips, chopped coarsely
2 tablespoons olive oil, extra
1 large brown onion (150g), chopped finely
2 medium potatoes (200g), chopped coarsely
2 litre (8 cups) chicken stock
1½ cups (375ml) cream
1½ cups (375ml) milk
¼ cup finely chopped fresh garlic chives

1 Preheat oven to moderately hot.
2 Place whole unpeeled garlic bulbs in large shallow baking dish; roast, uncovered, in moderately hot oven 10 minutes. Add combined oil and parsnip; roast, uncovered, in moderately hot oven about 30 minutes or until garlic and parsnip are tender. When garlic is cool enough to handle, halve bulbs crossways; use fingers to squeeze garlic puree into small bowl. Reserve.
3 Heat extra oil in large saucepan; cook onion, stirring, until softened. Add parsnip with potato and stock. Bring to a boil then reduce heat; simmer soup, uncovered, stirring occasionally, about 20 minutes or until potato is softened.
4 Blend or process soup with reserved garlic puree, in batches, until smooth. Reheat soup in same pan, stir in cream and milk; bring to a boil. Ladle soup into serving bowls; sprinkle with chives.

Roast beef with yorkshire puddings

preparation time **35 minutes** (plus refrigeration and standing time)
cooking time **2 hours** serves **8**

2kg corner piece beef topside roast
1 cup (250ml) dry red wine
¼ cup (70g) wholegrain mustard
4 cloves garlic, sliced
4 sprigs fresh thyme
1 medium brown onion (150g), chopped coarsely
2 medium carrots (240g), chopped coarsely
2 trimmed celery stalks (200g), chopped coarsely
2 tablespoons olive oil
2 tablespoons plain flour
1½ cups (375ml) beef stock

Yorkshire puddings
1 cup (150g) plain flour
½ teaspoon salt
2 eggs, beaten lightly
½ cup (125ml) milk
½ cup (125ml) water

1 Combine beef, wine, mustard, garlic, thyme and onion in large bowl, cover; refrigerate 3 hours or overnight.
2 Preheat oven to moderate. Drain beef over medium bowl; reserve 1 cup of marinade. Combine carrot and celery in large baking dish, top with beef; brush beef with oil. Bake, uncovered, in moderate oven about 1½ hours or until browned and cooked as desired.
3 Remove beef from pan, wrap in foil; stand 20 minutes before serving. Remove vegetables with slotted spoon; discard vegetables. Pour pan juices into jug, stand 2 minutes, then pour off excess oil; reserve 1½ tablespoons oil for yorkshire puddings and 2 tablespoons of pan juices for gravy.
4 Heat reserved pan juices for gravy in same baking dish, add flour; cook, stirring, until bubbling. Gradually add reserved marinade and stock; cook, stirring, until mixture boils and thickens, strain gravy into jug.
5 Meanwhile, make yorkshire puddings; serve with beef and gravy.
Yorkshire puddings Sift flour and salt into bowl, make well in centre; add combined egg, milk and water. Using a wooden spoon, gradually stir in flour from side of bowl until batter is smooth. Cover; allow to stan0d 30 minutes. Divide the reserved oil among 16 holes of a mini (1½ tablespoons/30ml) muffin pans; heat in hot oven 2 minutes. Divide batter among pan holes. Bake in hot oven about 10 minutes or until puddings are puffed and golden.

...continued on next page

Middle-Eastern roasted pumpkin, carrot and potato

preparation time **20 minutes** cooking time **35 minutes** serves **8**

900g piece pumpkin, chopped coarsely
4 medium potatoes (800g), chopped coarsely
4 large carrots (720g), halved, sliced thickly
2 tablespoons olive oil
⅓ cup firmly packed fresh flat-leaf parsley leaves
¼ cup (40g) toasted pine nuts

Spice paste
2 cloves garlic, quartered
1 teaspoon cumin seeds
1 teaspoon coriander seeds
1 teaspoon sea salt
1 tablespoon olive oil
¼ cup (55g) firmly packed brown sugar
1½ cups (375ml) apple juice

1 Preheat oven to moderately hot.
2 Place pumpkin, potato, carrot and oil in large baking dish; toss vegetables to coat in oil. Roast, uncovered, in moderately hot oven about 35 minutes or until just tender.
3 Meanwhile, make spice paste.
4 Place vegetables, parsley and nuts in large bowl with spice mixture; toss gently to combine.

Spice paste Using mortar and pestle or small electric spice blender, crush garlic, cumin, coriander, salt and oil until mixture forms a thick paste. Cook paste in large frying pan, stirring, about 3 minutes or until fragrant. Add sugar and juice; bring to a boil. Cook, uncovered, stirring, about 10 minutes or until mixture thickens slightly.

Chocolate self-saucing pudding

preparation time **10 minutes** cooking time **40 minutes** (plus standing time)
serves **8**

1 cup (150g) self-raising flour
½ teaspoon bicarbonate of soda
½ cup (50g) cocoa powder
1 ¼ cups (275g) firmly packed brown sugar
80g butter, melted
½ cup (120g) sour cream
1 egg, beaten lightly
2 cups (500ml) boiling water

1 Preheat oven to moderate. Grease deep 1.5 litre (6-cup) ovenproof dish.
2 Sift flour, soda, half the cocoa and ½ cup of the sugar into medium bowl;
stir in combined butter, sour cream and egg.
3 Spread mixture into prepared dish. Sift remaining cocoa and remaining
sugar evenly over mixture; gently pour over the boiling water. Bake,
uncovered, in moderate oven about 40 minutes. Stand 5 minutes before
serving.

serving suggestion Serve pudding with vanilla ice-cream.

Brain food lunch before exams

Peach, apple and strawberry juice
Tuna, bean and tomato salad
Baked bean jaffles

Peach, apple and strawberry juice

preparation time **5 minutes** serves **1**

1 medium apple (150g), cut into wedges
1 medium peach (150g), cut into wedges
2 strawberries (40g)

1 Push ingredients through juice extractor into glass; stir to combine.

Tuna, bean and tomato salad

preparation time **10 minutes** serves **1**

100g canned tuna in springwater, drained
150g canned red kidney beans, rinsed, drained
100g cherry tomatoes, halved
¼ cup coarsely chopped fresh basil leaves
½ small (100g) avocado, sliced

Balsamic dressing
1 tablespoon olive oil
2 teaspoons balsamic vinegar

1 Combine tuna, beans, tomato, basil and avocado in medium bowl.
2 Whisk ingredients for balsamic dressing in medium bowl; drizzle over bean mixture. Mix well.

Baked bean jaffles

preparation time **10 minutes** Cooking time **5 minutes** makes **1**

1 bacon rashers, chopped finely
150g can baked beans
2 teaspoons sweet chilli sauce
2 slices white bread
5g butter, softened

1 Cook bacon in non-stick frying pan, stirring, until crisp.
2 Combine bacon, beans and sweet chilli sauce in small bowl.
3 Spread bread with butter on one side; top one bread slice with bean mixture. Top with remaining bread slice, buttered side up. Cook in sandwich maker until browned.

PASTA AND NOODLES

Fettuccine boscaiola with chicken

preparation time **10 minutes** cooking time **10 minutes** serves **4**

500g fettuccine
1 tablespoon olive oil
1 medium brown onion (150g), chopped finely
2 bacon rashers (140g), chopped finely
200g button mushrooms, sliced finely
¼ cup (60ml) dry white wine
⅔ cup (160ml) cream
1 cup (250ml) milk
1 cup (170g) thinly sliced cooked chicken
¼ cup (20g) finely grated parmesan
2 tablespoons coarsely chopped fresh flat-leaf parsley

1 Cook pasta in large saucepan of boiling water, uncovered, until just tender; drain, reserving ½ cup of cooking liquid.
2 Meanwhile, heat oil in large saucepan; cook onion, stirring, until soft. Add bacon and mushrooms; cook, stirring, 1 minute.
3 Add wine, cream and milk. Bring to a boil then reduce heat; simmer, stirring, 5 minutes. Add chicken; stir until combined.
4 Add pasta, cheese, parsley and reserved cooking liquid; toss gently over low heat until hot.

Fettuccine carbonara

preparation time **10 minutes** cooking time **10 minutes** serves **4**

4 bacon rashers (280g), chopped coarsely
375g fettuccine
3 egg yolks, beaten lightly
1 cup (250ml) cream
½ cup (30g) finely grated parmesan
2 tablespoons coarsely chopped fresh chives

1 Cook bacon in heated small frying pan, stirring, until crisp; drain on absorbent paper.
2 Just before serving, cook pasta in large saucepan of boiling water, uncovered, until just tender; drain.
3 Combine pasta in large bowl with egg yolks, cream and cheese; sprinkle with bacon and chives.

Gnocchi with burnt butter and tomato

preparation time **40 minutes** (plus refrigeration time)
cooking time **25 minutes** serves **4**

625g packaged potato gnocchi
100g butter, chopped coarsely
⅓ cup baby basil leaves
3 medium egg tomatoes (225g), chopped coarsely

1 Cook gnocchi, in batches, in large saucepan of boiling water about 3 minutes or until gnocchi float to surface. Remove with slotted spoon; drain.
2 Meanwhile, melt butter in medium frying pan, add basil leaves; cook until crisp. Remove basil from pan with slotted spoon; drain on absorbent paper. Add tomato; cook, stirring, until tomato softens.
3 Combine drained gnocchi and tomato mixture in large bowl, toss gently. Divide among serving dishes, sprinkle with basil.

serving suggestion Serve gnocchi topped with grated parmesan.

Beef and pasta bake

preparation time **15 minutes** cooking time **50 minutes** serves **4**

2 tablespoons olive oil
1 medium brown onion (150g), chopped
1 clove garlic, crushed
2 bacon rashers (140g), chopped finely
1 small carrot (70g), chopped finely
1 celery stalk, chopped
300g button mushrooms, chopped
500g minced beef
440g can tomato soup
2 tablespoons tomato paste
¼ cup (60ml) tomato sauce
½ teaspoon dried oregano leaves
150g spiral pasta
1 cup (125g) grated cheddar

1 Preheat oven to moderate.
2 Heat oil in large frying pan, add onion, garlic and bacon; cook, stirring, until onion is soft. Add carrot, celery and mushrooms; cook 3 minutes.
3 Add mince; cook, stirring, until well browned. Add undiluted soup, paste, sauce and oregano; simmer, covered, 20 minutes, stirring occasionally.
4 Cook pasta in large saucepan of boiling water, uncovered, until just tender; drain. Combine pasta and mince mixture, transfer to a 2-litre (8-cup) ovenproof dish; top with cheese. Bake in moderate oven about 15 minutes or until cheese is melted and lightly browned.

Tagliatelle puttanesca

preparation time **10 minutes** cooking time **20 minutes** serves **4**

2 teaspoons vegetable oil
1 large brown onion (200g), sliced thickly
3 cloves garlic, crushed
4 fresh red thai chillies, chopped finely
600ml bottled tomato pasta sauce
¼ cup (40g) drained capers
1 cup (160g) kalamata olives, seeded
8 drained anchovy fillets, halved
½ cup coarsely chopped fresh flat-leaf parsley
375g tagliatelle

1 Heat oil in large frying pan; cook onion, garlic and chilli, stirring, until onion softens. Add sauce, capers, olives and anchovies. Bring to a boil then reduce heat; simmer, uncovered, about 5 minutes or until sauce thickens slightly. Stir in parsley.
2 Cook pasta in large saucepan of boiling water, uncovered, until just tender; drain. Serve pasta with sauce.

Pasta with broccoli and anchovies

preparation time **10 minutes** cooking time **8 minutes** serves **4**

375g tagliatelle
600g broccoli, chopped coarsely
⅓ cup (80ml) extra virgin olive oil
2 cloves garlic, crushed
4 drained anchovy fillets, chopped
½ teaspoon dried chilli flakes

1 Cook pasta in large saucepan of boiling water, uncovered, until almost tender. Add broccoli; boil with pasta about 4 minutes or until both are tender. Drain
2 Heat oil in medium frying pan; cook garlic, anchovy and chilli until fragrant.
3 Combine anchovy mixture with pasta and broccoli; toss well.

Ravioli salad with spicy dressing

preparation time **10 minutes** cooking time **10 minutes** serves **2**

500g ravioli
125g cherry tomatoes
1 large (320g) avocado, chopped
1 medium (170g) red onion, chopped
¼ cup firmly packed fresh coriander leaves

Spicy dressing
¼ cup (60ml) vegetable oil
1 tablespoon white vinegar
¼ cup (60ml) mild sweet chilli sauce
1 clove garlic, crushed

1 Cook pasta in large saucepan of boiling water, uncovered, until just tender; drain. Rinse under cold water; drain.
2 Place ingredients for spicy dressing in screw-top jar; shake well.
3 Combine pasta with tomatoes, avocado, onion, coriander and spicy dressing in bowl; toss gently to combine.

Spaghetti bolognese

preparation time **15 minutes** cooking time **2 hours 15 minutes** serves **4**

2 tablespoons olive oil
1 large brown onion (200g), chopped finely
2 cloves garlic, crushed
750g minced beef
2 x 400g cans tomatoes
⅓ cup (95g) tomato paste
1 litre (4 cups) water
1 tablepoon finely shredded fresh basil
1 tablespoon finely chopped fresh oregano
375g spaghetti
Grated parmesan

1 Heat oil in medium frying pan; cook onion and garlic until soft. Add mince to pan; cook until mince is browned all over, mashing with fork occasionally to break up any lumps.
2 Push tomatoes with liquid through sieve; add to pan. Add paste and the

water. Bring to a boil then reduce heat; cook, very gently, uncovered, about 2 hours or until nearly all liquid is evaporated. Stir in herbs.

3 Cook pasta in large saucepan of boiling water, uncovered, until tender; drain.

4 Place pasta in individual serving bowls; top with sauce. Sprinkle with cheese.

tips Store single portions of bolognese in well-sealed containers; freeze up to three months.

Ricotta and spinach stuffed pasta shells

preparation time **10 minutes** cooking time **1 hour 10 minutes** serves **4**

Large pasta shells, also known as conchiglioni, are available from gourmet delicatessens; you can use 16 cannelloni shells instead.

32 large pasta shells (280g)
500g spinach
250g low-fat ricotta
500g low-fat cottage cheese
600ml tomato pasta sauce
1 cup (250ml) vegetable stock
1 tablespoon finely grated parmesan

1 Cook pasta in large saucepan of boiling water, uncovered, 3 minutes; drain. Cool slightly.

2 Preheat oven to moderate.

3 Boil, steam or microwave spinach until just wilted; drain. Chop spinach finely; squeeze out excess liquid.

4 Combine spinach in large bowl with cheeses; spoon mixture into pasta shells.

5 Combine sauce and stock in oiled 2-litre (8-cup) ovenproof dish. Place pasta shells in dish; sprinkle with parmesan.

6 Bake, covered, in moderate oven about 1 hour or until pasta is tender.

Spaghetti napoletana

preparation time **5 minutes** cooking time **25 minutes** serves **4**

2 teaspoons olive oil
1 small brown onion (80g), chopped finely
3 cloves garlic, crushed
2 x 400g cans tomatoes
¼ cup coarsely chopped fresh basil
⅓ cup coarsely chopped fresh flat-leaf parsley
375g spaghetti

1 Heat oil in medium saucepan; cook onion and garlic, stirring, until soft.
2 Add undrained crushed tomatoes, bring to a boil, then reduce heat; simmer, uncovered, about 20 minutes or until reduced by about a third. Stir in basil and parsley.
3 Meanwhile, cook pasta in large saucepan of boiling water, uncovered, until just tender; drain. Serve pasta topped with sauce.

Spaghetti alla vongole

preparation time **30 minutes** (plus soaking time) cooking time **40 minutes** serves **6**

1.5kg clams
1 tablespoon coarse cooking salt
¼ cup (60ml) olive oil
1 medium brown onion (150g), chopped finely
2 cloves garlic, crushed
2 anchovy fillets, drained, chopped finely
1 fresh red thai chilli, seeded, chopped finely
2 teaspoons chopped fresh thyme
20 medium egg tomatoes (1.5kg), peeled, seeded, chopped finely
2 tablespoons chopped fresh flat-leaf parsley
500g spaghetti

1 Rinse clams under cold water and place in large bowl. Sprinkle with salt, cover with cold water and soak for 2 hours (this purges them of any grit). Discard water, then rinse clams thoroughly; drain.
2 Heat 2 tablespoons of the oil in large saucepan; add clams, cover with tight-fitting lid. Cook over high heat about 8 minutes or until all clams have opened.

3 Strain clam cooking liquid through fine cloth or tea-towel. Return liquid to clean pan; cook, uncovered, until liquid is reduced to 1 cup (250ml). Reserve clam stock.

4 Heat remaining oil in another saucepan; add onion, garlic, anchovy, chilli and thyme. Cook, stirring, until onion is soft. Add tomato and reserved clam stock; cook, uncovered, about 10 minutes or until sauce is thickened. Add clams, stir until hot. Stir in parsley.

5 Meanwhile, cook pasta in large saucepan of boiling water, uncovered, until just tender; drain. Toss clam sauce through spaghetti.

Spaghetti and meatballs

preparation time **15 minutes**   cooking time **20 minutes**   serves **4**

500g pork mince
2 tablespoons coarsely chopped fresh flat-leaf parsley
1 clove garlic, crushed
1 egg
1 cup (70g) stale breadcrumbs
1 tablespoon tomato paste
2 tablespoons olive oil
400g can tomatoes
600ml bottled tomato pasta sauce
375g spaghetti
1/3 cup (25g) finely grated romano

1 Combine pork, parsley, garlic, egg, breadcrumbs and paste in large bowl; roll tablespoons of pork mixture into balls. Heat oil in large saucepan; cook meatballs, in batches, until browned all over.

2 Place undrained crushed tomatoes and sauce in same pan; bring to a boil. Return meatballs to pan, reduce heat; simmer, uncovered, about 10 minutes or until meatballs are cooked through.

3 Meanwhile, cook pasta in large saucepan of boiling water, uncovered, until just tender; drain. Divide pasta among serving bowls; top with meatballs, sprinkle with cheese.

tip Double the meatball quantities and freeze half of them after frying. Thaw meatballs overnight in refrigerator before adding to the sauce.

Bucatini with baked ricotta

preparation time **5 minutes** cooking time **20 minutes** serves **4**

2 x 270g jars marinated eggplant in oil
2 cloves garlic, crushed
375g bucatini
2 x 400g cans tomatoes
½ teaspoon cracked black pepper
300g baked ricotta, chopped coarsely

1 Cook undrained eggplant and garlic in large saucepan, stirring, until fragrant.
2 Meanwhile, cook pasta in large saucepan of boiling water, uncovered, until just tender; drain.
3 Stir pasta, undrained crushed tomatoes and pepper into eggplant mixture; toss over medium heat until combined, gently stir in ricotta.

Orecchiette with ham, artichokes and sun-dried tomatoes

preparation time **10 minutes** cooking time **15 minutes** serves **4**

375g orecchiette
500g leg ham, sliced thickly
400g can artichoke hearts in oil, drained, quartered
½ cup (75g) sun-dried tomatoes, halved
1 cup (80g) flaked parmesan
1 cup loosely packed fresh flat-leaf parsley
2 tablespoons lemon juice
1 tablespoon wholegrain mustard
1 tablespoon honey
1 clove garlic, crushed
½ cup (125ml) olive oil

1 Cook pasta in large saucepan of boiling water, uncovered, until just tender; drain.
2 Place pasta in large bowl with ham, artichoke, tomato, cheese, parsley and combined remaining ingredients; toss gently to combine.

Rigatoni with spicy pork sausages

preparation time **15 minutes** cooking time **15 minutes** serves **4**

300g thin spicy pork sausages
375g rigatoni
1 medium brown onion (150g), chopped finely
1 clove garlic, crushed
500g tomato and basil pasta sauce
½ cup (75g) seeded black olives
100g baby rocket leaves
⅓ cup (25g) grated parmesan

1 Cook sausages in large non-stick frying pan until browned all over and cooked through. Remove from pan, drain on absorbent paper. Slice thickly.
2 Meanwhile, cook pasta in large saucepan of boiling water, uncovered, until just tender. Reserve ½ cup (125ml) of the cooking liquid; drain pasta.
3 Cook onion and garlic in same frying pan until soft. Add pasta sauce, sausages and olives; simmer, uncovered, until hot.
4 Combine pasta, sauce and reserved cooking liquid in pan or warmed serving bowl; toss well. Add rocket; toss gently.
5 Serve pasta topped with parmesan.

tips Spciy beef or lamb sausages can also be used inthis recipe. Penne or tortoglioni can be used instead of rigatoni.

Cheese and spinach tortellini with gorgonzola sauce

preparation time **10 minutes** cooking time **10 minutes** serves **4**

750g cheese and spinach tortellini
30g butter
2 tablespoons plain flour
1 cup (250ml) milk
¾ cup (180ml) cream
100g gorgonzola, chopped coarsely
¼ cup loosely packed fresh flat-leaf parsley

1 Cook pasta in large saucepan of boiling water, uncovered, until just tender.
2 Meanwhile, melt butter in medium saucepan, add flour; cook, stirring, about 2 minutes or until mixture thickens and bubbles.
3 Gradually stir in milk and cream. Bring to a boil then reduce heat; simmer, uncovered, until sauce boils and thickens. Remove from heat; stir in cheese.
4 Combine drained pasta and sauce; sprinkle with parsley to serve.

tip You can substitute ravioli or gnocchi for the tortellini, if you prefer.

Bow ties and salmon in lemon sauce

preparation time **5 minutes** cooking time **20 minutes** serves **4**

375g bow tie pasta
1 medium lemon (140g)
415g can red salmon, drained, flaked
½ cup (125ml) cream
4 green onions, sliced thinly

1 Cook pasta in large saucepan of boiling water, uncovered, until just tender; drain.
2 Meanwhile, using zester, remove rind from lemon; squeeze juice from lemon. Place rind, juice and pasta in large saucepan with remaining ingredients; stir over low heat until hot.
3 Divide among serving bowls; sprinkle with grated parmesan, if desired.

Quick and easy lasagne

preparation time **25 minutes** cooking time **1 hour** serves **6**

1 tablespoon olive oil
1 medium brown onion (150g), chopped
1 clove garlic, crushed
500g minced beef
3 cups (750ml) bottled pasta sauce
16 instant lasagne pasta sheets
500g ricotta
½ cup (125ml) milk
250g mozzarella, grated
½ cup (125ml) cream
¼ cup (20g) grated parmesan

1 Preheat oven to moderate.
2 Heat oil in pan, add onion and garlic; cook, stirring, until onion is soft. Add mince; cook, stirring, until well browned. Stir in pasta sauce; cook until hot. Remove from heat.
3 Line oiled shallow 20cm x 30cm ovenproof dish with layer of pasta, top with one-third of meat mixture. Spread with one-third of combined ricotta and milk, sprinkle with one-third of mozzarella. Repeat layering, finishing with pasta; pour over cream, sprinkle with parmesan.
4 Bake, covered, in moderate oven 30 minutes. Remove cover, bake further 10 minutes or until top of lasagne is bubbling and browned.

Ravioli with spinach and sage

preparation time **15 minutes** cooking time **10 minutes** serves **4**

500g ricotta and spinach ravioli
300ml cream
¼ cup (20g) finely grated parmesan
100g baby spinach leaves
1 tablespoon small sage leaves
2 tablespoons toasted pine nuts
2 tablespoons parmesan flakes

1 Cook pasta in large saucepan of boiling water, uncovered, until tender; drain.
2 Meanwhile, place cream and grated parmesan in small saucepan. Bring to a boil then reduce heat; simmer, uncovered, about 5 minutes or until mixture thickens.
3 Toss pasta with cream mixture, spinach and sage; season with salt and freshly ground black pepper.
4 Divide among serving plates, top with nuts and parmesan flakes.

Creamy tomato pesto tortellini

preparation time **10 minutes** cooking time **20 minutes** serves **6**

1kg spinach and ricotta tortellini
⅓ cup (90g) red pesto
300ml cream
2 tablespoons shredded fresh basil
½ cup (40g) finely grated parmesan

1 Cook pasta in large saucepan of boiling water, uncovered, until just tender; drain.
2 Combine pesto, cream and basil in large frying pan. Bring to a boil then reduce heat; simmer, uncovered, 5 minutes. Add pasta to sauce; toss to combine. Serve topped with cheese.

Chicken and asparagus pasta salad

preparation time **10 minutes** cooking time **15 minutes** serves **4**

500g macaroni
250g asparagus, chopped coarsely
3 cups (480g) shredded cooked chicken
200g button mushrooms, sliced
1/3 cup coarsely chopped fresh chives

Dressing
1/3 cup (80g) sour cream
1/2 cup (150g) whole-egg mayonnaise
1 tablespoon lemon juice
1 tablespoon wholegrain mustard

1 Cook pasta in large saucepan of boiling water, uncovered, until just tender; drain.
2 Meanwhile, boil, steam or microwave asparagus until just tender; drain.
3 Combine ingredients fro dressing in small jug or bowl.
4 Combine pasta, asparagus, chicken, mushrooms and chives in large bowl; add dressing, toss gently.

tip Macaroni can be replaced with penne, bowties or spiral pasta.

Crunchy-topped tuna pasta

preparation time **20 minutes** cooking time **1 hour** serves **4**

250g macaroni
20g butter
1 small brown onion (80g), chopped
2 tablespoons plain flour
3 cups (750ml) milk
400g can tuna in brine, undrained
1½ cups (185g) grated cheddar
1 tablespoon coarsely chopped fresh parsley
6 slices white bread
80g butter, melted, extra
1 clove garlic, crushed

1 Preheat oven to moderate.
2 Cook pasta in large saucepan of boiling water, uncovered, until just tender; drain.
3 Heat butter in large pan, add onion and cook, stirring, until soft. Add flour and cook, stirring, until mixture bubbles. Remove from heat, gradually stir in milk; stir over heat until sauce boils and thickens.
4 Combine pasta, sauce, tuna, 1 cup of cheese and parsley in a large bowl. Season with freshly ground black pepper. Transfer pasta mixture to oiled 1.5-litre (6-cup capacity) ovenproof dish; sprinkle top with remaining cheese.
5 Remove crusts from bread and cut into cubes. Combine bread, extra butter and garlic in bowl; toss until coated. Sprinkle bread over pasta. Bake, covered, in moderate oven 20 minutes; uncover, bake further 20 minutes or until browned.

Tagliatelle, chicken and peas in mustard cream sauce

preparation time **10 minutes** cooking time **30 minutes** serves **4**

250g tagliatelle
1 tablespoon olive oil
1 medium brown onion (150g), chopped finely
2 cloves garlic, crushed
½ cup (125ml) dry white wine
1 tablespoon dijon mustard
1 cup (250ml) cream
2 cups (250g) frozen peas, thawed
2 cups (320g) shredded cooked chicken
¼ cup finely chopped fresh garlic chives

1 Cook pasta in large saucepan of boiling water, uncovered, until just tender; drain.
2 Meanwhile, heat oil in large saucepan; cook onion and garlic, stirring, until onion softens. Add wine and mustard. Bring to a boil then reduce heat; simmer, uncovered, 5 minutes. Stir in cream; return mixture to a boil then simmer again, uncovered, about 5 minutes or until sauce thickens slightly.
3 Stir in drained peas and chicken; stir over low heat until mixture is hot.
4 Place pasta and chives in pan with chicken and pea sauce; toss to combine.

Cauliflower chilli spaghetti

preparation time **15 minutes** cooking time **15 minutes** serves **4 to 6**

¼ cup (60ml) extra virgin olive oil
700g small cauliflower florets
375g spaghetti
⅓ cup (50g) pine nuts, chopped
2 cloves garlic, crushed
6 drained anchovies, chopped
½ teaspoon dried chilli flakes
1 tablespoon lemon juice
¼ cup coarsely chopped flat-leaf parsley
2 tablespoons extra virgin olive oil, extra

1 Heat oil in large frying pan; cook cauliflower, stirring, for about 10 minutes or until just tender and browned lightly.
2 Meanwhile, cook pasta in large saucepan of boiling water, uncovered, until just tender; drain.
3 Add pine nuts to pasta; cook, stirring, until nuts are browned lightly. Add garlic, anchovies and chilli to cauliflower mixture; cook, stirring, until mixture is fragrant. Stir in juice and parsley.
4 Toss cauliflower mixture with spaghetti and extra oil.

Macaroni cheese

preparation time **5 minutes** cooking time **30 minutes** serves **4**

250g elbow macaroni
60g butter
⅓ cup (50g) plain flour
3 cups (750ml) milk
2 cups (250g) pizza cheese

1 Cook pasta in large saucepan of boiling water, uncovered, until just tender; drain.
2 Meanwhile, melt butter in medium saucepan, add flour; cook, stirring, about 2 minutes or until mixture bubbles and thickens. Gradually stir in milk; cook, stirring, until sauce boils and thickens.

3 Stir pasta and 1 cup of cheese into sauce; pour mixture into shallow 2-litre (8-cup) baking dish. Sprinkle with remaining cheese; place under preheated grill until cheese melts and top is browned lightly.

Pasta primavera

preparation time **15 minutes**   cooking time **15 minutes**   serves **4**

375g small spirals
1 tablespoon olive oil
1 medium brown onion (150g), chopped finely
3 cloves garlic, crushed
300g yellow patty-pan squash, quartered
1 medium red capsicum (200g), sliced thinly
200g sugar snap peas
1 medium carrot (120g), cut into ribbons
300ml cream
1 tablespoon wholegrain mustard
2 tablespoons coarsely chopped fresh flat-leaf parsley

1 Cook pasta in large saucepan of boiling water, uncovered, until just tender; drain.
2 While pasta is cooking, heat oil in large saucepan; cook onion and garlic, stirring, until onion softens. Add squash; cook, stirring, until just tender. Add capsicum, peas and carrot; cook, stirring, until capsicum is just tender.
3 Place pasta in pan with vegetables, add combined remaining ingredients; stir over low heat until just hot.

Tomato and tortellini salad

preparation time **10 minutes** cooking time **25 minutes** serves **2**

400g tortellini
125g broccoli, chopped coarsely
3 bacon rashers, chopped coarsely
250g cherry tomatoes
2 tablespoons coarsely chopped fresh chives

Dressing
¼ cup (60ml) olive oil
2 tablespoons white vinegar
1 clove garlic, crushed

1 Cook pasta in large pan of boiling water, uncovered, until just tender; drain. Rinse under cold water; drain well.
2 Boil, steam or microwave broccoli until just tender, rinse under cold water; drain.
3 Cook bacon in small pan, stirring, until browned and crisp; drain on absorbent paper.
4 Place dressing ingredients in screw-top jar; shake well.
5 Combine tortellini, broccoli, bacon, tomatoes and chives in medium bowl, add dressing; mix well.

Creamy pasta with ham and peas

preparation time **5 minutes** cooking time **15 minutes** serves **4**

500g rigatoni
1 tablespoon olive oil
200g sliced smoked leg ham, chopped coarsely
1 medium brown onion (150g), sliced thinly
1 clove garlic, crushed
300ml cream
1 cup (125g) frozen peas
¾ cup (60g) flaked parmesan

1 Cook pasta, uncovered, in large saucepan of boiling well-salted water, until just tender.

2 Reserve ¼ cup (60ml) of cooking liquid; drain pasta and return to pan.
3 Meanwhile, heat oil in large frying pan, add ham; cook, stirring, until crisp. Remove from pan. Add onion and garlic to same pan, cook, stirring, until onion is soft.
4 Add cream, peas and reserved liquid to pan. Bring to the boil then reduce heat; simmer, uncovered, until sauce is slightly thickened.
5 Add sauce, ham and half the cheese to pasta; toss gently to combine. Serve sprinkled with remaining cheese; season with freshly ground black pepper.

Chicken, broccoli and pasta bake

preparation **10 minutes** cooking time **30 minutes** serves **4**

250g small rigatoni
2 cups (170g) small broccoli florets
3 cups (480g) shredded cooked chicken
½ cup (30g) semi-dried tomatoes, chopped coarsely
4 green onions, chopped finely
300g sour cream
½ cup (125ml) chicken stock
2 tablespoons wholegrain mustard
1 clove garlic, crushed
½ cup (50g) grated mozzarella
½ cup (40g) grated parmesan

1 Preheat oven to moderately hot.
2 Cook pasta, uncovered, in large saucepan of boiling water until almost tender. Add broccoli; cook, uncovered, about 4 minutes or until both are tender, drain.
3 Combine pasta and broccoli with chicken, tomato and onion in large bowl. Stir in combined cream, stock, mustard and garlic. Season to taste with salt and freshly ground black pepper.
4 Pour pasta mixture into 1.5 litre (6-cup) ovenproof dish. Top with combined cheeses. Bake in moderately hot oven about 20 minutes or until browned.

Chow mein

preparation time **30 minutes** cooking time **25 minutes** serves **4**

1 tablespoon vegetable oil
500g lean beef mince
1 medium brown onion (150g), chopped finely
2 cloves garlic, crushed
1 tablespoon curry powder
1 large carrot (180g), chopped finely
2 trimmed celery stalks (200g), sliced thinly
150g mushrooms, sliced thinly
1 cup (250ml) chicken stock
⅓ cup (80ml) oyster sauce
2 tablespoons soy sauce
450g fresh thin egg noodles
½ cup (60g) frozen peas
½ cup (55g) frozen sliced green beans
½ small chinese cabbage (400g), shredded coarsely

1 Heat oil in wok; stir-fry mince, onion and garlic until mince is browned. Add curry powder; stir-fry about 1 minute or until fragrant. Add carrot, celery and mushrooms; stir-fry until vegetables soften.
2 Add stock, sauces and noodles, stir-fry gently until combined; bring to a boil. Add peas, beans and cabbage, reduce heat; simmer, uncovered, tossing occasionally, about 5 minutes or until vegetables are just soft.

Pad thai

preparation time **20 minutes** (plus standing time) cooking time **10 minutes**
serves **4**

2 tablespoons tamarind concentrate
2 tablespoons grated palm sugar
⅓ cup (80ml) sweet chilli sauce
⅓ cup (80ml) fish sauce
375g rice stick noodles
12 uncooked medium prawns (500g)
2 cloves garlic, crushed
2 tablespoons finely chopped preserved turnip
2 tablespoons dried shrimp
1 tablespoon grated fresh ginger
2 fresh small red thai chillies, chopped coarsely
1 tablespoon peanut oil
250g pork mince
3 eggs, beaten lightly
2 cups (160g) bean sprouts
4 green onions, sliced thinly
⅓ cup coarsely chopped fresh coriander
¼ cup (35g) coarsely chopped toasted unsalted peanuts
1 lime, quartered

1 Combine tamarind, sugar and sauces in small bowl; reserve.
2 Meanwhile, place noodles in large heatproof bowl, cover with boiling water; stand until noodles just soften, drain.
3 Shell and devein prawns, leaving tails intact.
4 Blend or process garlic, turnip, shrimp, ginger and chilli to a paste.
5 Heat oil in wok; stir-fry spice paste until fragrant. Add pork; stir-fry until just cooked through. Add prawns; stir-fry 1 minute. Add egg; stir-fry until egg sets. Add noodles, tamarind mixture, sprouts and half the onion; stir-fry, tossing gently until combined. Remove from heat; toss remaining onion, coriander and nuts through pad thai. Serve with lime wedges.

Singapore noodles

preparation time **15 minutes** cooking time **10 minutes** serves **12**

200g thin dried noodles
2 tablespoons peanut oil
250g beef rump steak, sliced thinly
1 small brown onion (100g), sliced thinly
2 fresh long red chillies, chopped finely
1 medium red capsicum (200g), sliced thinly
1 tablespoon mild curry paste
4 green onions, sliced thinly
200g bean sprouts
100g snow peas, sliced thinly
200g chinese barbecue pork, chopped
2 tablespoons oyster sauce
⅓ cup (80ml) soy sauce

1 Cook noodles in large saucepan of boiling water, uncovered, until just tender; drain.

2 Meanwhile, heat half the oil in hot wok; stir-fry beef in batches until just tender. Remove from wok.

3 Reheat wok, add remaining oil. Stir-fry onion, chilli and capsicum about 1 minute or until softened. Add paste and stir-fry until fragrant.

4 Add green onion, sprouts, snow peas and pork; stir-fry 1 minute. Return beef to wok with sauces and noodles. Stir-fry until well combined and hot.

Hokkien mee noodles

preparation time **15 minutes** cooking time **5 minutes** serves **4**

600g hokkien noodles
2 tablespoons vegetable oil
2 cloves garlic, crushed
2 teaspoons grated fresh ginger
1 large red capsicum (350g), sliced thinly
1 bunch baby bok choy (500g), chopped coarsely
6 green onions, chopped coarsely
1 cup (80g) bean sprouts
1 teaspoon cornflour
⅓ cup (80ml) kecap manis
2 tablespoons sweet chilli sauce
1 teaspoon sesame oil
1 tablespoon water

1 Place noodles in large heatproof bowl, cover with boiling water; separate with fork, drain.
2 Meanwhile, heat vegetable oil in wok; stir-fry garlic, ginger, capsicum and bok choy 2 minutes or until vegetables are almost tender.
3 Add onion, sprouts and noodles; stir to combine. Blend cornflour with kecap manis, sauce, sesame oil and the water. Add to wok; cook, stirring, until mixture boils and thickens slightly.

tip You could substitute chinese cabbage or any other asian green for the baby bok choy if not available.

Chiang mai noodles

preparation time **20 minutes** cooking time **20 minutes** serves **4**

Vegetable oil, for deep-frying
500g fresh egg noodles
1 large brown onion (200g), sliced thinly
2 green onions, sliced thinly
¼ cup loosely packed fresh coriander leaves
¼ cup (75g) red curry paste
2 cloves garlic, crushed
¼ teaspoon ground turmeric
2 cups (500ml) water
400ml can coconut milk
500g chicken breast fillets, sliced thinly
¼ cup (60ml) fish sauce
1 tablespoon soy sauce
2 tablespoons grated palm sugar
2 teaspoons lime juice
2 tablespoons coarsely chopped fresh coriander
1 fresh long red thai chilli, sliced thinly

1 Heat oil in wok; deep-fry about 100g of noodles, in batches, until crisp. Drain on absorbent paper.

2 Using same heated oil, deep-fry brown onion, in batches, until lightly browned and crisp. Drain on absorbent paper. Combine fried noodles, fried onion, green onion and coriander leaves in small bowl. Cool oil; remove from wok and reserve for another use.

3 Place remaining noodles in large heatproof bowl, cover with boiling water; separate with fork, drain.

4 Cook paste, garlic and turmeric in same cleaned wok; add the water and coconut milk. Bring to a boil then reduce heat; simmer, stirring, 2 minutes. Add chicken; cook, stirring, about 5 minutes or until chicken is cooked through. Add sauces, sugar and juice; cook, stirring, until sugar dissolves. Stir in chopped coriander.

5 Divide drained noodles among serving bowls; spoon chicken curry mixture into each bowl, top with fried noodle mixture. Sprinkle chilli slices over bowls.

Char kway teow

preparation time **25 minutes** cooking time **10 minutes** serves **6**

1kg fresh rice noodles
500g uncooked small prawns
2 tablespoons peanut oil
340g chicken breast fillets, chopped coarsely
4 fresh red thai chillies, chopped finely
2 cloves garlic, crushed
2 teaspoons grated fresh ginger
5 green onions, sliced thinly
2 cups (160g) bean sprouts
1/3 cup (80ml) soy sauce
1/4 teaspoon sesame oil
1 teaspoon brown sugar

1 Place noodles in large heatproof bowl, cover with boiling water; separate with fork, drain.
2 Shell and devein prawns, leaving tails intact; halve prawns crossways.
3 Heat 1 tablespoon of peanut oil in wok; stir-fry chicken, chilli, garlic and ginger until chicken is cooked through. Remove from wok.
4 Heat remaining peanut oil in wok; stir-fry prawns until they just change colour. Remove from wok. Stir-fry onion and sprouts in wok until onion is soft. Add noodles and combined remaining ingredients; stir-fry 1 minute.
5 Return chicken mixture and prawns to wok; stir-fry until hot.

Rice noodles with beef and black bean sauce

preparation time **15 minutes** cooking time **15 minutes** serves **4**

250g dried rice stick noodles
1 tablespoon peanut oil
400g beef mince
1 medium onion (150g), sliced thinly
2 medium red chillies, sliced thinly
350g choy sum, chopped coarsely
150g sugar snap peas, trimmed
2 tablespoons black bean sauce
2 tablespoons sweet soy sauce
⅓ cup (80ml) beef stock
4 green onions, sliced thinly

1 Place noodles in large heatproof bowl, cover with boiling water, stand 5 minutes; drain.
2 Meanwhile, heat oil in wok; stir-fry mince, onion and chilli 5 minutes or until mince is browned and cooked through.
3 Add choy sum and peas; stir-fry until just tender.
4 Add noodles and combined sauces, stock and green onions. Stir-fry until combined and hot.

tip This dish is not suitable to freeze or microwave.

Mee goreng

preparation time **15 minutes** cooking time **15 minutes** serves **4**

600g hokkien noodles
1 tablespoon peanut oil
3 eggs, beaten lightly
500g beef strips
2 cloves garlic, crushed
2cm piece fresh ginger (10g), grated
500g baby bok choy, chopped coarsely
4 green onions, sliced thinly
¼ cup coarsely chopped fresh coriander
¼ cup (60ml) kecap manis
2 teaspoons chilli paste
¼ cup (60ml) beef stock
½ cup (75g) toasted unsalted peanuts

1 Place noodles in large heatproof bowl; cover with boiling water, separate with fork, drain.
2 Heat a quarter of the oil in wok; cook half the egg, tilting pan, until egg mixture is almost set. Remove omelette from wok; repeat with another quarter of the oil and remaining egg. Roll omelettes; slice thinly.
3 Heat remaining oil in same wok; stir-fry beef, garlic and ginger, in batches, until beef is browned all over. Place bok choy in same wok; stir-fry until just wilted. Return beef mixture to wok with noodles, onion, coriander and combined kecap manis, chilli paste and stock; stir-fry until hot.
4 Serve topped with omelette and peanuts.

tip You could substitute chinese cabbage or any other asian green for the baby bok choy if not available.

Pasta toppings

Each of the following five recipes will top 500g spaghetti, fettuccine, tagliatelle or penne, cooked in a large saucepan of boiling water, uncovered, until tender.

Traditional tapenade

makes ½ **cup (125g)**

1 tablespoon drained capers
3 anchovy fillets, drained
½ cup (60g) seeded black olives
¼ cup (60ml) extra virgin olive oil

1 Blend or process combined ingredients until smooth.

Sun-dried tomato and olive tapenade

makes 1 **cup (250g)**

¾ cup (105g) sun-dried tomatoes
⅓ cup (80ml) extra virgin olive oil
2 tablespoons red wine vinegar
1 tablespoon brown sugar
1 tablespoon coarsely chopped fresh oregano
⅔ cup (70g) toasted pecans
⅓ cup (50g) seeded black olives

1 Blend or process combined ingredients until smooth.

Coriander pesto

makes ⅔ **cup (175g)**

2 tablespoons unsalted toasted peanuts
½ cup firmly packed fresh coriander leaves
2 cloves garlic, quartered
½ cup (125ml) peanut oil

1 Blend or process combined ingredients until smooth.

Traditional pesto

makes 1 ¼ cups (310g)

2 cups firmly packed fresh basil leaves
½ cup (80g) toasted pine nuts
2 cloves garlic, crushed
½ cup (125ml) olive oil
½ cup (25g) grated parmesan

1 Process basil, nuts and garlic until finely chopped.
2 With moter operating, add oil in thin stream; process until combined.
3 Add cheese, process mixture until well combined.

Mint pistachio pesto

makes 1 cup (220g)

1 cup firmly packed fresh mint leaves
⅓ cup (50g) toasted pistachios
⅓ cup (25g) coarsely grated parmesan
2 cloves garlic, quartered
1 tablespoon lemon juice
¼ cup (60ml) olive oil
2 tablespoons water, approximately

1 Blend or process mint, nuts, cheese, garlic and juice until almost smooth.
2 With motor operating, gradually add oil and just enough water to give pesto desired consistency.

GRAINS AND LEGUMES

Mixed mushroom risotto

preparation time **15 minutes** cooking time **40 minutes** serves **4**

1 litre (4 cups) chicken stock
1 ½ cups (375ml) water
40g butter
2 tablespoons olive oil
2 medium brown onions (300g), chopped finely
200g mixed mushrooms, sliced thinly
2 cups (400g) arborio rice
1 cup (80g) finely grated parmesan

1 Bring stock and the water to a boil in medium saucepan; reduce heat, cover, keep hot.
2 Heat butter and oil in large saucepan; cook onion and mushrooms, stirring, until onion is soft. Add rice; stir to coat in oil mixture. Stir in 1 cup (250ml) of the stock mixture; cook over low heat, stirring, until liquid is absorbed.
3 Continue adding stock mixture, in 1-cup batches, stirring after each addition until liquid is absorbed. Total cooking time should be about 35 minutes or until rice is just tender. Stir in cheese to serve.

Asparagus risotto

preparation time **15 minutes** cooking time **45 minutes** serves **4**

500g fresh asparagus
30g butter
1 tablespoon olive oil
1 large brown onion (200g), chopped
1 clove garlic, crushed
1 ¾ cups (350g) arborio rice
3 cups (750ml) vegetable stock
3 cups (750ml) water
¾ cup (60g) grated parmesan
2 tablespoons chopped fresh flat-leaf parsley

1 Cut asparagus into 2.5cm lengths. Boil, steam or microwave asparagus until just tender; drain, rinse under cold water, drain well.
2 Heat butter and oil in large saucepan, add onion and garlic; cook, stirring, until onion is soft. Add rice, stir to coat in oil mixture.
3 Meanwhile, combine stock and the water in another saucepan, bring to a boil; keep hot. Stir 1 cup (250ml) hot stock mixture into rice mixture; cook, stirring, over low heat until liquid is absorbed. Continue adding stock mixture, in 1-cup batches, stirring after each addition until liquid is absorbed. Total cooking time should be about 35 minutes or until rice is tender. Stir in asparagus, cheese and parsley; stir until hot.

serving suggestions Risotto can be served with grilled chicken breast fillets or salmon steakds.

Oven-baked risotto with italian-style sausages

preparation time **15 minutes** cooking time **40 minutes** serves **6**

1 litre (4 cups) chicken stock
6 spicy italian-style sausages (500g)
1 tablespoon olive oil
40g butter
2 large brown onions (400g), chopped
1 clove garlic, crushed
2 cups (400g) arborio rice
¾ cup (180ml) dry white wine
1 cup (160g) drained semi-dried tomatoes
¼ cup fresh basil leaves
¼ cup (20g) grated parmesan

1 Preheat oven to moderate.
2 Add stock to medium saucepan; bring to the boil.
3 Meanwhile, heat 2-litre (8-cup) flameproof dish on stove top; add sausages and cook until browned all over and cooked through. Remove from dish; slice thickly.
4 Heat oil and butter in same dish; cook onion and garlic, stirring, until soft. Add rice; stir to coat in onion mixture. Add wine, bring to the boil then reduce heat; simmer, uncovered, for 1 minute. Add stock, sausages and tomatoes; cover with lid and cook in moderate oven about 25 minutes or until liquid is absorbed and rice is just tender. Stir once during cooking time.
5 Gently stir in basil and cheese.

Roasted pumpkin and spinach risotto

preparation time **15 minutes** cooking time **45 minutes** serves **4**

500g pumpkin, chopped coarsely
2 tablespoons olive oil
1.25 litres (5 cups) water
1½ cups (375ml) vegetable stock
1 large brown onions (200g), chopped coarsely
2 cloves garlic, crushed
2 cups (400g) arborio rice
½ cup (125ml) dry white wine
250g spinach, chopped coarsely
½ cup (80g) toasted pine nuts
½ cup (40g) finely grated parmesan
½ cup (125ml) cream

1 Preheat oven to hot.
2 Combine pumpkin and half the oil in medium baking dish; roast, uncovered, in hot oven about 20 minutes or until tender.
3 Meanwhile, combine the water and stock in large saucepan; bring to a boil then reduce heat, simmer, covered.
4 Heat remaining oil in large saucepan; cook onion and garlic, stirring, until onion softens. Add rice; stir to coat rice in oil mixture. Add wine; cook, stirring, until liquid is almost evaporated. Stir in 1 cup (250ml) hot stock mixture; cook, stirring, over low heat until liquid is absorbed. Continue adding stock mixture, in 1-cup batches, stirring after each addition until liquid is absorbed. Total cooking time should be about 35 minutes or until rice is just tender.
5 Add spinach, nuts, cheese and cream to risotto; cook, stirring, until spinach wilts. Add pumpkin; stir gently.

Risotto milanese

preparation time **15 minutes** cooking time **40 minutes** serves **2**

3 cups (750ml) chicken stock
½ cup (125ml) dry white wine
¼ teaspoon saffron
50g butter
1 large brown onion (200g), chopped finely
1¾ cups (350g) arborio rice
2 tablespoons grated parmesan

1 Bring stock, wine and saffron to a boil in medium saucepan then reduce heat; simmer, covered.
2 Heat half the butter in large saucepan; cook onion, stirring, until soft. Add rice; stir to coat in butter mixture. Stir in 1 cup (250ml) of hot stock mixture; cook, stirring, over low heat until liquid is absorbed. Continue adding stock mixture in 1-cup batches, stirring after each addition until liquid is absorbed. Total cooking time should be about 35 minutes or until rice is tender.
3 Stir in remaining butter and cheese.

Combination fried rice

preparation time **10 minutes** (plus refrigeration time)
cooking time **10 minutes** (plus cooling time) serves **4**

You will need to cook about 1⅓ cups (260g) long-grain rice for this recipe.

2 teaspoons peanut oil
3 eggs, beaten lightly
1 tablespoon peanut oil, extra
2 cloves garlic, crushed
2 teaspoons grated fresh ginger
6 green onions, sliced thinly
4 cups cooked white long-grain rice
200g cooked shelled small prawns
200g chinese barbecued pork, sliced thinly
¾ cup (90g) frozen peas, thawed
1 cup (80g) bean sprouts
2½ tablespoons light soy sauce

1 Heat 1 teaspoon of oil in wok, add half the egg; swirl wok so egg forms an omelette over base. Cook omelette until set; remove, cool. Repeat with remaining 1 teaspoon of oil and remaining egg. Roll omelettes, slice thinly.
2 Heat extra oil in same wok; stir-fry garlic, ginger and onion until fragrant. Add rice, omelette, prawns, pork, peas, sprouts and sauce; stir-fry until hot.

Hummus

preparation time **10 minutes** (plus standing time) cooking time **50 minutes**
makes **2 cups**

450g canned chickpeas, drained, rinsed
1 teaspoon salt
1 clove garlic, quartered
⅓ cup (90g) tahini
¼ cup (60ml) lemon juice
¼ cup (60ml) water
Pinch cayenne pepper
1 tablespoon finely chopped fresh flat-leaf parsley
2 teaspoons extra virgin olive oil

1 Blend or process chickpeas with salt, garlic, tahini, juice and the water until almost smooth.
2 Spoon mixture into serving bowl; sprinkle with pepper and parsley. Drizzle with olive oil.

tip Store hummus in refrigerator for up to one week.

Chicken and thai basil fried rice

preparation time **15 minutes** cooking time **10 minutes** serves **4**

You will need to cook about 2 cups (400g) of jasmine rice the day before you want to make this recipe.

¼ cup (60ml) peanut oil
1 medium brown onion (150g), chopped finely
3 cloves garlic, crushed
2 long green thai chillies, chopped finely
1 tablespoon brown sugar
500g chicken breast fillets, chopped coarsely
2 medium red capsicums (400g), sliced thinly
200g green beans, chopped coarsely
4 cups cooked jasmine rice
2 tablespoons fish sauce
2 tablespoons soy sauce
½ cup loosely packed fresh thai basil leaves

1 Heat oil in wok; stir-fry onion, garlic and chilli until onion softens. Add sugar; stir-fry until dissolved. Add chicken; stir-fry until lightly browned. Add capsicum and beans; stir-fry until vegetables are just tender and chicken is cooked through.

2 Add rice and sauces; stir-fry, tossing gently to combine. Remove from heat; add basil, toss gently to combine.

Tunisian spicy nut pilaf

preparation time **10 minutes** cooking time **20 minutes** (plus standing time)
serves **4**

2 tablespoons (40g) unsalted butter
1 clove garlic, crushed
2 teaspoons ground cinnamon
½ teaspoon turmeric
1 tablespoon ground cumin
2 cups (400g) basmati rice
2 cups (500ml) vegetable stock
2 cups (500ml) water
2 large brown onions (400g), sliced thinly
2 medium carrots (240g), sliced thickly
¼ cup (35g) shelled pistachios, toasted
¼ cup (40g) pine nuts, toasted

1 Melt half the butter in large saucepan; cook garlic and spices, stirring, until
fragrant. Stir in rice; cook, stirring, 1 minute.
2 Stir in stock and the water. Bring to a boil then reduce heat; simmer,
covered, 15 minutes or until rice is just tender. Remove from heat; stand,
covered, 10 minutes.
3 Meanwhile, melt remaining butter in medium frying pan; cook onion,
stirring, until golden brown. Remove from pan.
4 Cook carrot in same pan, stirring, until just tender.
5 Stir onion, carrot and nuts through pilaf.

Chicken jambalaya

preparation time **15 minutes** cooking time **30 minutes** serves **4**

1 tablespoon olive oil
1 medium brown onion (150g), chopped coarsely
1 medium red capsicum (200g), chopped coarsely
1 clove garlic, crushed
2 trimmed celery stalks (150g), sliced thinly
2 fresh red thai chillies, sliced thinly
1½ cups (300g) basmati rice
½ cup (125ml) dry white wine
2½ cups (625ml) chicken stock
425g can crushed tomatoes
1 tablespoon tomato paste
700g chicken and herb sausages
⅓ cup coarsely chopped fresh coriander

1 Heat oil in large saucepan; cook onion, capsicum, garlic, celery and chilli, stirring, until vegetables soften. Stir in rice, wine, stock, undrained tomatoes and paste. Bring to a boil then reduce heat; simmer, covered, about 20 minutes or until liquid is absorbed.

2 Meanwhile, cook sausages, uncovered, in large frying pan until browned and cooked through. Drain on absorbent paper; slice thickly.

3 Stir sausage and coriander into jambalaya mixture just before serving.

Nasi goreng

preparation time **10 minutes** cooking time **10 minutes** serves **4**

You will need to cook about 1½ cups (300g) white long-grain rice for this recipe.

1 small brown onion (100g), chopped coarsely
2 cloves garlic, quartered
1 teaspoon shrimp paste
2 tablespoons peanut oil
4 eggs
125g small shelled uncooked prawns
4 cups cooked white long-grain rice
3 green onions, sliced thinly
125g chinese barbecued pork, sliced thinly
2 tablespoons light soy sauce

1 Blend or process brown onion, garlic and paste until almost smooth.
2 Heat half the oil in medium frying pan, break eggs into pan; cook, uncovered, until egg white has set and yolk is cooked as desired.
3 Meanwhile, heat remaining oil in wok or large frying pan; stir-fry onion mixture until fragrant. Add prawns; stir-fry until prawns just change colour.
4 Add rice, green onion, pork and sauce; stir-fry until hot. Serve nasi goreng with the eggs.

Rice with mushrooms and spinach

preparation time **15 minutes** cooking time **25 minutes** serves **4**

3 cups (750ml) vegetable stock
¼ cup (60ml) dry white wine
1 tablespoon finely grated lemon rind
1 medium brown onion (150g), chopped finely
2 cloves garlic, crushed
250g swiss brown mushrooms, halved
150g button mushrooms, halved
1½ cups (300g) white medium-grain rice
2 tablespoons lemon juice
1 cup (250ml) water
100g baby spinach leaves, torn
½ cup (40g) finely grated parmesan
2 tablespoons shredded fresh basil

1 Heat 1 tablespoon of stock with wine and rind in large saucepan, add onion and garlic; cook, stirring, until onion softens. Add mushrooms; cook, stirring, 5 minutes.

2 Stir in rice, juice, the water and remaining stock. Bring to a boil then reduce heat; simmer, covered, about 20 minutes or until rice is tender. Just before serving, stir in spinach, cheese and basil.

Italian brown rice salad

preparation time **15 minutes** cooking time **1 hour** serves **4**

3 cups (750ml) vegetable stock
2 teaspoons olive oil
1 small brown onion (80g), chopped finely
1 ½ cups (300g) brown medium-grain rice
⅓ cup (45g) toasted slivered almonds
100g sun-dried tomatoes, chopped coarsely
½ cup (60g) seeded black olives, chopped coarsely
½ cup coarsely chopped fresh basil

Lime and mustard dressing
¼ cup (60ml) lime juice
1 tablespoon olive oil
2 cloves garlic, crushed
2 teaspoons dijon mustard

1 Place stock in medium saucepan. Bring to a boil then reduce heat; simmer, covered.
2 Meanwhile, heat oil in large saucepan; cook onion, stirring, until soft. Add rice; stir to coat rice in onion mixture.
3 Add stock. Bring to a boil then reduce heat; simmer, covered, about 50 minutes or until rice is tender and liquid is absorbed.
4 Place ingredients for lime and mustard dressing in screw-top jar; shake well.
5 Add remaining ingredients and dressing to rice mixture in pan; toss gently to combine.

Balti biryani

preparation time **20 minutes** (plus refrigeration time)
cooking time **1 hour 30 minutes** serves **4**

750g skirt steak, cut into 2cm cubes
¾ cup (225g) curry paste
2 cups (400g) basmati rice
1 tablespoon vegetable oil
2 cloves garlic, crushed
4 cardamom pods, bruised
4 cloves
1 cinnamon stick
3 green onions, sliced thinly
2 cups (500ml) beef stock
¾ cup (100g) toasted slivered almonds
¼ cup loosely packed fresh coriander leaves
2 fresh red thai chillies, sliced thinly

1 Combine steak and curry paste in medium bowl, cover; refrigerate 1 hour.
2 Meanwhile, place rice in medium bowl, cover with water; stand 30 minutes.
Drain rice in strainer; rinse under cold water, drain.
3 Heat oil in large saucepan; cook garlic, cardamom, cloves, cinnamon
and onion, stirring, until fragrant. Add steak mixture, reduce heat; simmer,
covered, stirring occasionally, about 45 minutes or until steak is tender.
4 Add rice with stock to pan; simmer, covered, stirring occasionally, about
15 minutes or until rice is just tender.
5 Add almonds and coriander to biryani, cover; stand 5 minutes. Sprinkle
biryani with chilli.

serving suggestion Serve biryani with raita and naan.

Brown rice pilaf

preparation time **15 minutes** cooking time **1 hour** serves **1**

1 small sweet potato (250g), chopped coarsely
Cooking-oil spray
1½ cups (375ml) vegetable stock
1 teaspoon olive oil
1 small brown onion (80g), chopped finely
1 clove garlic, crushed
1 trimmed celery stalk (100g), chopped finely
70g mushrooms, chopped coarsely
¾ cup (150g) brown medium-grain rice
1 tablespoon finely grated lemon rind
¼ cup loosely packed fresh flat-leaf parsley leaves

1 Preheat oven to moderate.
2 Place sweet potato on lightly oiled oven tray; spray with oil. Roast, uncovered, about 25 minutes or until tender.
3 Meanwhile, bring stock to a boil in small saucepan then reduce heat; simmer, uncovered.
4 Heat oil in medium saucepan; cook onion, garlic and celery, stirring, until onion softens. Add mushrooms and rice; cook, stirring, 2 minutes. Add stock, reduce heat; simmer, covered, about 50 minutes or until stock is absorbed and rice is tender. Stir in sweet potato, rind and parsley.

Cheesy rice croquettes

preparation time **20 minutes** (plus refrigeration time)
cooking time **25 minutes** serves **6**

2 tablespoons olive oil
1 small brown onion (80g), chopped finely
1 clove garlic, crushed
300g minced pork and veal
400g can tomatoes
½ cup (100g) short-grain rice
1½ cups (375ml) chicken stock
2 tablespoons tomato paste
1 tablespoon chopped fresh basil
3 cups (210g) stale breadcrumbs
100g mozzarella
Plain flour
2 eggs, lightly beaten
1 tablespoon milk
1¼ cups (125g) packaged breadcrumbs
Oil for deep-frying

1 Heat oil in saucepan, add onion and garlic; cook, stirring, until onion is soft. Add mince, cook, stirring, until browned. Stir in undrained crushed tomatoes, rice, stock, paste and basil. Bring to boil then reduce heat; simmer, uncovered, about 12 minutes or until rice is tender and mixture is thick. Cool; stir in stale breadcrumbs, refrigerate until cold.

2 Cut cheese into 1cm x 5cm pieces. Roll 2 tablespoons mince mixture into log; press one piece of cheese in centre, roll into croquette shape to enclose cheese. Repeat, using remaining mince mixture and cheese.

3 Toss croquettes in flour, shake away excess flour. Dip into combined egg and milk, toss in breadcrumbs. Deep-fry in hot oil until browned; drain on absorbent paper.

Mixed dhal

preparation time **15 minutes** cooking time **1 hour 15 minutes** serves **8**

60g unsalted butter
2 medium brown onions (300g), chopped finely
2 cloves garlic, crushed
1 tablespoon grated fresh ginger
2 tablespoons black mustard seeds
2 tablespoons ground cumin
1 tablespoon ground coriander
2 teaspoons ground turmeric
¾ cup (150g) brown lentils
¾ cup (150g) red lentils
¾ cup (150g) yellow split peas
¾ cup (150g) green split peas
2 x 400g cans tomatoes
1 litre (4 cups) vegetable stock
⅔ cup (160ml) coconut cream
½ cup coarsely chopped fresh coriander

1 Heat butter in large heavy-base saucepan; cook onion, garlic and ginger, stirring, until onion is soft. Add seeds and spices; cook, stirring, until fragrant.
2 Add lentils and peas to pan; stir to combine. Add undrained crushed tomatoes and stock. Bring to a boil then reduce heat; simmer, covered, about 1 hour, stirring occasionally, until lentils are tender and mixture thickens.
3 Just before serving, add coconut cream and coriander; stir over low heat until dhal is hot.

tip Leftover dhal can be stored in refrigerator for up to one week.

Mexican broad bean burgers

preparation time **30 minutes** (plus refrigeration time)
cooking time **1 hour 20 minutes** makes **6**

1 tablespoon olive oil
2 medium red onions (340g), sliced thinly
6 hamburger buns
1 medium avocado (250g), sliced thinly
2 medium tomatoes (300g), sliced thickly
½ cup (125ml) sour cream
½ cup (125ml) mild chilli sauce

Broad bean patties
½ cup (100g) pearl barley
1kg frozen broad beans
1 medium white onion (150g), grated
1¾ cups (120g) stale breadcrumbs
2 eggs
1 tablespoon milk
100g cheese-flavoured corn chips, crushed finely

1 Make broad bean patties. Preheat oven to moderately hot. Bake patties, uncovered, about 25 minutes or until firm.
2 Heat oil in small frying pan; cook onion, stirring, until soft.
3 Split and toast buns. Fill buns with broad bean patties, avocado, tomato, onion, sour cream and sauce.

Broad bean patties Place barley in large saucepan of boiling water. Boil, uncovered, about 40 minutes or until tender; drain. Pour boiling water over beans in medium heatproof bowl. Stand 2 minutes; drain. Remove skins from beans; blend or process beans until smooth. Combine barley, bean puree, onion, 1 cup of breadcrumbs and one egg in large bowl; mix well. Shape mixture into six patties; dip in combined remaining egg and milk. Press on combined corn chips and remaining breadcrumbs. Place patties on oiled oven tray. Cover; refrigerate 1 hour.

tip Broad bean patties can be made one day ahead and stored, covered, in the refrigerator.

Felafel

preparation time **45 minutes** (plus standing time) cooking time **20 minutes**
makes **15**

1 cup (200g) dried chickpeas
1 small brown onion (80g), chopped coarsely
1 clove garlic, quartered
¼ cup coarsely chopped fresh flat-leaf parsley
1 teaspoon ground coriander
1 teaspoon ground cumin
½ teaspoon bicarbonate of soda
1 tablespoon plain flour
½ teaspoon salt
Vegetable oil, for deep-frying

1 Place chickpeas in large bowl, cover with cold water; stand overnight, drain.
2 Combine chickpeas, onion, garlic, parsley and spices in large bowl. Blend
or process, in two batches, until almost smooth; return mixture to large bowl.
3 Add soda, flour and salt to chickpea mixture; knead on lightly floured
surface 2 minutes. Stand 30 minutes.
4 Roll heaped tablespoons of mixture into balls; stand 10 minutes. Deep-fry
felafel in hot oil, in batches, until golden brown.

serving suggestion Serve felafel with a bowl of plain yogurt for dipping.

Barley and burghul fennel pilaf

preparation time **10 minutes** cooking time **40 minutes** serves **4**

1 tablespoon olive oil
1 medium brown onion (150g), sliced thinly
2 cloves garlic, crushed
2 teaspoons caraway seeds
2 teaspoons ground cumin
1½ cups (300g) pearl barley
2 cups (500ml) vegetable stock
2½ cups (625ml) water
1 cup (160g) burghul
40g butter
2 baby fennel bulbs (260g), trimmed, sliced thinly
200g char-grilled capsicum, drained, sliced thinly
⅓ cup (95g) yogurt

1 Heat oil in large saucepan; cook onion, garlic, caraway and cumin, stirring, until onion softens.
2 Add barley; cook, stirring, 1 minute. Add stock and the water. Bring to a boil then reduce heat, simmer, covered, 20 minutes.
3 Stir in burghul; cook, covered, about 10 minutes or until burghul and barley are tender.
4 Heat butter in medium frying pan; cook fennel, stirring, until tender.
5 Just before serving, toss capsicum and fennel into barley mixture. Top with yogurt.

Rice with chicken and soy

preparation time **10 minutes** cooking time **25 minutes** serves **4**

500g chicken breast fillets, sliced thinly
2cm piece fresh ginger (10g), grated
2 tablespoons soy sauce
½ teaspoon sesame oil
½ teaspoon cornflour
½ teaspoon white sugar
1 teaspoon chinese cooking wine
1 tablespoon water
1½ cups (300g) jasmine rice
2 cups (500ml) water, extra
1 chinese sausage, sliced thinly
150g button mushrooms, sliced thinly
2 green onions, sliced thinly

1 Combine chicken, ginger, sauce, oil, cornflour, sugar, wine and the water in large bowl.

2 Rinse rice in strainer under cold water until water runs clear.

3 Place rice and the extra water in large saucepan. Bring to the boil then reduce heat to low; cook, covered tightly, 10 minutes. Do not remove lid or stir during cooking time.

4 Drain chicken, reserve marinade. Place chicken, sausage and mushrooms on rice, cook, covered tightly, about 5 minutes or until chicken is cooked.

5 Meanwhile, place reserved marinade in small saucepan, bring to the boil.

6 Drizzle sauce over chicken and rice, sprinkle with onions. Stir to combine. .

tip Chinese cooking wine is available from asian food stores; substitute dry sherry, if desired.

Pearl barley salad

preparation time **10 minutes** cooking time **25 minutes** serves **1**

½ cup (100g) pearl barley
125g asparagus, trimmed, cut into 4cm lengths
125g cherry tomatoes, halved
½ lebanese cucumber (65g), sliced thinly
¾ cup (45g) finely shredded iceberg lettuce
2 tablespoons coarsely chopped fresh basil
2 tablespoons fresh lemon juice

1 Cook barley in small saucepan of boiling water, uncovered, about 25 minutes or until tender; drain. Cool 10 minutes.
2 Meanwhile, boil, steam or microwave asparagus until just tender; drain.
3 Place barley and asparagus in medium bowl with remaining ingredients; toss gently to combine.

Moroccan chicken with couscous

preparation **10 minutes** cooking **10 minutes** serves **4**

½ cup (125ml) vegetable stock
¾ cup (150g) couscous
1 small red onion (100g), sliced thinly
1½ cups (240g) shredded cooked chicken
¼ cup (35g) coarsely chopped dried apricots
¼ cup (40g) sultanas
¼ cup finely chopped fresh mint
1 tablespoon pine nuts
1 teaspoon cumin seeds
½ cup (125ml) bottled fat-free french dressing

1 Bring stock to a boil in large saucepan; remove from heat. Stir in couscous. Cover; stand about 5 minutes or until stock is absorbed, fluffing with fork. Stir in onion, chicken, apricot, sultanas and mint.
2 Meanwhile, stir pine nuts and seeds in small frying pan over low heat until just fragrant. Add to couscous with dressing; toss gently to combine.

Fried rice with sausages and salami

preparation time **15 minutes** cooking time **30 minutes** serves **2**

This recipe can be prepared several hours ahead.

1 cup (200g) white long-grain rice
250g beef sausages
100g sliced hot salami
1 tablespoon oil
1 medium brown onion (80g), chopped
1 clove garlic, crushed
1 medium zucchini (125g), sliced
1 cup (125g) frozen peas
1 teaspoon paprika
1 tablespoon chopped fresh flat-leaf parsley
1 medium ripe tomato (200g), seeded, chopped

1 Cook rice in large saucepan of boiling water, stirring occasionally, until just tender; drain.
2 Meanwhile, cook sausages in large frying pan until browned and cooked through. Remove from pan, drain on absorbent paper. Slice sausages. Drain fat from pan; add salami and cook, stirring, until salami is crisp; remove from pan.
3 Add oil to same pan; cook onion and garlic, stirring, until soft. Add zucchini and peas, cook, stirring, until tender. Return sausages to pan with rice, paprika and parsley; stir until hot. Stir in salami.
4 Serve sprinkled with tomato.

Borlotti bean, brown rice and almond salad

preparation time **10 minutes** (plus standing time) cooking time **20 minutes**
serves **1**

¼ cup (50g) dried borlotti beans
¼ cup (50g) brown long-grain rice
½ small red onion (50g), chopped finely
¼ cup finely chopped fresh flat-leaf parsley
¼ cup finely chopped fresh mint
1 medium tomato (150g), chopped finely
1 tablespoon toasted slivered almonds
2 tablespoons fresh lemon juice
2 teaspoons olive oil

1 Place beans in small bowl, cover with water; stand overnight, drain. Rinse under cold water; drain.

2 Cook beans in small saucepan of boiling water, uncovered, until just tender; drain. Rinse under cold water; drain.

3 Meanwhile, cook rice in small saucepan of boiling water, uncovered, until rice is tender; drain. Rinse under cold water; drain.

4 Place beans and rice in medium bowl with remaining ingredients; toss gently to combine.

tip to save time, use a 400g can of borlotti beans. Drain and rinse beans before adding to salad.

Chickpea, watercress and capsicum salad

preparation time **15 minutes** (plus standing time) cooking time **30 minutes**
serves **1**

¼ cup (50g) dried chickpeas
100g watercress
1 tablespoon water
1 clove garlic, quartered
¼ cup (35g) toasted pine nuts
¼ cup (60ml) fresh lemon juice
½ small red capsicum (75g), sliced thinly

1 Place chickpeas in small bowl, cover with water; stand overnight, drain.
Rinse under cold water; drain.
2 Cook chickpeas in small saucepan of boiling water, uncovered, until just
tender; drain. Rinse under cold water; drain.
3 Trim watercress; reserve stalks. Blend or process watercress stalks with
the water, garlic, a third of the chickpeas, 1 tablespoon of the nuts and
2 tablespoons of the juice until smooth. Transfer to medium bowl; stir in
remaining chickpeas and remaining nuts.
4 Place watercress leaves and capsicum in medium bowl with remaining
juice; toss gently to combine. Top with chickpea mixture.

tips To save time, use a 400g can of chickpeas. Drain and rinse chickpeas
before adding to salad.
Use rocket instead of watercress, if desired.

VEGETARIAN

Baked potatoes

preparation time **5 minutes** cooking time **1 hour** makes **4**

4 large potatoes (1.4kg), unpeeled

1 Preheat oven to moderate.
2 Pierce skin of each potato with fork; wrap each potato in foil, place on oven tray. Bake in moderate oven about 1 hour or until tender. Top with one of the variations below.

Toppings

preparation time **5 minutes**

Each of these toppings is enough to top the four potatoes above.

Cream cheese and pesto

Combine ¹/₃ cup spreadable cream cheese, ¼ teaspoon cracked black pepper and 2 tablespoons pesto in small bowl; refrigerate until required.

Lime and chilli yogurt

Combine ¹/₃ cup yogurt, 1 tablespoon coarsely chopped fresh coriander, 1 finely chopped fresh red thai chilli and ½ teaspoon finely grated lime rind in small bowl; refrigerate until required.

Mustard and walnut butter

Mash 30g softened butter, ½ teaspoon wholegrain mustard and 1 tablespoon finely chopped toasted walnuts in small bowl until mixture forms a paste; refrigerate until required.

Burghul and fetta salad

preparation time **10 minutes** (plus standing time) cooking time **5 minutes**
serves **4**

1½ cups (240g) burghul
200g green beans
⅓ cup (80ml) french dressing
2 tablespoons lemon juice
1½ cups firmly packed fresh flat-leaf parsley leaves
½ cup chopped fresh mint
4 green onions, sliced
250g cherry tomatoes, halved
200g fetta, crumbled

1 Place burghul in large bowl; cover with boiling water, set aside 10 minutes
or until burghul is just tender, drain. Using absorbent paper, pat burghul dry.
2 Meanwhile, cut beans into thirds. Boil, steam or microwave until beans
are just tender; drain.
3 Combine burghul, beans and remaining ingredients in large bowl; toss gently.

Yellow curry

preparation time **15 minutes** cooking time **30 minutes** serves **4**

¼ cup (60g) yellow curry paste
1⅔ cups (400ml) light coconut milk
1 cup (250ml) salt-reduced vegetable stock
1 large kumara (500g), chopped coarsely
200g green beans, trimmed
150g firm tofu, diced into 2cm cubes
2 tablespoons lime juice
¼ cup coarsely chopped fresh coriander

1 Cook curry paste in large saucepan, stirring, until fragrant. Add coconut
milk and stock. Bring to a boil then reduce heat; simmer, stirring, 5 minutes.
2 Add kumara to pan; simmer, covered, about 10 minutes or until kumara
is tender. Add beans, tofu and juice; cook, stirring, until beans are tender.
Stir in coriander.

serving suggestion Serve curry with steamed rice.

Mixed mushroom ragout with soft polenta

preparation time **20 minutes** cooking time **40 minutes** serves **4**

1 medium brown onion (150g), chopped coarsely
1 clove garlic, crushed
1 tablespoon plain flour
300g mixed mushrooms
1 tablespoon tomato paste
¼ cup (60ml) dry red wine
1 cup (250ml) water
1 cup (250ml) vegetable stock
1 teaspoon finely chopped fresh thyme
½ cup (85g) polenta
¼ cup (60ml) low-fat milk
2 tablespoons finely grated parmesan

1 Cook onion and garlic in large lightly oiled frying pan, stirring, until onion softens. Add flour; cook, stirring, until mixture bubbles. Add mushrooms; cook, stirring, until mushrooms are just tender.

2 Add tomato paste and wine to mushroom mixture. Bring to a boil then reduce heat; simmer, uncovered, until liquid reduces by half. Add half the combined water and stock. Return to a boil then reduce heat; simmer, uncovered, 20 minutes. Stir in thyme.

3 Meanwhile, combine the remaining water and remaining stock in another large saucepan; bring to a boil. Add polenta; cook, stirring, until polenta boils and thickens. Add milk and cheese; cook, stirring, until cheese has melted.

4 Serve ragout on polenta.

Vegetable tagine

preparation time **15 minutes** cooking time **40 minutes** serves **2**

2 teaspoons vegetable oil
1 clove garlic, crushed
1 medium brown onion (150g), chopped finely
2 teaspoons ground coriander
2 teaspoons ground cumin
1 teaspoon sweet paprika
1 tablespoon tomato paste
1 cup (250ml) water
400g can diced tomatoes
250g pumpkin, chopped coarsely
4 yellow patty-pan squash (120g), quartered
100g baby green beans, trimmed, halved
300g can chickpeas, rinsed, drained

1 Heat oil in large saucepan; cook garlic and onion, stirring, until onion softens. Add spices; cook, stirring, until fragrant.
2 Add paste, the water, undrained tomatoes and pumpkin. Bring to a boil then reduce heat; simmer, uncovered, 20 minutes. Stir in squash, beans and chickpeas; simmer, covered, about 10 minutes or until squash is tender.

serving suggestion Serve tagine with couscous.

Barbecued vegetarian pizza

preparation time **15 minutes** cooking time **55 minutes** serves **4**

4 small uncooked beetroot (400g), peeled, sliced thickly
2 medium red onions (340g), sliced thinly
1 tablespoon olive oil
2 tablespoons red wine vinegar
1 teaspoon brown sugar
2 cloves garlic, sliced thinly
6 sprigs fresh thyme
100g fetta, crumbled
²/₃ cup (170g) bottled tomato pasta sauce
4 pocket pittas
¼ cup finely shredded fresh basil

1 Preheat oven to moderately hot.
2 Combine beetroot, onion, oil, vinegar, sugar, garlic and thyme in oiled large baking dish. Roast, uncovered, in moderately hot oven about 50 minutes or until beetroot is tender, stirring halfway through cooking. Stir in cheese.
3 Spread pasta sauce equally over pittas; top each with beetroot mixture.
4 Cover barbecue flat plate with double thickness of lightly oiled foil; place pizzas on foil. Cook, covered, on medium heat, about 5 minutes or until pizzas are hot and base is crisp. Top with basil.

Stir-fried greens with green beans

preparation time **10 minutes** cooking time **10 minutes** serves **4**

1 tablespoon sesame oil
2 cloves garlic, crushed
1 teaspoon crushed ginger
300g green beans, halved
8 green onions, chopped coarsely
500g spinach, chopped coarsely
600g baby bok choy, chopped coarsely
2 tablespoons soy sauce
1 tablespoon sweet chilli sauce
2 tablespoons finely chopped fresh coriander

1 Heat oil in wok; stir-fry garlic, ginger, beans and onion until beans are just tender.
2 Add spinach and bok choy; stir-fry until bok choy is just wilted. Add combined sauces; stir-fry until hot. Serve sprinkled with coriander.

Sweet chilli tofu stir-fry

preparation time **10 minutes** cooking time **10 minutes** serves **4**

300g firm tofu
2 tablespoons kecap manis
2 tablespoons peanut oil
500g hokkien noodles
2 cloves garlic, crushed
2 medium carrots (240g), sliced thinly
300g broccoli, chopped
6 green onions, chopped coarsely
½ cup (125ml) sweet chilli sauce
1 tablespoon lime juice
⅓ cup (50g) salted peanuts, chopped coarsely
2 tablespoons coarsely chopped fresh coriander

1 Cut tofu into 3cm cubes; place in medium bowl with half the kecap manis. Toss to coat tofu in kecap manis.
2 Heat half the oil in wok; stir-fry tofu gently, in batches, until browned all over. Cover to keep warm.
3 Place noodles in medium heatproof bowl; cover with boiling water, separate with fork, drain.
4 Heat remaining oil in same cleaned wok; stir-fry garlic and carrot until just tender. Add broccoli; stir-fry until just tender.
5 Add green onion, noodles, sauce, remaining kecap manis and juice; stir-fry until hot. Stir in tofu, peanuts and coriander.

Pumpkin, pea and smoked cheddar risotto

preparation time **15 minutes** cooking time **50 minutes** serves **4**

8 whole unpeeled cloves garlic
500g butternut pumpkin, peeled, chopped coarsely
1 teaspoon fresh thyme leaves
¼ cup (60ml) olive oil
1 litre (4 cups) salt-reduced chicken stock
2 cups (500ml) water
1 medium brown onion (150g), chopped finely
2 cups (400g) arborio rice
½ cup (125ml) dry white wine
1 cup (125g) frozen peas
30g butter, chopped
1 cup (125g) grated smoked cheddar

1 Preheat oven to hot.
2 Combine garlic, pumpkin, thyme and 1 tablespoon of oil in medium baking dish. Bake, uncovered, in hot oven about 20 minutes, turning once, or until pumpkin is just tender.
3 Meanwhile, place stock and the water in medium saucepan. Bring to the boil, reduce heat; simmer, covered.
4 Heat remaining oil in large saucepan; cook onion, stirring, until soft. Add rice; stir to coat in oil mixture. Add wine, cook, stirring, until almost evaporated.
5 Add hot stock mixture in 1-cup batches to rice; cook, stirring after each addition until stock mixture is absorbed. Total cooking time should be about 25 minutes. After 20 minutes, stir peas through rice.
6 Add butter and cheese, season with freshly ground black pepper; cook, stirring, until hot. Gently stir in pumpkin, top with garlic cloves.

Split pea patties with tomato salad

preparation time **20 minutes** cooking time **25 minutes** serves **4**

1 cup (200g) yellow split peas
3 cups (750ml) vegetable stock
¼ cup (25g) packaged breadcrumbs
1 medium potato (200g), grated coarsely
1 medium carrot (120g), grated coarsely
¼ cup (35g) sesame seeds, toasted
1 egg, beaten lightly
2 teaspoons curry powder

Tomato salad
4 medium egg tomatoes (300g), cut into wedges
4 green onions, chopped finely
2 tablespoons shredded fresh mint
¼ cup (60ml) olive oil
2 tablespoons lime juice

1 Combine peas and stock in large saucepan; simmer, covered, about 20 minutes or until peas are very soft and stock is absorbed. You need 2 cups of the pea mixture.
2 Combine pea mixture with remaining ingredients in large bowl. Using hands, shape mixture into 12 patties.
3 Cook patties on large oiled grill pan (or grill or barbecue) until browned both sides.
4 Combine ingredients for tomato salad in large bowl; serve with patties.

Potato and onion bhaji

preparation time **15 minutes** cooking time **15 minutes** serves **6**

45g unsalted butter
1 teaspoon brown mustard seeds
2 medium leeks (700g), sliced thinly
2 large brown onions (400g), sliced thinly
2 medium potatoes (400g), sliced thinly
1 medium carrot (120g), sliced thinly
1 teaspoon grated fresh ginger
½ teaspoon cumin seeds
½ teaspoon ground turmeric
¼ teaspoon chilli powder
1 teaspoon garam masala
1 teaspoon salt

1 Heat butter in large heavy-base frying pan, add mustard seeds; cook, stirring, 30 seconds.
2 Stir in leek, onion, potato, carrot, ginger, cumin seeds, turmeric and chilli powder; cook, stirring, 5 minutes.
3 Add garam masala and salt, cover; cook over low heat 10 minutes or until vegetables are tender.

Vegetarian burger

preparation time **10 minutes** cooking time **10 minutes** serves **6**

600g piece firm tofu
1 clove garlic, crushed
½ cup (125ml) barbecue sauce
2 tablespoons vegetable oil
1 large red onion (300g), sliced thinly
6 bread rolls
1 baby cos lettuce
2 medium tomatoes (380g), sliced

1 Cut tofu into 12 slices. Combine tofu, garlic and half the barbecue sauce in large shallow dish.
2 Heat half the oil on heated grill plate (or grill or barbecue); cook onion until soft, remove from grill plate.

3 Heat remaining oil on grill plate; cook tofu until browned both sides.
4 Split each roll in half, toast both sides. Top each base with lettuce, tofu, remaining sauce, tomato and onion; top with remaining bread half.

Free-form spinach and ricotta pie

preparation time **15 minutes** cooking time **30 minutes** serves **4**

200g spinach
2 tablespoons olive oil
1 medium brown onion (150g), chopped coarsely
1 clove garlic, crushed
2 teaspoons finely grated lemon rind
¼ cup coarsely chopped fresh flat-leaf parsley
¼ cup coarsely chopped fresh dill
2 tablespoons coarsely chopped fresh mint
1½ cups (300g) ricotta
2 sheets ready-rolled puff pastry

1 Preheat oven to very hot.
2 Boil, steam or microwave spinach until just wilted; drain on absorbent paper. Squeeze out excess liquid.
3 Heat oil in small frying pan, add onion and garlic; cook, stirring, until onion softens.
4 Combine spinach, onion mixture, rind, herbs and cheese in large bowl.
5 Oil two oven trays and place in oven about 5 minutes to heat. Place sheet of pastry on each tray, divide spinach mixture between sheets, leaving 3cm border. Using metal spatula, fold pastry roughly over edge of filling.
6 Bake pies in very hot oven about 20 minutes or until pastry browns.

Larb tofu

preparation time **15 minutes** (plus standing time) cooking time **5 minutes** serves **4**

900g fresh firm silken tofu
Peanut oil, for deep-frying
1 medium red onion (170g), chopped finely
½ cup coarsely chopped fresh coriander
1 tablespoon finely chopped fresh lemon grass
2 fresh red thai chillies, sliced thinly
2 tablespoons lemon juice
1 teaspoon grated palm sugar
1 tablespoon soy sauce
½ teaspoon sambal oelek
8 small chinese cabbage leaves (360g)

1 Pat tofu with absorbent paper; chop coarsely. Spread tofu, in single layer, on tray lined with absorbent paper; cover tofu with more absorbent paper, stand at least 20 minutes.
2 Heat oil in wok; deep-fry tofu, in batches, until lightly browned. Drain on absorbent paper.
3 Combine tofu in large bowl with onion, coriander, lemon grass and chilli.
4 Combine juice, sugar, sauce and sambal in small jug; stir until sugar dissolves. Pour dressing over tofu mixture; toss to combine.
5 Serve tofu mixture spooned into individual whole cabbage leaves.

tip It is important that the tofu is well drained before it is deep-fried. If you have time, pat the piece of tofu with absorbent paper then place it in a strainer or colander that has been lined with absorbent paper and set over a large bowl. Weight the tofu piece with an upright saucer topped with a heavy can; allow to drain this way for up to 3 hours.

Potato lentil patties

preparation time **15 minutes** cooking time **45 minutes** makes **12**

1kg potatoes
½ cup (100g) red lentils
2 teaspoons olive oil
1 small brown onion (80g), chopped finely
1 clove garlic, crushed
1 egg, beaten lightly
2 tablespoons finely chopped fresh chives
1 tablespoon finely shredded fresh basil
⅓ cup (25g) finely grated parmesan
½ cup (125ml) sweet chilli sauce

1 Preheat oven to moderately hot.
2 Boil, steam or microwave potatoes until tender; drain, mash.
3 Meanwhile, cook lentils in small saucepan of boiling water, uncovered, about 8 minutes or until tender. Drain lentils, rinse under cold water; drain.
4 Heat oil in small non-stick frying pan; cook onion and garlic, stirring, until onion is soft.
5 Combine potato, lentils, onion mixture, egg and herbs in large bowl. Using hands, shape mixture into 12 patties.
6 Place patties on oven tray lined with baking paper; sprinkle with cheese. Bake, uncovered, in moderately hot oven about 30 minutes or until lightly browned; serve with chilli sauce.

Dhal with egg and eggplant

preparation time **20 minutes** cooking time **1 hour** serves **4**

2 cups (400g) red lentils
2 teaspoons vegetable oil
1 medium brown onion (150g), chopped finely
1 clove garlic, crushed
2 teaspoons ground cumin
½ teaspoon cumin seeds
1 tablespoon tomato paste
1 litre (4 cups) water
2 cups (500ml) vegetable stock
1 large tomato (250g), chopped coarsely
3 baby eggplant (180g), chopped coarsely
4 hard-boiled eggs

1 Rinse lentils in large colander under cold water until water runs clear.
2 Heat oil in large heavy-base saucepan; cook onion, garlic, ground cumin, seeds and paste, stirring, 5 minutes. Add lentils with the water and stock. Bring to a boil then reduce heat; simmer, uncovered, about 40 minutes or until dhal mixture thickens slightly, stirring occasionally.
3 Add tomato and eggplant; simmer, uncovered, about 20 minutes or until dhal is thickened and eggplant is tender, stirring occasionally. Add whole eggs; stir gently until eggs are hot.

Vegetable couscous

preparation time **20 minutes** cooking time **30 minutes** serves **4**

350g kumara, peeled
80g butter
4 baby eggplant (240g), sliced thinly
1 large brown onion (200g), sliced thinly
¼ teaspoon cayenne pepper
2 teaspoons ground cumin
1½ cups (375ml) vegetable stock
2 cups (400g) couscous
2 cups (500ml) boiling water
400g can chickpeas, drained, rinsed
2 tablespoons lemon juice
100g baby spinach leaves
¼ cup loosely packed fresh flat-leaf parsley leaves

1 Chop kumara into 1cm cubes. Heat half the butter in large frying pan; cook kumara with eggplant and onion, stirring, until vegetables brown.
2 Add spices; cook about 2 minutes or until just fragrant. Stir in stock. Bring to a boil then reduce heat; simmer, uncovered, about 15 minutes or until vegetables are just tender.
3 Meanwhile, combine couscous in large heatproof bowl with half the remaining butter and the water. Cover; stand about 5 minutes or until water is absorbed, occasionally fluffing couscous with fork.
4 Add chickpeas and remaining butter to vegetable mixture; cook, stirring, until butter melts. Stir in couscous, juice, spinach and parsley.

Lentil cottage pie

preparation time **20 minutes** cooking time **40 minutes** (plus standing time)
serves **4**

800g medium new potatoes, quartered
40g butter
1 medium brown onion (150g), chopped finely
1 clove garlic, crushed
415g can crushed tomatoes
1 cup (250ml) vegetable stock
1 cup (250ml) water
2 tablespoons tomato paste
⅓ cup (80ml) dry red wine
⅔ cup (130g) red lentils
1 medium carrot (120g), chopped finely
½ cup (60g) frozen peas, thawed
⅓ cup coarsely chopped fresh flat-leaf parsley

1 Preheat oven to hot.
2 Boil, steam or microwave potato until tender; drain. Mash in large bowl with half the butter.
3 Melt remaining butter in medium frying pan; cook onion and garlic, stirring, until onion softens. Add undrained tomatoes, stock, the water, paste, wine, lentils and carrot. Bring to a boil then reduce heat; simmer, uncovered, 15 minutes, stirring occasionally. Add peas and parsley; cook, uncovered, 5 minutes. Spoon lentil mixture into shallow 1-litre (4-cup) ovenproof dish.
4 Spread mash on top. Bake, uncovered, in hot oven 20 minutes. Stand pie 10 minutes before serving.

Chickpea patties

preparation time **10 minutes** (plus refrigeration time)
cooking time **40 minutes** makes **2**

1 medium potato (200g)
300g can chickpeas, rinsed, drained
1 clove garlic, crushed
1 green onion, sliced thinly
⅓ cup coarsely chopped fresh coriander
1 tablespoon polenta
¼ cup (70g) plain yogurt

1 Preheat oven to moderate.
2 Boil, steam or microwave potato until tender; drain. Mash potato and chickpeas in medium bowl; stir in garlic, onion and coriander. Using hands, shape mixture into two patties. Coat with polenta; refrigerate 1 hour.
3 Cook patties in lightly oiled medium frying pan until browned lightly. Transfer to oven tray; bake in preheated moderate oven about 15 minutes or until patties are hot. Serve with yogurt.

serving suggestion Serve patties with salad greens.

Roasted vegetable and balsamic salad

preparation time **20 minutes** cooking time **20 minutes** serves **4**

¼ cup (60ml) olive oil
1 clove garlic, crushed
2 large zucchini (300g)
4 medium flat mushrooms (500g), quartered
4 large egg tomatoes (360g), quartered
1 medium red onion (170g), cut into wedges
150g lamb's lettuce, trimmed
⅓ cup coarsely chopped fresh basil

Dressing
¼ cup (60ml) olive oil
2 tablespoons balsamic vinegar
½ teaspoon dijon mustard
1 clove garlic, crushed

1 Preheat oven to hot. Combine oil and garlic in small bowl.
2 Halve zucchini lengthways, chop into pieces on the diagonal.
3 Arrange vegetables, in single layer, on oven trays; brush with garlic-flavoured oil. Roast, uncovered, in hot oven about 20 minutes or until browned and just tender. Remove vegetables from oven; cool.
4 Place ingredients for dressing in screw-top jar; shake well.
5 Combine cold vegetables in large bowl with lettuce and basil. Add dressing; toss to combine.

tip Substitute baby spinach or rocket leaves for lamb's lettuce.

Risoni with mushrooms, zucchini and green onions

preparation time **10 minutes** cooking time **10 minutes** serves **4**

500g risoni
1 tablespoon olive oil
60g butter
500g zucchini, sliced thinly
300g button mushrooms, sliced thinly
2 cloves garlic, crushed
1 tablespoon coarsely chopped fresh oregano
1 tablespoon lemon juice
1 tablespoon red wine vinegar
200g green onions, sliced thinly
½ cup (40g) coarsely grated parmesan

1 Cook pasta in large saucepan of boiling water, uncovered, until just tender.
2 Meanwhile, heat oil with half the butter in large frying pan; cook zucchini, stirring, until tender and browned lightly. Add remaining butter with mushrooms, garlic and oregano; cook, stirring, 2 minutes. Stir in juice and vinegar. Remove from heat; stir in onion and cheese.
3 Place zucchini mixture in large serving bowl with drained pasta; toss gently to combine.

Vegetable and fetta freeform tarts

preparation time **30 minutes** (plus standing time) cooking time **50 minutes**
serves **4**

1 small eggplant (230g), chopped coarsely
Coarse cooking salt
1 tablespoon olive oil
1 medium brown onion (150g), sliced thinly
2 medium zucchini (240g), sliced thinly
4 sheets ready-rolled shortcrust pastry
¼ cup (65g) bottled pesto
120g piece fetta, crumbled
8 cherry tomatoes, halved
1 tablespoon finely chopped fresh basil
1 egg, beaten lightly

1 Place eggplant colander, sprinkle all over with salt; stand 15 minutes. Rinse
eggplant, drain; pat dry with absorbent paper.
2 Preheat oven to moderate.
3 Heat oil in large non-stick frying pan; cook onion, stirring, until softened.
Add eggplant and zucchini to pan; cook, stirring, until vegetables soften.
4 Using plate as guide, cut 20cm round from each pastry sheet; place rounds
on oven trays. Spread equal amounts of pesto in centre of each round, leaving
4cm border around outside edge.
5 Divide vegetables among rounds over pesto; top each with equal amounts
of cheese, tomato and basil. Using hands, turn 4cm edge on each round over
filling; brush around pastry edge with egg. Bake, uncovered, in moderate
oven about 40 minutes or until pastry is browned lightly.

tip Be sure to rinse eggplant well under cold running water to remove as
much of the salt as possible, and to dry it thoroughly with absorbent paper
before cooking it.

Chinese cabbage and tofu stir-fry

preparation time **15 minutes** cooking time **10 minutes** serves **4**

You will need one small chinese cabbage to make this recipe.

250g dried rice noodles
2 tablespoons peanut oil
300g firm tofu, chopped coarsely
1 clove garlic, crushed
1 fresh red thai chilli, sliced thinly
200g mushrooms, quartered
⅓ cup (80ml) black bean sauce
⅓ cup (80ml) vegetable stock
300g finely shredded chinese cabbage
1 cup (80g) bean sprouts
3 green onions, sliced thinly
2 tablespoons chopped fresh coriander

1 Place noodles in medium heatproof bowl, cover with boiling water, stand until tender; drain.

2 Meanwhile, heat half the oil in wok or frying pan; stir-fry tofu until browned all over. Drain on absorbent paper.

3 Heat remaining oil in wok; stir-fry garlic, chilli and mushrooms until tender. Stir in sauce and stock; bring to a boil. Add cabbage; stir-fry until just wilted.

4 Remove from heat; stir in tofu, sprouts, onion and coriander. Serve noodles topped with chinese cabbage and tofu stir-fry.

Roasted root vegetables

preparation time **15 minutes** cooking time **30 minutes** serves **2**

1 tablespoon olive oil
10 baby carrots (200g), peeled, halved lengthways
2 small parsnips (120g), peeled, quartered lengthways
8 baby potatoes (320g), halved
3 baby onions (75g), halved
1 clove garlic, crushed
1 tablespoon fresh rosemary
1 tablespoon honey
2 teaspoons wholegrain mustard
1 tablespoon lemon juice

1 Preheat oven to hot.
2 Heat oil in flameproof baking dish on stove top. Place carrot, parsnip, potato and onion in dish; cook, covered, until browned, turning occasionally.
3 Remove from heat; stir in garlic, rosemary, honey and mustard.
4 Bake in hot oven about 20 minutes or until vegetables are tender. Serve drizzled with lemon juice.

Rice and zucchini patties

preparation time **15 minutes** cooking time **10 minutes** serves **4**

You will need to cook about ¾ cup (150g) brown rice for this recipe.

1 ½ cups cooked brown rice
3 medium zucchini (300g), grated coarsely
1 medium brown onion (150g), chopped finely
2 tablespoons finely chopped fresh flat-leaf parsley
2 eggs, beaten lightly
1 cup (70g) stale breadcrumbs
130g can creamed corn
¼ cup (60ml) olive oil

1 Combine rice, zucchini, onion, parsley, egg, breadcrumbs and corn in large bowl. Using hands, shape mixture into 12 patties.
2 Heat oil in large frying pan. Cook patties until browned both sides and hot; drain on absorbent paper.

Tuscan white bean salad

preparation time **15 minutes** Serves **2**

400g can white beans, drained, rinsed
½ medium red onion (85g), chopped finely
⅓ cup (50g) drained semi-dried tomatoes
100g mozzarella, cut into 1cm pieces
¼ cup (30g) seeded kalamata olives
80g rocket

Oregano balsamic vinaigrette
1 clove garlic, crushed
2 teaspoons finely chopped fresh oregano
2 tablespoons balsamic vinegar
2 tablespoons extra virgin olive oil

1 Combine beans, onion, tomato, cheese and olives in medium bowl.
2 Place ingredients for oregano balsamic vinaigrette in screw-top jar; shake well.
3 Drizzle salad with vinaigrette; toss gently to combine. Serve salad with rocket.

tip Many varieties of cooked white beans are available canned, among them cannellini, butter and haricot beans; any of these are suitable for this salad.

Haloumi salad on turkish bread

preparation time **5 minutes** cooking time **10 minutes** serves **4**

250g antipasto char-grilled vegetables
180g jar marinated artichoke hearts
250g haloumi
½ long loaf turkish bread
200g baby rocket leaves
250g teardrop tomatoes
¼ cup (60ml) balsamic vinegar
2 tablespoons toasted pine nuts

1 Drain antipasto over bowl and reserve ⅓ cup (80ml) of the oil; slice vegetables. Drain artichokes; cut into quarters.

2 Cut cheese into eight slices; cook in heated oiled small frying pan until browned both sides.

3 Meanwhile, cut bread into 1cm slices; toast under preheated grill until browned both sides.

4 Divide toasted bread among four plates; top with rocket, antipasto, artichokes, cheese and tomatoes. Drizzle with combined reserved oil and vinegar; sprinkle with nuts.

tip Char-grilled vegetables can also be purchased from a delicatessen.

Steamed spinach dumplings with fresh tomato and herb sauce

preparation time **30 minutes** (plus standing time) cooking time **20 minutes**
serves **4**

2 x 250g packets frozen spinach, thawed
200g ricotta
1 clove garlic, crushed
1 egg white
1 tablespoon plain flour
¼ cup (20g) finely grated parmesan
1½ cups (110g) stale breadcrumbs
¼ teaspoon ground nutmeg
1 tablespoon finely chopped fresh chives
2 tablespoons finely grated parmesan, extra

Fresh tomato and herb sauce
½ cup (125ml) dry white wine
4 medium tomatoes (600g), chopped finely
2 tablespoons finely chopped fresh flat-leaf parsley
1 teaspoon white sugar

1 Squeeze excess liquid from spinach. Combine spinach in large bowl with ricotta, garlic, egg white, flour, parmesan, breadcrumbs, nutmeg and chives; roll level tablespoons of mixture into balls. Place balls, in single layer, about 2cm apart, in baking-paper-lined bamboo steamer fitted over large saucepan of boiling water. Steam, covered, about 10 minutes or until dumplings are hot.
2 Meanwhile, make fresh tomato and herb sauce.
3 Serve dumplings with sauce and extra parmesan.

Fresh tomato and herb sauce Bring wine to a boil in medium saucepan then reduce heat; simmer, uncovered, until reduced by half. Add tomato; return to a boil. Boil, uncovered, about 10 minutes or until thickened slightly. Stir in parsley and sugar.

Roasted vegetable lasagne

preparation time **40 minutes** (plus standing time) cooking time **1 hour**
serves **6**

3 medium red capsicums (600g)
2 medium eggplant (600g), sliced thinly
2 tablespoons coarse cooking salt
2 medium zucchini (240g), sliced thinly
600g kumara, sliced thinly
Cooking-oil spray
700g bottled tomato pasta sauce
4 fresh lasagne sheets
150g ricotta, crumbled
1 tablespoon finely grated parmesan

White sauce
40g butter
¼ cup (35g) plain flour
1½ cups (375ml) low-fat milk
2 tablespoons coarsely grated parmesan

1 Preheat oven to very hot.
2 Quarter capsicums; discard seeds and membranes. Roast, uncovered, in very hot oven, skin-side up, about 5 minutes or until skin blisters and blackens. Cover capsicum pieces in plastic or paper 5 minutes; peel away skin.
3 Reduce oven to moderately hot. Place eggplant in colander, sprinkle all over with salt; stand 20 minutes. Rinse eggplant under cold water; pat dry with absorbent paper.
4 Place eggplant, zucchini and kumara in single layer on oven trays; spray with oil. Roast, uncovered, about 15 minutes or until tender.
5 Meanwhile, make white sauce.
6 Oil deep rectangular 2.5-litre (10-cup) ovenproof dish. Spread 1 cup pasta sauce over base of prepared dish; top with half the eggplant and half the capsicum. Layer with lasagne sheet; top with ½ cup of pasta sauce, ricotta, kumara and zucchini. Layer with another lasagne sheet; top with remaining pasta sauce, remaining eggplant and remaining capsicum. Layer remaining lasagne sheet over vegetables; top with white sauce, sprinkle with parmesan.
7 Bake, uncovered, about 45 minutes or until browned lightly. Stand lasagne 5 minutes before serving.

White sauce Melt butter in small saucepan, add flour; cook, stirring, until mixture thickens and bubbles. Remove from heat, gradually stir in milk; cook, stirring, until sauce boils and thickens. Remove from heat; stir in cheese.

Pumpkin and haloumi salad

preparation time **15 minutes** cooking time **10 minutes** serves **4**

650g pumpkin, cut into thin wedges
200g green beans, halved
2 tablespoons olive oil
2 tablespoons red wine vinegar
¾ cup loosely packed fresh coriander leaves
¾ cup loosely packed fresh flat-leaf parsley leaves
100g baby spinach leaves
⅓ cup (55g) toasted pepitas
250g haloumi, sliced thickly

1 Boil, steam or microwave pumpkin and beans, separately, until almost tender; drain. Rinse under cold water; drain. Place pumpkin on heated oiled grill plate; cook, uncovered, until wedges are tender.
2 Meanwhile, place oil, vinegar, coriander, parsley, spinach and pepitas in large bowl; toss gently to combine.
3 Cook cheese on heated oiled grill plate, uncovered, until browned both sides. Add cheese, pumpkin and beans to bowl with spinach mix; toss gently to combine.

Vietnamese omelette

preparation time **15 minutes** (plus standing time) cooking time **30 minutes**
serves **4**

5 dried shiitake mushrooms
8 eggs
½ cup (125ml) milk
1 tablespoon finely chopped fresh vietnamese mint
1 tablespoon peanut oil
5 green onions, sliced thinly
2 cloves garlic, crushed
230g can sliced bamboo shoots, drained
1 medium carrot (120g), sliced thinly
1 large red capsicum (350g), sliced thinly
1 cup (80g) bean sprouts
1 tablespoon mild chilli sauce
2 tablespoons light soy sauce
1 tablespoon finely chopped fresh coriander

1 Place mushrooms in small heatproof bowl, cover with boiling water; stand 20 minutes, then drain. Discard stems; slice caps thinly.
2 Meanwhile, whisk eggs, milk and mint in medium bowl until combined.
3 Heat half the oil in medium frying pan; cook onion, garlic and bamboo shoots, stirring, until onion softens. Add carrot and capsicum; cook, stirring, until carrot is just tender. Add mushrooms, sprouts, sauces and coriander; cook, stirring, until hot. Remove from pan; keep warm.
4 Heat remaining oil in pan. Add quarter of egg mixture; cook over medium heat, tilting pan, until egg mixture is almost set. Place quarter of vegetable mixture evenly over half the omelette.
5 Fold omelette over to enclose filling; slide onto serving plate. Repeat with remaining egg and vegetable mixture.

Vegetarian skewers

preparation time **10 minutes**   cooking time **10 minutes**   serves **4**

You need to soak 12 bamboo skewers in cold water before use to prevent them splintering or scorching.

2 tablespoons sun-dried tomato pesto
¼ cup (60ml) lemon juice
2 tablespoons olive oil
1 small red onion (100g), quartered
1 small green capsicum (150g), chopped coarsely
6 vegetarian sausages (300g), sliced thickly
250g cherry tomatoes, halved
100g ciabatta, diced into 2cm pieces
8 cherry bocconcini (80g)

1 Combine pesto, juice and oil in small bowl.

2 Thread onion, capsicum, sausage and half the tomato, alternately, onto eight skewers. Thread bread, cheese and remaining tomato, alternately, onto four skewers.

3 Brush skewers with pesto mixture. Cook, uncovered, on heated oiled grill plate, brushing occasionally with some of remaining pesto mixture, until skewers are browned lightly. Divide skewers among serving plates; drizzle with remaining pesto mixture.

Black-eyed beans with kumara, shallots and garlic

preparation time **20 minutes** (plus standing time) cooking time **35 minutes**
serves **1**

⅓ cup (65g) dried black-eyed beans
1 teaspoon olive oil
5 shallots (125g)
5 cloves garlic, unpeeled
1 small kumara (250g), chopped coarsely
2 tablespoons fresh lemon juice
1 small radicchio, shredded finely
1 tablespoon finely chopped fresh flat-leaf parsley

1 Place beans in small bowl, cover with water; stand overnight. Drain, then rinse under cold water; drain.
2 Preheat oven to moderately hot.
3 Combine oil, shallots, garlic and kumara on oven tray. Roast, uncovered, about 20 minutes or until garlic softens. Remove garlic from tray. Return remaining vegetables to oven; roast, uncovered, about 15 minutes or until vegetables are browned lightly.
4 Meanwhile, place beans in small saucepan of boiling water. Bring to a boil then reduce heat; simmer, covered, about 25 minutes or until beans are tender. Drain.
5 Using fingers, squeeze garlic from skins into medium bowl; stir in juice.
6 Add beans, vegetables, radicchio and parsley; toss gently to combine.

Baked potato with guacamole

preparation time **15 minutes** cooking time **1 hour** serves **1**

1 medium potato (200g)
1 small avocado (200g)
½ small red onion (50g), chopped finely
1 small tomato (90g), seeded, chopped finely
1 tablespoon finely chopped fresh coriander
1 tablespoon fresh lime juice
50g mesclun

1 Preheat oven to moderately hot.
2 Pierce potato skin in several places with fork, wrap potato in foil; place on oven tray. Bake about 1 hour or until tender.
3 Mash avocado coarsely in small bowl; stir in onion, tomato, coriander and lime juice.
4 Cut deep cross in potato; serve potato topped with guacamole and accompanied with mesclun.

Chickpea corn enchiladas

preparation time **15 minutes** cooking time **10 minutes** serves **4**

1 tablespoon olive oil
1 small white onion (80g), chopped coarsely
1 clove garlic, crushed
½ teaspoon ground chilli
1 teaspoon ground cumin
400g can tomato puree
300g can chickpeas, rinsed, drained
1 tablespoon coarsely chopped fresh coriander
8 corn tortillas
1 small red onion (100g), chopped coarsely
1 medium tomato (190g), chopped coarsely
1 small avocado (200g), chopped coarsely
½ cup (60g) coarsely grated cheddar
½ cup loosely packed, finely shredded iceberg lettuce

1 Heat oil in medium saucepan; cook onion and garlic, stirring, until onion softens. Add spices; cook, stirring, 2 minutes. Add puree. Bring to a boil then reduce heat; cook, stirring, until hot.
2 Soften tortillas in microwave oven on HIGH (100%) 30 seconds. Divide onion mixture and remaining ingredients among tortillas; fold enchiladas to enclose filling.

tip You can also soften tortillas by wrapping them in foil and heating them in a moderate oven about 5 minutes or until hot.

Mushroom burgers with the lot

preparation time **10 minutes** cooking time **15 minutes** serves **1**

10g baby spinach leaves
1 teaspoon lemon juice
1 teaspoon olive oil
½ teaspoon dijon mustard
1 thick slice ciabatta
½ small brown onion (40g), sliced thickly
1 large flat mushroom (100g), halved
½ small tomato (90g), sliced thinly
1 egg

1 Place spinach and combined juice, oil and mustard in medium bowl; toss gently to combine.
2 Toast ciabatta, both sides, on heated oiled grill plate (or grill or barbecue); cook onion, mushroom and tomato on same heated oiled grill plate, uncovered, until vegetables are just tender.
3 Meanwhile, cook egg in lightly oiled egg ring on heated oiled flat plate, uncovered, until cooked as desired.
4 Top ciabatta with mushroom, onion, tomato, egg and spinach mixture.

tip Substitute turkish bread or focaccia for ciabatta, if you prefer.

Roasted root vegetables with yogurt

preparation time **15 minutes** cooking time **35 minutes** serves **1**

1 small parsnip (120g), chopped coarsely
100g celeriac, chopped coarsely
150g pumpkin, chopped coarsely
1 medium potato (200g), chopped coarsely
2 cloves garlic, crushed
1 teaspoon finely chopped fresh rosemary
2 teaspoons olive oil
½ small red capsicum (75g), chopped finely
1 tablespoon coarsely chopped fresh chives
2 tablespoons goat's milk yogurt

1 Preheat oven to moderately hot.
2 Combine parsnip, celeriac, pumpkin, potato, garlic, rosemary and oil on oven tray. Roast, uncovered, about 35 minutes or until vegetables are tender. Add capsicum and chives; toss gently to combine.
3 Serve vegetables topped with yogurt.

Zucchini fritters

preparation time **10 minutes** cooking time **10 minutes** makes **10**

5 large zucchini (750g), grated coarsely
1 medium white onion (150g), chopped finely
½ cup (75g) plain flour
3 eggs, beaten lightly
1 tablespoon chopped fresh oregano
1 tablespoon chopped fresh basil
1 tablespoon chopped fresh flat-leaf parsley
Vegetable oil, for shallow-frying

1 Combine zucchini, onion, flour, egg and herbs in medium bowl.
2 Cook ¼-cup measures of zucchini mixture, in batches, in hot oil until fritters are browned both sides and cooked through; drain on absorbent paper.

Eggplant, fetta and capsicum stack with mesclun salad

preparation time **15 minutes** cooking time **15 minutes** serves **4**

2 medium red capsicums (400g)
¼ cup (60ml) olive oil
2 tablespoons lemon juice
1 clove garlic, crushed
1 large eggplant (500g)
1 cup (150g) drained sun-dried tomatoes, chopped coarsely
¼ cup (50g) seeded kalamata olives, chopped coarsely
½ cup loosely packed fresh basil leaves, torn
100g mesclun
2 tablespoons red wine vinegar
200g fetta, cut into 8 slices
1 tablespoon small whole fresh basil leaves, extra

1 Quarter capsicums; discard seeds and membranes. Cook capsicum on heated oiled grill plate (or grill or barbeuce), skin-side down, until skin blisters and blackens. Cover with plastic wrap 5 minutes; peel away skin.

2 Meanwhile, combine 2 tablespoons of oil in small bowl with juice and garlic. Cut eggplant lengthways into eight slices, brush slices both sides with oil mixture; cook on same heated oiled grill plate, uncovered, brushing occasionally with oil mixture, until just tender.

3 Combine tomato, olives and basil in small bowl. Place mesclun in medium bowl, drizzle with vinegar and remaining oil; toss gently to combine.

4 Place one slice of eggplant on each serving plate; top each with two slices of cheese, two pieces of capsicum and one remaining eggplant slice. Top with tomato mixture, sprinkle with extra basil leaves; serve with salad.

CURRIES AND STEWS

Chickpea, pumpkin and eggplant curry

preparation time **15 minutes** cooking time **40 minutes** serves **4**

1 tablespoon vegetable oil
1 medium brown onion (150g), chopped coarsely
2 cloves garlic, crushed
4 baby eggplant (200g), chopped coarsely
¼ cup (75g) medium curry paste
½ cup (600g) butternut pumpkin, peeled, chopped coarsely
½ cauliflower (500g), chopped
1½ cups (375ml) vegetable stock
425g can crushed tomatoes
400g can chickpeas, drained, rinsed
1 cup (280g) plain yogurt
½ cup finely shredded fresh mint

1 Heat oil in large saucepan, add onion, garlic and eggplant; cook, stirring, until just tender. Add curry paste; cook, stirring, until fragrant.
2 Add pumpkin, cauliflower, stock and undrained tomatoes. Bring to a boil then reduce heat; simmer, covered, 20 minutes. Add chickpeas; simmer, covered, 10 minutes or until vegetables are tender.
3 Meanwhile, combine yogurt and mint in small bowl. Serve curry with yogurt mixture.

Rogan josh

preparation time **10 minutes**   cooking time **2 hours 10 minutes**   serves **6**

2 teaspoons ground cardamom
1 teaspoon ground fennel
2 teaspoons ground cumin
2 teaspoons ground coriander
1.4kg trimmed diced lamb shoulder
¼ cup (60ml) vegetable oil
2 medium brown onions (300g), chopped finely
2 tablespoons grated fresh ginger
6 fresh red thai chillies, sliced thinly
4 cloves garlic, crushed
400g can tomatoes
¼ teaspoon saffron threads
2 bay leaves
2 cinnamon sticks
¼ cup (40g) poppy seeds
1 cup (280g) thick yogurt
2 teaspoons brown sugar
¼ cup fresh coriander leaves

1 Combine ground spices in medium bowl, add lamb; toss to cover lamb in spice mix.

2 Heat half the oil in large saucepan, add lamb; cook, in batches, until browned all over.

3 Heat remaining oil in same pan, add onion, ginger, chilli and garlic; cook, stirring, until onion is soft. Return lamb to pan with undrained crushed tomatoes, saffron, bay leaves, cinnamon sticks and poppy seeds. Add yogurt, 1 tablespoon at a time, stirring well between each addition.

4 Bring to a boil then reduce heat to very low; cook, covered, 1 ¾ hours or until lamb is very tender. Stir in brown sugar; cook, uncovered, 10 minutes or until curry has thickened.

5 Sprinkle with fresh coriander leaves to serve.

tip Freeze leftover curry in single portions for up to two months.

Red chicken curry

preparation time **15 minutes** cooking time **40 minutes** serves **4**

750g chicken thigh fillets
1 ²/₃ cups (410ml) coconut milk
200g green beans, halved
4 kaffir lime leaves, torn
1 medium red capsicum (200g), chopped coarsely

Curry paste
3 cloves garlic, chopped coarsely
2 tablespoons coarsely chopped fresh lemon grass
1 tablespoon grated fresh galangal
4 green onions, chopped coarsely
1 teaspoon shrimp paste
5 fresh red thai chillies, chopped coarsely
1 teaspoon hot paprika
¼ cup (60ml) peanut oil

1 Blend or process ingredients for curry paste until smooth.
2 Cut chicken into 3cm-thick slices. Cook curry paste in heated large frying pan about 3 minutes or until fragrant. Add chicken; cook, stirring, until browned. Stir in coconut milk, beans and lime leaves. Bring to a boil then reduce heat; simmer, uncovered, 20 minutes. (Can be made three days ahead to this stage and refrigerated, covered.)
3 Add capsicum; simmer, uncovered, about 10 minutes or until capsicum is just tender. Discard lime leaves before serving.

tips You can use ¹/₃ cup packaged red curry paste in this recipe.
Freeze leftover curry in single portions for up to two months.

Beef rendang

preparation time **15 minutes** cooking time **15 minutes** serves **4**

2 medium brown onions (300g)
2 cloves garlic, quartered
4cm piece fresh ginger (20g), peeled
1 tablespoon coarsely chopped lemon grass
1 tablespoon peanut oil
1kg beef fillet, sliced thinly
1 cinnamon stick
2 whole cloves
1 tablespoon ground coriander
1 tablespoon ground cumin
½ cup (45g) desiccated coconut
1 tablespoon tamarind concentrate
¼ cup (60ml) coconut cream

1 Blend or process one quartered onion, garlic, ginger and lemon grass until mixture is almost smooth. Finely chop remaining onion.
2 Heat oil in wok; stir-fry beef and remaining onion, in batches, until beef is browned all over. Remove beef mixture from pan.
3 Add onion mixture to wok with spices and coconut; stir-fry until fragrant.
4 Return beef mixture to wok with tamarind and coconut cream; stir-fry until rendang is almost dry.

serving suggestion Beef rendang is traditionally eaten with sticky rice cooked in coconut milk; steamed or boiled rice is just as good.

Pork vindaloo

preparation time **15 minutes** (plus refrigeration time)
cooking time **1 hour 15 minutes** serves **6**

2 teaspoons cumin seeds
2 teaspoons garam masala
1 tablespoon grated fresh ginger
6 cloves garlic, crushed
8 fresh red thai chillies, chopped finely
1 tablespoon white vinegar
1 tablespoon tamarind concentrate
1kg diced pork
2 tablespoons unsalted butter
2 large brown onions (400g), chopped coarsely
2 cinnamon sticks
6 whole cloves
2 teaspoons plain flour
1 litre (4 cups) beef stock
8 curry leaves
2 tablespoons finely chopped palm sugar

1 Cook cumin and garam masala in large heated dry saucepan, stirring until fragrant; cool.
2 Combine cumin mixture with ginger, garlic, chilli, vinegar, tamarind and pork in large bowl; cover, refrigerate 1 hour.
3 Heat butter in same pan; cook onion, cinnamon and cloves, stirring, until onion is lightly browned. Add pork mixture; cook, stirring, about 5 minutes or until pork is lightly browned. Stir in flour.
4 Add stock gradually, stir in leaves; simmer, covered, 30 minutes. Remove cover; simmer about 30 minutes or until pork is tender and sauce thickened. Add palm sugar; stir until dissolved.

tip Freeze leftover curry in single portions for up to two months.

Coconut chicken masala

preparation time **15 minutes** cooking time **35 minutes** serves **4**

2 tablespoons peanut oil
1 large brown onion (200g), sliced thinly
2 cloves garlic, crushed
1 tablespoon coriander seeds
1 tablespoon ground cumin
1 teaspoon ground turmeric
1 teaspoon ground ginger
1 teaspoon garam masala
2 teaspoons chilli powder
1 teaspoon coarsely ground black pepper
1.5kg chicken breast fillets, chopped coarsely
¼ cup (70g) tomato paste
1½ cups (375ml) chicken stock
½ cup (125ml) water
1 teaspoon cornflour
¾ cup (180ml) coconut cream
2 tablespoons coarsely chopped fresh coriander

1 Heat oil in large saucepan; cook onion and garlic, stirring, until onion softens. Add coriander seeds; cook, stirring, about 1 minute or until seeds start to pop. Add remaining spices; cook, stirring, until mixture is fragrant.
2 Add chicken to pan, turning to coat pieces in spice mixture; cook, stirring, until chicken is just browned.
3 Stir in tomato paste, stock and the water. Bring to a boil then reduce heat; simmer, covered, about 20 minutes or until chicken is cooked through.
4 Blend cornflour with coconut cream in small bowl; stir into chicken curry. Bring to a boil; cook, stirring, until mixture thickens slightly. Just before serving, stir in fresh coriander.

tip Freeze leftover curry in single portions for up to two months.

Bombay potato masala

preparation time **10 minutes** cooking time **15 minutes** serves **6**

1.5kg potatoes
20g butter
1 large brown onion (200g), sliced thinly
3 cloves garlic, crushed
1 teaspoon yellow mustard seeds
3 teaspoons garam masala
2 teaspoons ground coriander
2 teaspoons ground cumin
½ teaspoon chilli powder
¼ teaspoon ground turmeric
400g canned tomatoes

1 Cut potatoes into wedges. Boil, steam or microwave potato until just tender; drain.
2 Heat butter in large frying pan; cook onion and garlic, stirring, until onion is soft. Add seeds and spices; cook, stirring, until fragrant.
3 Stir in undrained crushed tomatoes; cook, stirring, 2 minutes or until sauce thickens slightly. Add potato; gently stir until hot.

Dry beef curry

preparation time **15 minutes** cooking time **1 hour 50 minutes** serves **4**

2 tablespoons peanut oil
2 large brown onions (400g), chopped
3 cloves garlic, crushed
1 tablespoon grated fresh ginger
1 teaspoon ground turmeric
½ teaspoon chilli powder
2 tablespoons chopped fresh lemon grass
1.5kg chuck steak, cubed
1¼ cups (310ml) water

1 Heat oil in large frying pan; cook onion, garlic, ginger, turmeric, chilli and lemon grass, stirring, until onion is soft. Add steak; cook, stirring, over high heat about 5 minutes or until steak is browned.

2 Stir in the water. Bring to a boil then reduce heat; simmer, covered, about 1½ hours or until steak is tender.

3 Remove lid, stir over high heat until liquid has evaporated.

Sour duck curry

preparation time **15 minutes** (plus standing time) cooking time **50 minutes** serves **4**

1.6kg whole duck
1 large brown onion (200g), chopped finely
1 tablespoon ground coriander
1 teaspoon ground ginger
½ teaspoon ground turmeric
½ teaspoon ground cardamom
¼ teaspoon paprika
1 teaspoon tamarind concentrate
2 cups (500ml) chicken stock
2 tablespoons water
1 tablespoon cornflour
1 tablespoon chopped fresh coriander

1 Cut duck into serving-size pieces. Cook duck, in batches, in large heated pan until browned both sides.

2 Remove from pan; drain on absorbent paper.

3 Drain fat from pan, reserving 1 tablespoon. Heat reserved fat in same pan; cook onion, stirring, 1 minute. Add ground coriander, ginger, turmeric, cardamom and paprika; cook, stirring, until spices become fragrant. Stir in tamarind and stock.

4 Return duck to pan. Bring to boil then reduce heat; simmer, uncovered, 30 minutes or until duck is tender.

5 Combine the water and flour in small bowl; stir into duck mixture. Stir over medium heat until sauce boils and thickens. Stir through fresh coriander just before serving.

tip Freeze leftover curry in single portions for up to two months.

Potato and pea curry

preparation time **15 minutes** cooking time **20 minutes** serves **4**

¼ cup (60ml) vegetable oil
1 medium brown onion (150g), chopped finely
2 cloves garlic, crushed
1 teaspoon ground cumin
½ teaspoon ground coriander
½ teaspoon ground fennel
½ teaspoon ground turmeric
¼ teaspoon cayenne pepper
1 teaspoon garam masala
4 medium potatoes (800g), peeled, chopped
400g can tomatoes
½ cup (125ml) water
1 cup (125g) frozen peas

1 Heat oil in large pan; cook onion and garlic, stirring, until onion is soft.
Add spices and potato; cook 2 minutes.
2 Stir in undrained crushed tomatoes and the water. Bring to boil then reduce
heat; simmer, stirring occasionally, about 20 minutes or until potato is tender.
3 Add peas; cook, stirring, about 3 minutes or until peas are hot.

Fish cutlets with coconut

preparation time **10 minutes** (plus cooling time) cooking time **25 minutes**
serves **4**

2 tablespoons desiccated coconut
1 tablespoon coriander seeds
2 teaspoons cumin seeds
1 fresh red thai chilli, chopped finely
2 cloves garlic, crushed
1 teaspoon grated fresh ginger
2 tablespoons tamarind concentrate
1 tablespoon peanut oil
1 medium brown onion (150g), chopped finely
1½ cups (375ml) coconut cream
4 x 250g white fish cutlets

1 Stir coconut in small frying pan over medium heat until browned lightly; remove from pan. Add seeds to pan; stir over medium heat, about 2 minutes or until lightly browned. Remove from pan; cool.

2 Blend or process coconut, seeds, chilli, garlic, ginger and tamarind until smooth and paste-like.

3 Heat oil in medium frying pan; cook onion, stirring, over medium heat, about 2 minutes or until onion is soft. Stir in coconut mixture; stir over medium heat, 1 minute.

4 Stir in coconut cream. Bring to a boil then reduce heat; add fish, simmer, uncovered, about 8 minutes or until fish is tender. Turn fish halfway through cooking time.

tip Freeze leftover curry in single portions for up to two months.

Lamb korma meatballs

preparation time **30 minutes** (plus standing time) cooking time **30 minutes**
serves **4**

500g lamb mince
1 large brown onion (200g), grated
½ cup (35g) stale breadcrumbs
1 egg, beaten lightly
¼ cup (75g) korma curry paste
2 tablespoons vegetable oil
1 cup (250ml) beef stock
200g spinach leaves, sliced thinly
200g plain yogurt

1 Combine lamb, onion, breadcrumbs, egg and 2 tablespoons of curry paste in large bowl. Roll level tablespoons of lamb mixture into balls.

2 Heat half the oil in non-stick frying pan; add meatballs, cook until browned. Remove meatballs from pan, drain on absorbent paper.

3 Heat remaining oil in same pan; cook remaining curry paste, stirring, until fragrant. Add stock, bring to a boil then return meatballs to pan; simmer, covered, until meatballs are cooked through.

4 Add spinach, stir until just wilted. Remove from heat; stand 2 minutes. Stir in yogurt, season with salt and freshly ground black pepper.

tip Freeze leftover curry in single portions for up to two months.

Braised beef curry

preparation time **15 minutes** (plus refrigeration time)
cooking time **2 hours 30 minutes** serves **8**

1 tablespoon peanut oil
2 medium brown onions (300g), chopped coarsely
2 cloves garlic, crushed
1 fresh red thai chilli, chopped finely
1 teaspoon finely grated fresh ginger
2 teaspoons garam masala
2 tablespoons ground cumin
2 tablespoons ground coriander
4 cardamom pods, bruised
3 cinnamon sticks, broken
2 cups (500ml) water
2kg beef chuck steak, cut into 2cm pieces
3 cups (750ml) beef stock
½ cup (125ml) coconut milk
⅓ cup coarsely chopped fresh coriander

1 Heat oil in large heavy-base saucepan; cook onion, garlic, chilli and ginger, stirring, until onion is soft. Stir in spices; cook, stirring, until fragrant.
2 Gradually stir ¼ cup (60ml) of the water into onion mixture until it forms a paste; cook, stirring, 2 minutes. Add beef; stir to coat in paste.
3 Add the remaining water and stock. Bring to a boil then reduce heat; simmer, covered, stirring occasionally, about 1½ hours or until beef is tender. Refrigerate overnight, to allow flavours to develop.
4 Add coconut milk; simmer, uncovered, about 30 minutes or until thickened slightly. Discard cardamom pods and cinnamon sticks. Stir in coriander.

serving suggestion Serve curry with cooked red lentils, if desired.

tip Freeze leftover curry in single portions for up to two months.

Dry squid curry

preparation time **15 minutes** cooking time **10 minutes** serves **4**

500g squid hoods
2 tablespoons mild chilli powder
1 teaspoon ground turmeric
1 tablespoon tamarind concentrate
2 tablespoons hot water
2 tablespoons vegetable oil
2 medium white onions (300g), chopped finely
4 cloves garlic, crushed
2 tablespoons tomato sauce
1 teaspoon soy sauce
1 tablespoon fish sauce
½ teaspoon white sugar
⅓ cup (80ml) lemon juice

1 Cut squid into rings. Combine squid, chilli powder and turmeric in large bowl; mix well. Place tamarind concentrate and the water in small bowl.
2 Heat oil in large frying pan. Cook squid mixture, stirring, until squid changes colour; remove from pan.
3 Cook onion and garlic in pan, stirring, until onion is soft. Add tamarind mixture, sauces and sugar; cook, stirring occasionally, 4 minutes.
4 Return squid to pan. Add juice; stir until squid is tender.

serving suggestion Serve squid curry sprinkled with fried onions.

Green lamb curry

preparation time **10 minutes** cooking time **1 hour 45 minutes** serves **4**

1 tablespoon vegetable oil
1 kg diced lamb
1 large brown onion (200g), sliced thinly
⅓ cup (80g) green curry paste
3 cups (750ml) chicken stock
2 bay leaves
1⅔ cups (410ml) coconut cream
1 large green capsicum (350g), sliced thinly
100g snow peas, trimmed
425g can whole baby corn, drained
2 tablespoons finely chopped fresh coriander
½ cup (40g) bean sprouts

1 Heat oil in large saucepan. Cook lamb, in batches, until browned all over; remove from pan. Cook onion and paste in pan, stirring, until onion is soft. Return lamb to pan; add stock and bay leaves. Bring to a boil then reduce heat; simmer, uncovered, 1½ hours or until lamb is tender.
2 Add coconut cream, capsicum, snow peas, corn and coriander; stir until hot. Serve topped with sprouts.

tip Freeze leftover curry in single portions for up to two months.

Malaysian fish curry

preparation time **25 minutes** cooking time **35 minutes** serves **4**

6 fresh red thai chillies, chopped coarsely
2 cloves garlic, quartered
10 french shallots (120g), chopped coarsely
½ cup coarsely chopped fresh lemon grass
5cm piece galangal (25g), quartered
1 teaspoon curry powder
1 teaspoon ground coriander
¼ teaspoon ground turmeric
2 tablespoons vegetable oil
1 tablespoon fish sauce
1⅔ cups (400ml) coconut milk
1⅔ cups (400ml) coconut cream
4 x 220g firm white fish fillets
¼ cup (10g) flaked coconut, toasted

1 Blend or process chilli, garlic, shallot, lemon grass, galangal, curry powder, coriander, turmeric and half the oil until mixture forms a paste.
2 Heat remaining oil in large frying pan; cook paste, stirring, over medium heat, about 3 minutes or until fragrant. Add sauce, coconut milk and coconut cream. Bring to a boil then reduce heat; simmer, uncovered, about 15 minutes or until mixture thickens slightly.
3 Cook fish on heated oiled grill plate, in batches, until browned both sides and cooked as desired.
4 Divide fish among serving bowls; top with sauce, sprinkle with coconut.

tips If you cannot find french shallots, substitute a medium brown onion and a small clove of crushed garlic; galangal can be replaced with fresh ginger.

Green chilli beef stew

preparation time **15 minutes** cooking time **2 hours** serves **4**

2 tablespoons olive oil
1kg beef chuck steak, cut into 3cm cubes
1 large brown onion (200g), sliced thinly
2 cloves garlic, sliced thinly
2 teaspoons ground cumin
2 long green chillies, sliced thinly
2 cups (500ml) beef stock
1 tablespoon tomato paste
3 large egg tomatoes (270g), chopped coarsely
500g baby new potatoes, halved
¼ cup coarsely chopped fresh coriander

1 Preheat oven to moderate.
2 Heat half the oil in large flameproof baking dish; cook beef, in batches, stirring, until browned all over. Remove from dish.
3 Heat remaining oil in same dish; cook onion, garlic, cumin and chilli, stirring, until onion softens. Add stock and paste; bring to a boil, stirring. Return beef to dish; cook, covered, in moderate oven 45 minutes.
4 Add tomato and potato; cook, covered, in moderate oven 35 minutes. Uncover; cook 20 minutes. Stir coriander into stew.

serving suggestion Serve stew with warmed wheat flour tortillas.

tip Freeze leftover stew in single portions for up to two months.

Beef and horseradish stew

preparation time **40 minutes** cooking time **3 hours 30 minutes** serves **6**

2 tablespoons olive oil
1.5kg beef chuck steak, cut into 5cm cubes
3 medium brown onions (450g), sliced into wedges
3 cloves garlic, crushed
8cm piece fresh ginger (40g), grated
2 teaspoons curry powder
¼ cup (35g) plain flour
3 cups (750ml) beef stock
1 tablespoon worcestershire sauce
2 tablespoons horseradish cream
¼ cup coarsely chopped fresh flat-leaf parsley

1 Preheat oven to very slow.
2 Heat oil in large flameproof casserole dish; cook beef, in batches, until browned. Remove from dish.
3 Cook onion, garlic and ginger in same dish, stirring, about 5 minutes or until onion softens. Add curry powder and flour; cook, stirring, 5 minutes.
4 Return beef to dish with stock and worcestershire sauce; stir over heat until mixture boils and thickens. Cover dish tightly; cook in very slow oven for 3 hours, stirring occasionally.
5 Stir horseradish cream and parsley through beef mixture off heat, just before serving.

serving suggestion Serve stew with mashed potato.

tip Freeze leftover stew in single portions for up to two months.

Cauliflower, pea and fried tofu curry

preparation time **15 minutes** cooking time **20 minutes** serves **4**

You will need a small cauliflower weighing approximately 1kg to make this recipe.

2 tablespoons peanut oil
1 medium brown onion (150g), chopped coarsely
2 cloves garlic, crushed
900g cauliflower florets
1 teaspoon ground cumin
½ teaspoon ground coriander
½ teaspoon ground turmeric
¼ teaspoon ground cayenne pepper
1 teaspoon garam masala
400g can tomatoes
1 cup (250ml) vegetable stock
400g firm tofu
¼ cup (60ml) vegetable oil
1 cup (125g) frozen peas, thawed

1 Heat peanut oil in wok; stir-fry onion and garlic until onion softens. Add cauliflower and spices; cook, stirring, 2 minutes.

2 Add undrained crushed tomatoes and stock, stir to combine. Bring to a boil then reduce heat; simmer, covered, 10 minutes or until cauliflower softens.

3 Meanwhile, cut tofu into 1cm cubes. Heat vegetable oil in medium frying pan; cook tofu, in batches, until lightly coloured and crisp on all sides, drain on absorbent paper. Add tofu and peas to cauliflower curry.

Butter chicken

preparation time **20 minutes** (plus refrigeration time)
cooking time **50 minutes** serves **8**

1.5kg chicken thigh fillets, halved
4 cloves garlic, crushed
2 teaspoons garam masala
2 teaspoons ground coriander
2 teaspoons ground cumin
½ teaspoon chilli powder
2 teaspoons sweet paprika
½ cup (140g) plain yogurt
80g butter, chopped
2 tablespoons white vinegar
2 tablespoons tomato paste
410g can tomato puree
¾ cup (180ml) chicken stock
5 cardamom pods, bruised
1 cinnamon stick
300ml cream
⅓ cup coarsely chopped fresh coriander

1 Combine chicken, garlic, spices and yogurt in large bowl, cover; refrigerate
3 hours or overnight.
2 Melt butter in large saucepan; cook chicken mixture, stirring, about
10 minutes or until chicken browns lightly. Add vinegar, paste, puree,
stock, cardamom and cinnamon. Bring to a boil then reduce heat; simmer,
uncovered, stirring occasionally, about 30 minutes or until chicken is cooked
through. Add cream; stir until hot. Stir in coriander.

tip Freeze leftover curry in single portions for up to two months.

Lamb and spinach curry

preparation time **15 minutes** cooking time **35 minutes** serves **4**

2 tablespoons vegetable oil
750g lamb fillets, sliced thinly
2 medium brown onions (300g), chopped finely
3 cloves garlic, crushed
1 teaspoon finely grated fresh ginger
1 teaspoon chilli powder
1 cinnamon stick
5 cardamom pods, bruised
2 tablespoons garam masala
2 teaspoons black mustard seeds
2 tablespoons tomato paste
600ml buttermilk
½ cup (120g) sour cream
600g frozen spinach, thawed, drained

1 Heat half the oil in large saucepan; cook lamb, in batches, until browned. Remove from pan.
2 Heat remaining oil in same pan; cook onion, garlic and ginger, stirring, until onion softens. Add spices and paste; cook, stirring, until fragrant.
3 Return lamb to pan with remaining ingredients. Bring to a boil then reduce heat; simmer, uncovered, about 15 minutes or until sauce thickens.

tip Freeze leftover curry in single portions for up to two months.

Beef coconut curry

preparation time **10 minutes** cooking time **15 minutes** serves **4**

2 tablespoons peanut oil
500g beef strips
1 medium brown onion (150g), sliced thinly
2 teaspoons grated fresh ginger
1 clove garlic, crushed
⅓ cup (100g) mild curry paste
1⅔ cups (400ml) coconut milk
1 medium yellow capsicum (200g), sliced thinly
150g green beans, halved

1 Heat half the oil in wok; stir-fry beef, in batches, until browned. Remove from wok.
2 Heat remaining oil in wok, stir-fry onion until soft. Add ginger, garlic and paste; stir-fry until fragrant. Stir in coconut milk; bring to a boil.
3 Return beef to wok with remaining ingredients; stir-fry until vegetables are tender.

tip Freeze leftover curry in single portions for up to two months.

Chicken, capsicum and caper stew

preparation time **35 minutes** cooking time **45 minutes** serves **4**

8 chicken drumsticks (1.2kg)
¼ cup (35g) plain flour
1 teaspoon paprika
2 tablespoons olive oil
1 medium red capsicum (200g), chopped coarsely
1 medium yellow capsicum (200g), chopped coarsely
1 medium brown onion (150g), chopped coarsely
100g button mushrooms, halved
2 cloves garlic, crushed
1¾ cups (430ml) chicken stock
¼ cup (60ml) dry white wine
2 bay leaves
2 tablespoons drained tiny capers

1 Remove skin from chicken. Toss chicken in combined flour and paprika; shake away excess flour mixture.
2 Heat half the oil in large saucepan; cook chicken, in batches, until browned all over. Remove from pan.
3 Heat remaining oil in pan; cook capsicums, onion, mushrooms and garlic, stirring, until onion is soft.
4 Return chicken to pan. Add stock, wine, bay leaves and capers; simmer, covered, 20 minutes, stirring occasionally.
5 Remove cover; simmer 10 minutes or until chicken is tender. Discard bay leaves before serving.

tip Freeze leftover stew in single portions for up to two months.

Chicken and bean madras

preparation time **10 minutes** cooking time **20 minutes** serves **4**

1 tablespoon peanut oil
1 large white onion (200g), sliced thinly
700g chicken thigh fillets, sliced thinly
¼ cup (75g) madras curry paste
200g green beans, chopped coarsely
½ cup (125ml) chicken stock
1 tablespoon tomato paste

1 Heat oil in wok; stir-fry onion and chicken, in batches, until chicken is just browned. Remove from pan.
2 Heat curry paste in wok; stir-fry until fragrant. Return chicken mixture to wok with beans, stock and tomato paste; stir-fry until sauce thickens slightly and chicken is cooked through.

serving suggestion Serve curry with steamed basmati rice.

tip Freeze leftover curry in single portions for up to two months.

Oxtail stew

preparation time **25 minutes** cooking time **2 hours** serves **6**

2kg oxtails, cut into 5cm pieces
Plain flour
60g unsalted butter
2 large brown onions (400g), sliced thinly
2 cloves garlic, crushed
2 teaspoons coarsely chopped fresh rosemary
¼ cup (60ml) dry red wine
2 large parsnips (360g), sliced thickly
2 medium carrots (240g), sliced thickly
3 cups (750ml) beef stock
1 teaspoon freshly ground black pepper
2 medium zucchini (240g), sliced thickly
1 cup (250ml) tomato puree
1 tablespoon coarsely chopped fresh parsley

1 Toss oxtail in flour; shake away excess flour. Heat butter in large saucepan; cook oxtail, in batches, until browned all over. Drain on absorbent paper.
2 Add onion, garlic and rosemary to pan; cook, stirring, until onion is soft.
3 Add wine; cook, stirring, until liquid reduces by half.
4 Return oxtail to pan; add parsnip, carrot, stock and black pepper. Cook, covered, 1¼ hours.
5 Add zucchini, puree and parsley; cook, uncovered, 20 minutes or until oxtail is tender.

tip Freeze leftover stew in single portions for up to two months.

Spicy caribbean-style chicken stew

preparation time **45 minutes** cooking time **50 minutes** serves **6**

1kg chicken thigh fillets
2 teaspoons ground allspice
1 teaspoon ground cinnamon
Pinch ground nutmeg
1 tablespoon finely chopped fresh thyme
¼ cup (60ml) olive oil
2 medium brown onions (300g), sliced thinly
2 cloves garlic, crushed
1 tablespoon grated fresh ginger
1 teaspoon sambal oelek
5 medium tomatoes (650g), peeled, seeded, chopped finely
2 tablespoons brown sugar
2 teaspoons grated orange rind
2 tablespoons soy sauce
1 medium kumara (400g), chopped coarsely
2 fresh corn cobs, sliced thickly
125g baby spinach leaves

1 Cut chicken into 2cm strips. Toss chicken in combined spices and thyme.

2 Heat half the oil in large saucepan; cook chicken, in batches, stirring, until browned. Drain on absorbent paper.

3 Heat remaining oil in pan. Cook onion, garlic, ginger and sambal, stirring, until onion is soft.

4 Add tomato, sugar, rind, sauce, kumara, corn and chicken; cook, covered, about 15 minutes or until chicken and vegetables are tender. Remove cover; simmer 5 minutes.

5 Remove from heat. Add spinach; stir until spinach is wilted.

tip Freeze leftover stew in single portions for up to two months.

Chicken gumbo

preparation time **30 minutes** cooking time **1 hour 30 minutes** serves **6**

400g okra
12 chicken thigh cutlets (2kg)
2 tablespoons olive oil
2 medium brown onions (300g), chopped finely
3 cloves garlic, crushed
1 medium green capsicum (200g), chopped coarsely
1 medium red capsicum (200g), chopped coarsely
1 ½ teaspoons cajun seasoning
½ teaspoon ground cumin
¼ teaspoon cayenne pepper
2 bay leaves
2 cups (500ml) chicken stock
2 x 400g cans tomatoes
2 teaspoons worcestershire sauce

1 Trim stems from okra. Remove skin from chicken.
2 Heat oil in large saucepan; cook chicken, in batches, until browned all over. Drain on absorbent paper.
3 Add onion, garlic and okra to pan; cook, stirring, until onion is soft.
4 Return chicken to pan with capsicums, spices and bay leaves; cook, stirring, until fragrant.
5 Add stock, undrained crushed tomatoes and sauce; simmer, covered, 1 hour.
6 Remove cover; simmer further 10 minutes or until thickened slightly. Discard bay leaves before serving.

tip Freeze leftover stew in single portions for up to two months.

Beef bourguignon

preparation time **35 minutes** cooking time **2 hours 30 minutes** serves **4**

1 kg beef chuck steak
8 baby onions (200g)
3 bacon rashers (210g)
300g button mushrooms
1 tablespoon olive oil
30g butter
1 clove garlic, crushed
¼ cup (35g) plain flour
1 cup (250ml) beef stock
1 cup (250ml) dry red wine
1 tablespoon brown sugar
2 tablespoons chopped fresh oregano

1 Cut away and discard as much fat as possible from beef; cut into 3cm pieces. Peel onions, leaving root end trimmed but intact so onion remains whole during cooking. Cut off and discard rind from bacon; coarsely chop bacon. Trim mushroom stems.
2 Heat oil in large heavy-base flameproof casserole dish; cook beef, in batches, stirring, until browned all over. Remove from dish.
3 Heat butter in same dish; cook onions, bacon, mushrooms and garlic, stirring, until onions are browned all over.
4 Sprinkle flour over onion mixture; cook, stirring, until flour is browned lightly. Remove dish from heat; gradually stir in stock, then wine.
5 Return dish to heat; cook, stirring, until mixture boils and thickens. Return beef with any juices to dish, add sugar. Bring to a boil then reduce heat; simmer, covered, about 2 hours or until beef is tender, stirring every 30 minutes. Stir in oregano.

serving suggestion Serve stew with crusty bread or buttered noodles.

tip Freeze leftover stew in single portions for up to two months.

Irish stew with herb dumplings

preparation time **30 minutes** cooking time **1 hour 45 minutes** serves **4**

1kg diced lamb
2 tablespoons plain flour
1 teaspoon freshly ground black pepper
2 large brown onions (400g), sliced
2 large potatoes (600g), sliced
1 large carrot (180g), sliced
½ cup (100g) pearl barley
2 teaspoons finely chopped fresh thyme
1½ cups (375ml) beef stock
1 litre (4 cups) hot water

Herb dumplings
1 cup (150g) self-raising flour
50g cold butter, chopped
1 tablespoon finely chopped fresh parsley
1 tablespoon finely chopped fresh thyme
1 egg, beaten
¼ cup (60ml) milk, approximately

1 Toss lamb in large bowl with combined flour and pepper.
2 Layer half the onion, potato, carrot and lamb in large heavy-base pan; repeat layering with remaining vegetables and lamb. Sprinkle with barley and thyme; pour over combined stock and water. Bring to boil; skim surface of stew. Reduce heat, simmer, covered, for 1½ hours.
3 Make herb dumplings.
4 Uncover stew; drop heaped tablespoons of dumpling mixture, 2cm apart, on top. Cover stew; simmer about 15 minutes or until dumplings are cooked.

Herb dumplings Sift flour into medium bowl; rub in butter. Stir in herbs, egg and enough milk to mix to soft, sticky dough.

ROASTS, BAKES AND GRILLS

Traditional beef pot roast

preparation time **20 minutes** (plus standing time) cooking time **3 hours**
serves **6**

1 tablespoon olive oil
125g butter
2kg corner piece beef topside roast
4 medium carrots (680g), chopped
2 large potatoes (600g), chopped
1 large brown onion (200g), sliced
3 medium parsnips (375g), chopped
¼ cup (35g) plain flour
1 litre (4 cups) beef stock
½ cup (125ml) dry red wine
¼ cup (60ml) tomato paste
¼ cup (60ml) worcestershire sauce

1 Heat oil and 20g of butter in large pan, add roast; cook until browned all over. Remove from pan. Melt another 20g of butter in same pan; add carrot, potato, onion and parsnip. Cook, stirring, until vegetables are just soft and browned lightly; remove from pan.
2 Heat remaining butter in same pan, add flour; cook, stirring, until browned lightly. Remove pan from heat, gradually stir in stock and wine; stir over heat until sauce boils and thickens. Return roast and any juices to pan; add paste and sauce. Simmer, covered, about 2 hours or until roast is tender, turning occasionally. Return vegetables to pan; simmer, uncovered, 20 minutes or until sauce thickens slightly. Stand beef, covered, 10 minutes before carving.

Roast chicken and beetroot pesto butter

preparation time **25 minutes** (plus standing time)
cooking time **1 hour 30 minutes** serves **4**

1.6kg chicken
1 medium brown onion (150g), quartered
1 bulb garlic, cloves separated
Cooking-oil spray
1 teaspoon salt
8 small fresh beetroot

Pesto butter
125g butter, softened
1 tablespoon lemon juice
⅓ cup coarsely chopped fresh basil
2 tablespoons toasted pine nuts
2 cloves garlic, crushed
2 tablespoons grated parmesan

1 Make pesto butter.
2 Preheat oven to moderate.
3 Wash cavity of chicken under cold water; pat dry with absorbent paper. Tuck wings under chicken. Loosen skin of chicken by sliding fingers carefully between skin and meat. Spread half the pesto butter under skin; spread mixture evenly over breast by pressing with fingers. Place onion and two garlic cloves inside chicken cavity. Tie legs of chicken together with kitchen string.
4 Place chicken, breast-side up, on wire rack in large baking dish. Spray chicken all over with cooking-oil spray; sprinkle with salt. Roast, uncovered, in moderate oven 45 minutes. Add unpeeled beetroot to dish; roast, uncovered, further 15 minutes. Add remaining unpeeled garlic cloves to dish; roast further 30 minutes or until chicken and beetroot are cooked when tested. Cover loosely with foil if chicken starts to overbrown.
5 Cover chicken to keep warm; stand 10 minutes. Meanwhile, peel beetroot.
6 Serve chicken with beetroot, garlic and remaining pesto butter.

Pesto butter Process butter, lemon juice, basil, nuts, garlic and parmesan until almost smooth.

Roast chicken with 40 cloves of garlic

preparation time **20 minutes** (plus standing time)
cooking time **1 hour 20 minutes** (plus cooking time) serves **4**

3 bulbs garlic
60g butter, softened
1.5kg chicken
2 teaspoons salt
2 teaspoons cracked black pepper
1 cup (250ml) water

Roasted potatoes
1kg baby new potatoes
Cooking-oil spray

1 Preheat oven to moderately hot. Wash cavity of chicken under cold water; pat dry with absorbent paper.
2 Separate cloves from garlic bulb, leaving peel intact. Rub butter over outside of chicken and inside cavity; press combined salt and pepper onto skin and inside cavity. Place half the garlic inside cavity; tie chicken legs together with kitchen string.
3 Place remaining garlic cloves, in single layer, in medium baking dish; place chicken on garlic. Pour the water carefully into dish; roast chicken, uncovered, in moderately hot oven, brushing occasionally with pan juices, about 1 hour 20 minutes or until cooked as desired.
4 Meanwhile, make roasted potatoes.
5 Stand chicken on platter, covered with foil, 15 minutes; serve with garlic and roasted potatoes.

Roasted potatoes Boil, steam or microwave potatoes 5 minutes; drain. Pat dry with absorbent paper; cool 10 minutes. Place potatoes, in single layer, in large oiled baking dish; spray with cooking-oil spray. Roast, uncovered, in moderately hot oven for about the last 30 minutes of chicken cooking or until potatoes are tender.

Roast leg of lamb with garlic and rosemary

preparation time **10 minutes** (plus standing time)
cooking time **1 hour 30 minutes** serves **6**

2kg leg of lamb
2 sprigs fresh rosemary, chopped coarsely
8 cloves garlic, sliced thinly
20g butter, softened
1 teaspoon cracked black pepper

1 Preheat oven to moderately hot. Pierce lamb all over with sharp knife; place in large baking dish.
2 Press rosemary and garlic firmly into cuts; rub combined butter and pepper over lamb. Bake lamb, uncovered, in moderately hot oven 15 minutes.
3 Reduce heat to moderate; bake lamb, uncovered, about 1 ¼ hours or until cooked as desired. Stand, covered, 10 minutes before carving.

Roast chicken with thai flavours

preparation time time **10 minutes** cooking time time **1 hour 30 minutes** serves **4**

1.5kg chicken
100g fresh coriander, roots intact
20cm stalks lemon grass (40g), chopped coarsely
2 limes, quartered
Cooking-oil spray
1 teaspoon salt

1 Preheat oven to moderately hot. Wash cavity of chicken under cold water; pat dry with absorbent paper.
2 Chop coriander roots, stems and leaves; place all of the coriander, lemon grass and four lime quarters inside chicken cavity. Tuck wings under chicken; trim skin around chicken neck, secure to underside of chicken with toothpicks. Tie legs together using kitchen string.
3 Place chicken, breast-side up, on rack inside large baking dish. Spray chicken all over with cooking-oil spray; sprinkle with salt. Place enough water in baking dish to come to 1cm depth. Bake chicken, uncovered, in moderately hot oven for 1 ½ hours; cover loosely with foil after 1 hour if chicken starts to overbrown. Discard cavity filling; serve chicken with remaining lime quarters.

Roast beef and vegetables in an oven bag

preparation time **15 minutes** (plus standing time)
cooking time **1 hour 40 minutes** serves **6**

4 cloves garlic, peeled
1.8kg corner piece beef topside roast
12 small sprigs fresh thyme
6 medium carrots (720g), halved
12 baby onions (300g), peeled
1 tablespoon wholegrain mustard
¼ cup (90g) honey
1 tablespoon olive oil

1 Preheat oven to moderate.
2 Cut each garlic clove into three slices. Make 12 small slits on fat side of beef; insert garlic and thyme into slits. Cut narrow strip from top of 35cm x 48cm oven bag to use as tie. Place beef, carrot and onion in bag. Add combined remaining ingredients to bag, close end with tie; gently turn bag to coat beef and vegetables.
3 Place bag in large baking dish, pierce three holes near tie end; bake in moderate oven about 1½ hours or until beef is cooked as desired. Carefully remove beef and vegetables from bag; stand, covered, in warm place, 10 minutes before serving.
4 Meanwhile, pour juices from oven bag into baking dish; simmer, uncovered, until reduced to ½ cup (125ml). Serve beef and vegetables drizzled with baking juices.

Honey chicken with roasted capsicum

preparation **10 minutes** cooking time **1 hour 30 minutes** serves **4**

1.5kg chicken
2 medium red capsicums (400g)
2 medium yellow capsicums (400g)

Honey glaze
½ cup (175g) honey
¼ cup (60ml) soy sauce
1 tablespoon grated fresh ginger
½ teaspoon sesame oil
½ teaspoon five-spice powder

1 Preheat oven to moderate.
2 Combine ingredients for honey glaze in small bowl.
3 Place chicken in baking dish, brush with honey glaze; cover with oiled foil. Bake in moderate oven 45 minutes.
4 Cut capsicum into 3cm pieces, add to dish; bake, covered, 30 minutes. Remove foil; bake, uncovered, 15 minutes or until chicken is cooked through, brushing occasionally with pan juices during cooking time.
5 Serve chicken with capsicum and pan juices.

Spicy roast spatchcocks

preparation **15 minutes** (plus refrigeration time) cooking time **30 minutes**
serves **4**

4 x 500g spatchcocks
2 teaspoons sweet paprika
2 cloves garlic, crushed
1 teaspoon cumin seeds
2 teaspoons yellow mustard seeds
2 tablespoons finely chopped fresh coriander
2 green onions, chopped finely
⅓ cup (110g) mango chutney
2 tablespoons olive oil

Vinaigrette
⅓ cup (80ml) olive oil
2 tablespoons lemon juice
½ teaspoon sugar

1 Using kitchen scissors, cut along each side of spatchcock backbone;
discard backbones. Cut spatchcocks in half along breastbones.
2 Combine spatchcocks in large bowl with paprika, garlic, seeds, coriander,
onion, chutney and oil. Cover, refrigerate 3 hours or overnight.
3 Preheat oven to hot. Drain spatchcocks; reserve marinade.
4 Place spatchcocks, skin-side up, on rack in baking dish. Bake, uncovered,
in hot oven about 30 minutes or until cooked through, brushing with
marinade several times during cooking.
5 Place ingredients for vinaigrette in screw-top jar; shake well.
6 Serve spatchcocks drizzled with vinaigrette.

Baked fish with ginger and soy

preparation time **10 minutes** cooking time **25 minutes** serves **2**

800g whole snapper
1 tablespoon grated fresh ginger
1 tablespoon peanut oil
¼ cup (60ml) chinese rice wine
¼ cup (60ml) soy sauce
½ teaspoon white sugar
3 green onions, sliced thinly

1 Preheat oven to moderately hot. Cut three deep slits in each side of fish; place fish in oiled baking dish.
2 Rub ginger into fish; drizzle with combined oil, wine, sauce and sugar. Bake, covered, in moderately hot oven about 25 minutes or until fish is cooked.
3 Serve fish drizzled with some of the pan juices and topped with onion.

Crumbed smoked haddock florentine

preparation time **10 minutes** cooking time **1 hour** serves **4**

600g smoked haddock
400g spinach, trimmed
1 cup (125g) coarsely grated cheddar
⅓ cup finely chopped fresh chives
⅔ cup (160ml) cream
1 cup (70g) stale breadcrumbs
40g butter

1 Place fish in large pan; cover with cold water, bring to boil, drain. Repeat process; chop fish coarsely. Boil, steam or microwave spinach until just wilted; drain. Squeeze excess liquid from spinach; chop coarsely. (Recipe can be made ahead to this stage.)
2 Preheat oven to hot. Place half the fish in oiled 1.25-litre (5-cup capacity) ovenproof dish; top with half the spinach, third of the cheese, half the chives and half the cream. Repeat layering, finishing with remaining cream. Sprinkle with combined breadcrumbs and remaining cheese; drizzle with melted butter. Bake, uncovered, in hot oven about 40 minutes or until browned.

Barbecue glazed meatloaf

preparation time **20 minutes** (plus standing time) cooking time **40 minutes**
serves **4**

400g beef mince
150g sausage mince
1 medium brown onion (150g), chopped finely
2 cloves garlic, crushed
¼ cup (25g) packaged breadcrumbs
1 egg, beaten lightly
1 tablespoon coarsely chopped fresh oregano
8 bacon rashers (560g), rinds removed, sliced lengthways

Barbecue glaze
¼ cup (60ml) water
1 tablespoon tomato paste
1 tablespoon red wine vinegar
2 tablespoons brown sugar

1 Preheat oven to moderate. Line 8cm x 25cm bar cake pan with plastic
wrap. Lightly oil 25cm x 30cm swiss roll pan.
2 Combine minces, onion, garlic, breadcrumbs, egg and oregano in large
bowl. Press meatloaf mixture into prepared bar cake pan.
3 Turn pan onto prepared swiss roll pan; remove plastic wrap from meatloaf.
Cover top and sides of meatloaf with bacon, overlapping bacon.
4 Bake, uncovered, in moderate oven 15 minutes.
5 Make barbecue glaze.
6 Pour off any excess fat from meatloaf, brush with glaze; bake, uncovered,
about 25 minutes or until meatloaf is cooked through. Stand 10 minutes
before slicing.

Barbecue glaze Combine ingredients in small saucepan. Bring to a boil
then reduce heat; simmer, uncovered, 5 minutes.

Pork burgers
with caramelised pears

preparation time **15 minutes** cooking time **15 minutes** serves **4**

500g pork mince
2 cloves garlic, crushed
3 green onions, chopped finely
1 fresh red thai chilli, chopped finely
1 egg
2 tablespoons barbecue sauce
½ cup (35g) stale breadcrumbs
4 small pears (720g), sliced thinly
1 medium red onion (170g), sliced thinly
¼ cup (60ml) balsamic vinegar
1 tablespoon brown sugar
1 long french bread stick (350g)
2 tablespoons dijonnaise
50g mizuna

1 Using hands, combine mince, garlic, green onion, chilli, egg, sauce and breadcrumbs in medium bowl; shape mixture into four burgers. Cook burgers on heated oiled flat plate, uncovered, until cooked through.
2 Meanwhile, cook pear and red onion on heated oiled flat plate, uncovered, until onion softens. Sprinkle combined vinegar and sugar over pear and red onion; cook, turning, about 10 minutes or until mixture caramelises.
3 Cut bread into quarters; split quarters in half horizontally. Spread dijonnaise on cut sides; sandwich mizuna, burgers, and caramelised pear and red onion between bread pieces.

tip Mizuna can be replaced with rocket leaves or mesclun.

Barbecue spare ribs

preparation time **25 minutes** (plus refrigeration time)
cooking time **2 hours 10 minutes** serves **2**

800g slabs of american-style pork spare ribs

Barbecue sauce
½ **cup (125ml) tomato sauce**
⅓ **cup (80ml) apple cider vinegar**
1 **tablespoon olive oil**
2 **tablespoons worcestershire sauce**
2 **tablespoons firmly packed brown sugar**
1 **tablespoon american-style mustard**
2 **fresh red thai chillies, chopped finely**
2 **cloves garlic, crushed**

1 Make barbecue sauce.
2 Place slabs of ribs in large deep baking dish; brush both sides of each slab with sauce. Pour remaining sauce over slabs, cover; refrigerate overnight.
3 Preheat oven to moderately slow. Drain slabs, reserving sauce. Place ribs onto wire rack over large shallow baking dish. Roast, covered, in moderately slow oven 1½ hours, uncovering to brush with sauce every 20 minutes. Turn slabs midway through cooking.
4 Increase oven temperature to hot. Uncover slabs; bake in hot oven, brushing frequently with sauce, until slabs are browned and cooked through, turning after 15 minutes.
5 Place remaining barbecue sauce in small saucepan. Bring to a boil then reduce heat; simmer, stirring, about 4 minutes or until sauce thickens slightly. Using scissors, cut slabs in portions of two or three ribs; serve ribs with hot barbecue sauce.

Barbecue sauce Combine ingredients in medium saucepan; bring to a boil. Remove from heat; cool before brushing over ribs.

tip You'll save on cleaning time if you line the bases of the baking dish with baking paper.

Tex-mex spare ribs with grilled corn salsa

preparation time **15 minutes** cooking time **25 minutes** serves **4**

2 tablespoons brown sugar
1 tablespoon cajun seasoning
2 teaspoons cracked black pepper
¼ cup (60ml) water
2 tablespoons vegetable oil
1.5kg american-style pork spare ribs
3 trimmed corn cobs (750g)
2 medium tomatoes (300g), seeded, chopped finely
1 long green chilli, chopped finely
1 medium red onion (170g), chopped finely
¼ cup coarsely chopped fresh coriander
2 tablespoons lime juice
1 tablespoon olive oil

1 Combine sugar, seasoning, pepper, the water and oil in large bowl; add pork, rub spice mixture all over pork. Cook pork on heated oiled flat plate, uncovered, until cooked as desired.

2 Meanwhile, cook corn on heated oiled grill plate (or grill or barbecue), uncovered, until tender. When cool enough to handle, cut kernels from cobs. Place kernels in medium bowl with remaining ingredients; toss salsa gently to combine. Serve with pork.

Pork satay with grilled baby bok choy

preparation time **10 minutes** cooking time **25 minutes** serves **4**

1 tablespoon peanut oil
1 small brown onion (80g), chopped finely
2 cloves garlic, crushed
2 fresh red thai chillies, chopped finely
½ cup (140g) peanut butter
1 tablespoon soy sauce
⅔ cup (100ml) coconut cream
½ cup (125ml) orange juice
½ cup (75g) coarsely chopped unsalted toasted peanuts
800g pork fillets
800g baby bok choy, halved lengthways

1 Heat half the oil in medium saucepan; cook onion, garlic and chilli, stirring, until onion softens. Add peanut butter, sauce, coconut cream, juice and nuts. Bring to a boil then reduce heat; simmer, uncovered, about 5 minutes or until mixture thickens slightly. Cover to keep warm.
2 Cook pork on heated oiled grill plate (or grill or barbecue), uncovered, until cooked as desired. Cover pork; stand 5 minutes, slice thickly.
3 Meanwhile, boil, steam or microwave bok choy until leaves just wilt; drain. Brush bok choy with remaining oil; cook on heated oiled grill plate, uncovered, until tender.
4 Serve pork and bok choy with satay sauce.

serving suggestion Serve pork satay with steamed jasmine rice.

Margarita-marinated pork chops

preparation time **15 minutes** (plus refrigeration time)
cooking time **15 minutes** serves **4**

¼ cup (60ml) lime juice
2 fresh red thai chillies, chopped finely
2 cloves garlic, crushed
½ cup (170g) orange marmalade
⅓ cup finely chopped fresh coriander
½ cup (125ml) tequila
8 pork loin chops (2.2kg)

1 Combine juice, chilli, garlic, marmalade, coriander and tequila, add pork;
toss pork to coat in marinade. Cover; refrigerate overnight.
2 Drain pork; reserve marinade. Cook pork on heated oiled grill plate
(or grill or barbecue), uncovered, brushing occasionally with marinade,
until cooked as desired.

Stuffed chicken breast with spinach salad

preparation time **10 minutes** cooking time **20 minutes** serves **4**

4 single chicken breast fillets (680g)
80g fontina cheese, sliced thinly
4 slices bottled char-grilled red capsicum (170g)
100g baby spinach leaves
1 medium lemon (140g)
2 medium oranges (480g)
1 small red onion (100g), sliced thinly
1 tablespoon olive oil

1 Using tip of small knife, slit pocket in one side of each fillet, taking care not
to cut all the way through. Divide cheese, capsicum and a few spinach leaves
among pockets; secure with toothpicks.
2 Cook chicken on heated oiled grill plate (or grill or barbecue), uncovered,
until cooked through. Cover chicken; stand 10 minutes. Remove toothpicks;
slice thickly.
3 Meanwhile, segment lemon and orange over large bowl. Add onion, oil and
remaining spinach; toss to combine. Serve with chicken.

Chilli and lemon grass marinated lamb chops

preparation time **10 minutes** (plus refrigeration time)
cooking time **10 minutes** serves **4**

1 clove garlic, crushed
5cm (10g) stick finely chopped fresh lemon grass
1 teaspoon ground coriander
2 tablespoons fish sauce
1 fresh red thai chilli, chopped finely
2 tablespoons peanut oil
4 forequarter lamb chops (760g)

1 Combine garlic, lemon grass, coriander, sauce, chilli and oil in large bowl; add chops, turn to coat in marinade. Cover; refrigerate 3 hours or overnight.
2 Cook drained lamb on heated oiled grill plate (or grill or barbecue) until browned both sides and cooked as desired.

Beef spare ribs

preparation time **10 minutes** (plus refrigeration time)
cooking time **20 minutes** serves **4**

2 cups (500ml) tomato sauce
½ cup (125ml) worcestershire sauce
¾ cup (180ml) vegetable oil
½ cup (125ml) water
¼ cup (60ml) white vinegar
⅓ cup (75g) firmly packed brown sugar
1 medium brown onion (150g), chopped finely
1.5kg beef spare ribs

1 Combine sauces, oil, the water, vinegar, sugar and onion in large shallow dish; add ribs. Cover; refrigerate 3 hours or overnight.
2 Drain ribs; reserve marinade.
3 Place reserved marinade in small saucepan. Bring to a boil then reduce heat; simmer, uncovered, until thickened slightly.
4 Cook ribs on heated oiled grill plate (or grill or barbecue), uncovered, until cooked as desired. Pour sauce over ribs.

Hamburger with a twist

preparation time **15 minutes** cooking time **10 minutes** serves **4**

80g gorgonzola, crumbled
¼ cup (60g) sour cream
400g beef mince
120g sausage mince
1 small brown onion (80g), chopped finely
1 tablespoon barbecue sauce
2 teaspoons worcestershire sauce
½ cup (75g) drained sun-dried tomatoes in oil, chopped finely
4 hamburger buns
50g baby rocket leaves
170g marinated artichoke hearts, drained, quartered

1 Combine cheese and cream in a small bowl.
2 Using hands, combine minces, onion, sauces and tomato in medium bowl; shape mixture into four hamburger patties.
3 Cook patties on heated oiled grill plate (or grill or barbecue) until browned both sides and cooked as desired.
4 Meanwhile, halve buns; toast, cut-side up. Sandwich rocket, patties, gorgonzola cream and artichoke in toasted buns.

Five-spice pork belly ribs

preparation time **10 minutes** (plus refrigeration time)
cooking time **20 minutes** serves **4**

3 cloves garlic, crushed
3cm piece fresh ginger (15g), grated
1 ½ teaspoons five-spice powder
¼ cup (85g) orange marmalade
¼ cup (90g) honey
2 tablespoons kecap manis
1.5kg pork belly ribs

1 Combine garlic, ginger, five-spice, marmalade, honey and kecap manis in large bowl, add pork; toss to coat in marinade. Cover; refrigerate overnight.
2 Drain pork; reserve marinade. Cook pork on heated oiled grill plate, uncovered, brushing occasionally with reserved marinade, until cooked through.

Meat lover's pizza

preparation time **10 minutes** cooking time **25 minutes** serves **4**

Pizzas can be prepared several hours ahead; cook just before serving.

2 teaspoons olive oil
1 small brown onion (80g), chopped finely
1 clove garlic, crushed
250g lean beef mince
1 teaspoon paprika
⅓ cup (80ml) barbecue sauce
2 x 335g pizza crusts (26cm round)
2 tablespoons tomato paste
2 cups (200g) pizza cheese
1 stick (100g) cabanossi, sliced coarsely
50g sliced spicy salami, chopped coarsely

1 Preheat the oven to hot. Heat oil in non-stick frying pan; cook onion and garlic, stirring, until soft. Add mince; cook, stirring, until well browned. Stir in paprika and 1 tablespoon of barbecue sauce. Remove from heat.
2 Meanwhile, place pizza crusts on baking trays. Combine tomato paste with remaining barbecue sauce and spread evenly over crusts. Sprinkle pizzas with half the cheese. Top with mince mixture, cabanossi, spicy salami and remaining cheese.
3 Cook in hot oven about 15 minutes or until crusts are crisp and topping is browned lightly.

Grilled chicken with herbed butter, almonds and gruyère

preparation time **15 minutes** cooking time **15 minutes** serves **4**

80g butter, softened
1 tablespoon finely chopped fresh flat-leaf parsley
2 teaspoons lemon juice
4 single chicken breast fillets (680g)
3 medium carrots (360g), cut into 8cm matchsticks
250g baby green beans
¼ cup (35g) toasted slivered almonds
¼ cup (30g) finely grated gruyère

1 Combine butter, parsley and juice in small bowl, cover; refrigerate.

2 Cook chicken on heated oiled grill plate (or grill or barbecue) until browned both sides and cooked through. Cover loosely to keep warm.

3 Meanwhile, boil, steam or microwave carrot and beans, separately, until tender; drain.

4 Serve chicken on vegetables; divide parsley butter among chicken pieces, sprinkle with nuts and cheese.

Steak sandwich revisited

preparation time **10 minutes** cooking time **35 minutes** serves **4**

4 thin fillet steaks (650g)
8 thick slices crusty white bread
2 tablespoons olive oil
60g rocket, trimmed
⅓ cup (80ml) sweet chilli sauce

Caramelised leek
30g butter
1 medium leek (350g), sliced thinly
2 tablespoons brown sugar
2 tablespoons dry white wine

1 Make caramelised leek.

2 Cook steaks on heated oiled grill plate (or grill or barbecue) until browned both sides and cooked as desired.

3 Meanwhile, brush both sides of bread slices with oil; toast both sides under hot grill. Sandwich rocket, steaks, chilli sauce and caramelised leek between bread slices.

Caramelised leek Melt butter in medium frying pan; cook leek, stirring, until softened. Add sugar and wine; cook, stirring occasionally, about 20 minutes or until leek is caramelised.

Baked fish with tomatoes and olives

preparation time **15 minutes** cooking time **20 minutes** serves **4**

2 medium green capsicums (400g)
2 tablespoons olive oil
1 small brown onion (80g), chopped finely
1 clove garlic, crushed
1 long red chilli, chopped finely
400g can whole peeled tomatoes
²/₃ cup (100g) green olives
½ teaspoon dried oregano leaves
2 tablespoons coarsely chopped fresh flat-leaf parsley
4 firm white fish fillets (600g)

1 Preheat oven to hot.
2 Quarter capsicums, remove seeds and membrane; place in small baking dish, brush with half the oil. Bake capsicum in hot oven 10 minutes.
3 Heat remaining oil in medium frying pan; cook onion, garlic and chilli, stirring, until onion is soft. Add undrained crushed tomatoes, olives, oregano and parsley. Stir until hot; remove from heat.
4 Place fish in lightly oiled small ovenproof dish; pour over tomato mixture.
5 Place fish in oven with capsicum; bake a further 8 minutes or until fish is cooked as desired and capsicum is tender.
6 Serve fish with sauce and capsicum.

serving suggestion Serve baked fish with crusty bread.

Mustard rosemary chicken

preparation time **15 minutes** cooking time **20 minutes** serves **4**

2 tablespoons lemon juice
2 tablespoons olive oil
2 cloves garlic, crushed
3 tablespoons finely chopped fresh rosemary
¼ cup (60g) wholegrain mustard
1kg chicken thigh fillets
½ cup (125ml) dry white wine
300ml cream
1 teaspoon cornflour
1 teaspoon water

1 Combine juice, oil, garlic, 2 tablespoons of the rosemary, mustard and chicken in medium bowl; stir until chicken is well coated in mixture.
2 Drain chicken over small bowl; reserve liquid. Cook chicken on heated oiled grill plate (or grill or barbecue) until browned and cooked as desired.
3 Place reserved liquid and wine in small saucepan. Bring to a boil then reduce heat; simmer until reduced by half. Stir in cream, then blended cornflour and water; bring to a boil, stirring until mixture thickens slightly. Serve chicken with sauce; sprinkle with remaining rosemary.

Grilled fish with corn salsa

preparation time **20 minutes** cooking time **25 minutes** serves **6**

6 firm white fish fillets (1.2kg)

Corn salsa
2 trimmed corn cobs (500g)
2 medium red capsicums (400g)
1 small red onion (100g), chopped finely
1 fresh red thai chilli, chopped finely
1 tablespoon olive oil
¼ cup chopped fresh coriander

1 Make corn salsa.
2 Cook fish on heated oiled grill plate (or grill or barbecue) until browned both sides and cooked as desired.
3 Serve fish with corn salsa.

Corn salsa Cook corn on heated oiled grill plate (or grill or barbecue), covered loosely with piece of foil, about 20 minutes or until browned and tender. Using sharp knife, cut kernels from cobs. Quarter capsicums; remove and discard seeds and membranes. Cook on same heated oiled grill plate until skin blisters and blackens. Cover capsicum pieces with plastic or paper 5 minutes. Peel away and discard skin; chop capsicum flesh finely. Combine corn, capsicum, onion, chilli, oil and coriander in medium bowl.

Peri peri chicken

preparation time **10 minutes** (plus refrigeration time)
cooking time **25 minutes** serves **4**

⅓ cup (80ml) lemon juice
¼ cup (60ml) olive oil
6 small red chillies, chopped finely
2 teaspoons brown sugar
1 teaspoon sweet paprika
2 cloves garlic, crushed
2 teaspoons finely chopped fresh rosemary
2 teaspoons sea salt
1.5kg chicken pieces

1 Combine juice, oil, chilli, sugar, paprika, garlic, rosemary and salt in large bowl. Add chicken pieces, coat in marinade. Cover, refrigerate 3 hours.

2 Drain chicken from marinade; reserve marinade. Make deep cuts into chicken pieces on diagonal.

3 Cook chicken on heated oiled grill plate (or grill or barbecue), covered, about 25 minutes or until cooked as desired. Brush with reserved marinade frequently during cooking.

Thai fish burgers

preparation time **10 minutes** cooking time **15 minutes** serves **4**

500g blue-eye fillets, chopped coarsely
1 tablespoon fish sauce
1 tablespoon kecap manis
1 clove garlic, quartered
1 fresh red thai chilli, quartered
50g green beans, trimmed, chopped coarsely
¼ cup (15g) shredded coconut
¼ cup finely chopped fresh coriander
½ loaf turkish bread (215g)
100g mixed lettuce leaves
50g snow pea sprouts
⅓ cup (80ml) sweet chilli sauce

1 Blend or process fillets, sauce, kecap manis, garlic and chilli until smooth. Place in large bowl with beans, coconut and coriander; using hands, combine ingredients then shape mixture into four burgers.

2 Cook burgers on heated oiled flat plate, covered, about 15 minutes or until cooked as desired.

3 Cut bread in half; split halves horizontally. Toast, cut-side up. Divide bread among serving plates; top with lettuce, sprouts, burgers and chilli sauce.

Fish parcels with lime coriander dressing

preparation time **15 minutes** cooking time **30 minutes** serves **4**

4 x 200g thick white fish fillets
1 teaspoon cracked black peppercorns
1 medium carrot (120g), cut into thin strips
1 small red capsicum (150g), cut into thin strips
2 green onions, cut into thin strips

Lime coriander dressing
2 tablespoons lime juice
1 tablespoon soy sauce
1 teaspoon honey
½ teaspoon sesame oil
1 clove garlic, crushed
1 tablespoon chopped fresh coriander

1 Preheat oven to hot.
2 Place each fillet on large sheet of baking paper or foil, sprinkle with pepper; top with carrot, capsicum and onion. Seal ends to enclose fish and vegetables.
3 Place parcels on oven tray, bake in hot oven about 30 minutes or until fish is cooked through.
4 Place ingredients for lime coriander dressing in screw-top jar; shake well.
5 Open parcels, drain excess liquid; drizzle with dressing to serve.

Yakitori chicken

preparation time **10 minutes** (plus standing time) cooking time **10 minutes**
serves **4**

You can substitute sherry or sweet white wine for mirin, if you prefer.

1kg chicken breast fillets
¼ cup (60ml) mirin
½ cup (125ml) light soy sauce
2cm piece fresh ginger (10g), grated finely
2 cloves garlic, crushed
1 tablespoon white sugar

1 Cut chicken into 2cm pieces.
2 Combine chicken with remaining ingredients in large bowl; stand
10 minutes. Drain chicken over small bowl; reserve marinade.
3 Thread chicken onto 12 bamboo skewers. Cook skewers on heated oiled
grill plate (or grill or barbecue), turning and brushing with reserved marinade
occasionally, until browned and cooked as desired.

Tandoori lamb cutlets

preparation **10 minutes** (plus standing time) cooking time **15 minutes**
serves **4**

12 lamb cutlets (780g)
1 teaspoon finely grated lemon rind
1 tablespoon lemon juice
¼ cup (75g) tandoori paste
¼ cup (70g) plain yogurt
2 teaspoons brown sugar

1 Place lamb cutlets in large bowl with rind, juice, paste, yogurt and sugar.
Cover; stand 10 minutes.
2 Cook lamb on heated oiled grill plate (or grill or barbecue) until browned
both sides and cooked as desired.

serving suggestion Serve tandoori lamb cutlets with steamed basmati
rice and lemon wedges.

Fish with chermoulla

preparation time **10 minutes** cooking time **10 minutes** serves **4**

1kg snapper fillet

Chermoulla
3 cloves garlic, crushed
1 teaspoon ground cumin
½ teaspoon hot paprika
2 tablespoons coarsely chopped fresh coriander
2 tablespoons coarsely chopped fresh flat-leaf parsley
¼ cup (60ml) olive oil
2 teaspoons finely grated lemon rind
¼ cup (60ml) lemon juice

1 Cut fish into eight even-size pieces. Place in large shallow dish.
2 Combine ingredients for chermoulla in medium bowl; pour half over fish.
3 Cook fish on heated oiled grill plate (or grill or barbecue) until browned both sides and cooked as desired.
4 Serve fish drizzled with remaining chermoulla.

tip Fish can also be cooked under a preheated grill.

Homemade hamburgers with tomato relish

preparation time **15 minutes** cooking time **15 minutes** serves **4**

2 tablespoons olive oil
1 large brown onion (200g), sliced thinly
600g beef mince
1 small brown onion (80g), chopped finely
2 tablespoons worcestershire sauce
1 tablespoon finely chopped fresh parsley
4 round bread rolls, halved
4 leaves butter lettuce, halved
2 medium tomatoes (300g), sliced thickly
1 dill cucumber (45g), sliced thinly
⅓ cup (110g) tomato relish

1 Heat half the oil in large frying pan; add sliced onion, cook, stirring, until browned. Remove from pan; cover to keep warm.

2 Meanwhile, combine mince, chopped onion, sauce and parsley in large bowl; mix well. Shape mixture into four patties.

3 Heat remaining oil in same pan; cook patties until browned on both sides and cooked as desired.

4 Grill cut-side of bread rolls until toasted lightly.

5 Divide lettuce among bases of bread rolls; top with patties, tomato, cucumber, onion and tomato relish, then tops of bread rolls.

Butterflied pork steaks with pear and apple salsa

preparation time **15 minutes**   cooking time **10 minutes**   serves **4**

8 x 100g butterflied pork steaks, trimmed

Pear and apple salsa
1 tablespoon water
2 tablespoons lemon juice
2 teaspoons white sugar
1 medium green apple (150g), diced into 1cm pieces
1 medium red apple (150g), diced into 1cm pieces
1 small pear (180g), peeled, diced into 1cm pieces
1 long green chilli, chopped finely
1 tablespoon finely chopped fresh mint

1 Make pear and apple salsa.

2 Cook pork on heated lightly oiled grill plate (or grill or barbecue) until browned both sides and cooked as desired. Serve pork with salsa.

Pear and apple salsa Combine the water, juice and sugar in medium bowl, stirring, until sugar dissolves. Add apples, pear, chilli and mint; toss gently to combine.

Beef, tomato and pea pies

preparation time **15 minutes** (plus refrigeration time)
cooking time **45 minutes** (plus cooling time) makes **6**

1 tablespoon vegetable oil
1 small brown onion (80g), chopped finely
300g beef mince
400g can tomatoes
1 tablespoon tomato paste
2 tablespoons worcestershire sauce
½ cup (125ml) beef stock
½ cup (60g) frozen peas
3 sheets ready-rolled puff pastry
1 egg, beaten lightly

1 Heat oil in large saucepan; cook onion, stirring, until softened. Add beef; cook, stirring, until changed in colour. Stir in undrained crushed tomatoes, paste, sauce and stock. Bring to a boil then reduce heat; simmer, uncovered, about 20 minutes or until sauce thickens. Stir in peas. Cool.

2 Preheat oven to moderately hot. Oil six-hole (¾-cup/180ml) texas muffin pan.

3 Cut two 13cm rounds from opposite corners of each pastry sheet; cut two 9cm rounds from remaining corners of each sheet. Place the six large rounds in muffin pan holes to cover bases and sides; trim any excess pastry. Lightly prick bases with fork; refrigerate 30 minutes. Cover the six small rounds with a damp cloth.

4 Cover pastry-lined muffin pan holes with baking paper; fill holes with uncooked rice or dried beans. Bake, uncovered, in moderately hot oven, 10 minutes; remove paper and rice. Cool.

5 Spoon mince filling into holes; brush edges with a little egg. Top pies with small pastry rounds; gently press around edges to seal.

6 Brush pies with remaining egg; bake, uncovered, in moderately hot oven about 15 minutes or until browned lightly. Stand 5 minutes before serving.

Salmon and potato bake

preparation time **15 minutes** cooking time **40 minutes** serves **4**

1kg baby new potatoes
415g can pink salmon, drained
4 green onions, chopped finely
1 teaspoon finely grated lemon rind
300ml cream
1 cup (125g) pizza cheese

1 Boil, steam or microwave potatoes until tender, cool slightly; slice thinly.
2 Preheat oven to moderately hot. Layer half the potato slices into 2-litre (8-cup) oiled shallow ovenproof dish; top with combined salmon, onion and rind, then remaining potato slices. Pour over cream; sprinkle with cheese.
3 Bake, uncovered, about 30 minutes or until browned lightly and hot.

Mega beef burgers

preparation **15 minutes** cooking time **15 minutes** serves **6**

1kg beef mince
1 small brown onion (80g), grated
2 cloves garlic, crushed
2 tablespoons barbecue sauce
2 tablespoons worcestershire sauce
2 tablespoons chopped fresh flat-leaf parsley
½ cup (35g) stale breadcrumbs
1 egg, beaten lightly
2 large brown onions (400g), extra, sliced
12 rindless bacon rashers, halved
6 eggs, extra
6 hamburger buns
75g mesclun

1 Combine beef in large bowl with grated onion, garlic, sauces, parsley, breadcrumbs and egg; shape mixture into six patties.
2 Cook patties on oiled grill plate (or grill or barbecue) until browned both sides and cooked as desired. Cook sliced onion, bacon and extra eggs in large non-stick frying pan until onion is soft, bacon crisp and eggs cooked.
3 Split buns; toast both sides. Sandwich with mesclun, patties, onion, bacon and eggs between buns.

Chicken and vegie pie

preparation **15 minutes** cooking time **35 minutes** serves **4**

60g butter
1 medium leek (350g), sliced thinly
⅓ cup (50g) plain flour
¾ cup (180ml) milk
1 cup (250ml) chicken stock
3 cups (480g) shredded cooked chicken
2½ cups (350g) frozen mixed vegetables
¼ cup coarsely chopped fresh flat-leaf parsley
4 sheets fillo pastry
Cooking-oil spray

1 Preheat oven to hot.
2 Melt butter in large saucepan; cook leek, stirring, until softened. Add flour; cook, stirring, until mixture bubbles and thickens.
3 Gradually stir in milk and stock; heat, stirring, until mixture boils and thickens. Add chicken, vegetables and parsley; stir until heated through.
4 Spoon chicken pie filling into shallow 1.5-litre (6-cup) ovenproof dish.
5 Place one sheet of pastry over filling; spray with cooking-oil spray. Repeat process with remaining pastry, overlapping pastry around dish. Roll and fold pastry around edge of dish. Spray top of pastry with cooking-oil spray. Bake, uncovered, in hot oven 10 minutes.

Savoury corn slice

preparation **10 minutes** cooking time **35 minutes** serves **4**

2 bacon rashers (140g), chopped finely
2 small tomatoes (260g), seeded, chopped finely
310g can corn kernels, drained
2 teaspoons curry powder
1 cup (125g) coarsely grated cheddar
4 eggs, beaten lightly

1 Preheat oven to moderately hot. Oil 20cm-round sandwich pan; line base with baking paper.
2 Cook bacon in heated medium frying pan until crisp; drain on absorbent

paper. Combine bacon with remaining ingredients in large bowl; pour into prepared pan.

3 Bake, uncovered, in moderately hot oven about 30 minutes or until set.

Shepherd's pie

preparation time **20 minutes** cooking time **45 minutes** serves **4**

30g butter
1 medium brown onion (150g), chopped finely
1 medium carrot (120g), chopped finely
4 cups (750g) chopped cooked lamb
¼ cup (70g) tomato paste
¼ cup (60ml) tomato sauce
2 tablespoons worcestershire sauce
2 cups (500ml) beef stock
2 tablespoons plain flour
⅓ cup (80ml) water

Potato topping
5 medium potatoes (1kg), chopped
60g butter, chopped
¼ cup (60ml) milk

1 Preheat oven to moderately hot. Oil shallow 2.5-litre (10-cup) capacity ovenproof dish.

2 Make potato topping.

3 Meanwhile, heat butter in large saucepan; cook onion and carrot, stirring, until tender. Add lamb; cook, stirring, 2 minutes. Stir in paste, sauces and stock, then blended flour and water; stir over heat until mixture boils and thickens. Pour mixture into prepared dish.

4 Place heaped tablespoons of potato topping on lamb mixture. Bake, uncovered, in moderately hot oven about 20 minutes or until browned lightly and hot.

Potato topping Boil, steam or microwave potatoes until tender; drain. Mash with butter and milk until smooth.

Easy ham and zucchini pie

preparation time **15 minutes** cooking time **45 minutes** serves **4**

1.2 cup (50g) plain flour
1½cups (375ml) milk
3 eggs
3 slices (60g) ham, chopped coarsely
3 green onions, chopped finely
1 cup (125g) coarsely grated cheddar
1 medium zucchini (120g), grated coarsely
2 tablespoons chopped fresh flat-leaf parsley

1 Preheat oven to moderately slow. Oil 20cm-round ovenproof dish.
2 Whisk flour and milk in medium bowl until smooth; whisk in eggs. Stir in remaining ingredients; pour mixture into prepared dish.
3 Bake in moderately slow oven about 45 minutes or until filling is set.

serving suggestion Sprinkle pie with extra chopped parsley; serve with salad and bread.

Lamb patties with beetroot and tzatziki

preparation time **20 minutes** cooking time **10 minutes** serves **4**

500g lamb mince
1 small brown onion (80g), chopped finely
1 medium carrot (120g), grated coarsely
1 egg
2 tablespoons finely chopped fresh flat-leaf parsley
1 teaspoon finely grated lemon rind
2 cloves garlic, crushed
½ cup (140g) yogurt
1 lebanese cucumber (130g), seeded, chopped finely
1 tablespoon finely chopped fresh mint
1 loaf turkish bread (430g)
1 cup (60g) coarsely shredded cos lettuce
200g can sliced beetroot, drained
1 lemon (140g), cut into wedges

1 Using hands, combine lamb, onion, carrot, egg, parsley, rind and half the garlic in medium bowl; shape lamb mixture into four patties. Cook patties on heated oiled grill plate (or grill or barbecue) until cooked as desired.

2 Meanwhile, combine yogurt, cucumber, mint and remaining garlic in small bowl. Cut bread into four pieces; split each piece in half horizontally. Toast bread cut-side up.

3 Sandwich lettuce, patties, yogurt mixture and beetroot between bread pieces. Serve with lemon wedges.

Lamb pide

preparation time **10 minutes** cooking time **20 minutes** serves **4**

2 small brown onions (160g), chopped finely
2 cloves garlic, crushed
250g lamb mince
1 tablespoon tomato paste
¼ teaspoon hot paprika
1 teaspoon ground cumin
2 small pide
¼ cup (25g) finely grated low-fat mozzarella
2 tablespoons chopped fresh mint

1 Preheat oven to hot.

2 Cook onion and garlic in lightly oiled medium saucepan, stirring, until onion softens. Add lamb, paste, paprika and cumin; cook, stirring, until lamb is cooked as desired.

3 Split bread; place bases on oven tray. Spread with lamb mixture; sprinkle with cheese and mint. Replace tops; bake, uncovered, in hot oven about 10 minutes or until bread is crisp.

STIR-FRY AND PAN-FRY

Beef and bok choy with black bean sauce

preparation time **10 minutes** (plus refrigeration time)
cooking time **15 minutes** serves **4**

800g beef rump steak, thinly sliced
1 tablespoon sesame oil
1 tablespoon fish sauce
¼ cup (35g) cornflour
1 egg, lightly beaten
¼ cup (60ml) peanut oil
2 medium brown onions (300g), sliced
3 cloves garlic, crushed
1 tablespoon grated fresh ginger
1 bunch (340g) baby bok choy, chopped
250g asparagus, halved
2 tablespoons black bean sauce

1 Combine beef, sesame oil and fish sauce in bowl; mix well. Cover, refrigerate 30 minutes. Combine cornflour and egg with beef mixture; mix well.
2 Heat 1 tablespoon of peanut oil in wok; add half the beef mixture, stir-fry until browned. Drain on absorbent paper; keep warm. Repeat with another tablespoon of peanut oil and remaining beef mixture.
3 Heat remaining peanut oil in wok, add onions, garlic and ginger; stir-fry until onions are just soft. Add bok choy, asparagus, black bean sauce and beef mixture, stir-fry until hot.

Salt and pepper squid

preparation time **15 minutes** cooking time **5 minutes** serves **4**

500g squid hoods
¾ cup (110g) plain flour
2 tablespoons salt
2 tablespoons ground black pepper
Vegetable oil, for deep-frying

1 Cut squid in half lengthways; score inside surface of each piece. Cut into 2cm-wide strips.
2 Combine flour, salt and pepper in large bowl; add squid. Coat in flour mixture; shake off excess.
3 Heat oil in wok or large frying pan; deep-fry squid, in batches, until tender and browned all over. Drain on absorbent paper.

serving suggestion Serve squid with sweet chilli sauce and lime wedges.

Chicken and oyster sauce stir-fry

preparation time **15 minutes** cooking time **10 minutes** serves **4**

1 tablespoon sesame oil
1 tablespoon peanut oil
750g chicken thigh fillets, sliced thickly
175g broccolini, chopped coarsely
230g baby corn, halved lengthways
2 cloves garlic, crushed
½ cup (125ml) oyster sauce
2 tablespoons water
½ cup coarsely chopped fresh garlic chives

1 Heat half the combined oils in wok; stir-fry chicken, in batches, until cooked through.
2 Heat remaining oil in same wok; stir-fry broccolini, corn and garlic until vegetables are just tender. Return chicken to wok with combined sauce and the water; stir-fry until hot. Stir in chives.

Chilli pork with oyster sauce

preparation time **10 minutes** cooking time **15 minutes** serves **4**

1 tablespoon peanut oil
500g pork fillets, sliced thinly
1 clove garlic, crushed
1 medium white onion (150g), sliced thinly
1 large red capsicum (350g), sliced thinly
1 small green zucchini (90g), sliced thinly
1 small yellow zucchini (90g), sliced thinly
¼ cup (60ml) oyster sauce
1 tablespoon mild sweet chilli sauce
1 tablespoon coarsely chopped fresh coriander

1 Heat oil in wok; stir-fry pork, in batches, until browned.
2 Stir-fry garlic and onion until onion is just tender. Add capsicum and zucchini; stir-fry until tender.
3 Return pork to wok with combined sauces; stir-fry until hot. Serve sprinkled with coriander.

Almond chicken and noodles

preparation time **15 minutes** cooking time **10 minutes** serves **4**

700g chicken breast fillets, sliced thickly
2 cloves garlic, crushed
¼ cup (60ml) hoisin sauce
2 tablespoons soy sauce
2 tablespoons peanut oil
½ cup (80g) blanched almonds
4 green onions, sliced thinly
1 medium brown onion (150g), sliced thinly
420g fresh egg noodles
200g choy sum, chopped coarsely
½ cup (125ml) chicken stock

1 Combine chicken, garlic, 2 tablespoons of hoisin sauce and 1 tablespoon of soy sauce in medium bowl.
2 Heat 2 teaspoons of oil in wok; stir-fry almonds until browned. Remove from wok.

3 Heat remaining oil in wok; stir-fry chicken mixture and onions, in batches, until chicken is browned.

4 Place noodles in large heatproof bowl; cover with boiling water, stand 5 minutes or until just tender; drain.

5 Return chicken to wok with almonds, noodles, choy sum, stock and remaining sauces; stir-fry until choy sum is just wilted.

Beef kway teow

preparation time **15 minutes** cooking time **10 minutes** serves **4**

2 tablespoons peanut oil
500g beef strips
450g fresh wide rice noodles
3 cloves garlic, crushed
2cm piece fresh ginger (10g), grated
6 green onions, cut into 2cm pieces
1 small red capsicum (150g), sliced thinly
2 cups (160g) bean sprouts
¼ cup (75g) satay sauce
2 tablespoons fish sauce

1 Heat half the oil in wok; stir-fry beef, in batches, until browned all over.

2 Place noodles in large heatproof bowl; cover with boiling water, separate with fork; drain.

3 Heat remaining oil in wok; stir-fry garlic and ginger until fragrant. Add onion and capsicum; stir-fry until vegetables are just tender. Return beef to wok with noodles, sprouts and sauces; stir-fry until hot.

Teriyaki beef

preparation time **10 minutes** cooking time **10 minutes** serves **4**

½ cup (125ml) mirin
⅓ cup (80ml) light soy sauce
¼ cup (50g) firmly packed brown sugar
1 tablespoon grated fresh ginger
1 clove garlic, crushed
1 teaspoon sesame oil
1 tablespoon sesame seeds
700g beef strips
300g fresh baby corn, halved
2 green onions, sliced thinly

1 Combine mirin, sauce, sugar, ginger, garlic, oil and seeds in large bowl.
Stir in beef and corn; stand 5 minutes.
2 Drain beef mixture over medium saucepan; reserve marinade in pan.
Cook beef and corn, in batches, in heated wok until browned and cooked
as desired.
3 Meanwhile, bring marinade to a boil then reduce heat; simmer, uncovered,
5 minutes.
4 Serve beef and corn drizzled with hot marinade; sprinkle with onion.

tip Instead of mirin, you can use sherry or sweet wine.

Sticky pork and vegetable stir-fry

preparation time **10 minutes** cooking time **15 minutes** serves **4**

¼ cup (60ml) peanut oil
600g pork fillets, sliced thinly
1 medium brown onion (150g), sliced thinly
2 cloves garlic, crushed
300g broccoli, chopped coarsely
230g baby corn, halved lengthways
2 medium carrots (240g), sliced thinly
⅓ cup (80ml) sweet chilli sauce
1 tablespoon brown sugar
2 tablespoons soy sauce

1 Heat half the oil in wok; stir-fry pork, in batches, until browned all over.
2 Heat remaining oil in wok; stir-fry onion and garlic until tender. Add broccoli, corn and carrot; stir-fry until just tender.
3 Return pork to wok with remaining ingredients; stir-fry until the mixture boils and thickens slightly.

Lemon grass lamb in lettuce cups

preparation time **15 minutes** cooking time **15 minutes** serves **4**

8 iceberg lettuce leaves
100g rice vermicelli
2 tablespoons peanut oil
750g lamb strips
1 medium carrot (120g), sliced thinly
3 cloves garlic, crushed
2 teaspoon finely grated fresh ginger
2 tablespoons finely chopped fresh lemon grass
1 tablespoon lime juice
¼ cup (60ml) sweet chilli sauce
¼ cup (60ml) fish sauce
¼ cup coarsely chopped fresh chives

1 Place lettuce in large bowl of iced water; stand 10 minutes. Drain; pat dry with absorbent paper.
2 Meanwhile, place vermicelli in large heatproof bowl, cover with boiling water, stand until just tender; drain.
3 Heat half the oil in wok; stir-fry lamb, in batches, until browned and cooked as desired.
4 Heat remaining oil in wok; stir-fry carrot, garlic, ginger and lemon grass until carrot is tender. Return lamb to wok with vermicelli, juice, sauces and half the chives; stir-fry until hot.
5 Place two lettuce leaves on each serving plate; divide lamb mixture among leaves, sprinkle with remaining chives.

Satay pork and noodle stir-fry

preparation time **10 minutes** cooking time **15 minutes** serves **6**

500g fresh egg noodles
1 tablespoon vegetable oil
500g pork fillet, sliced thinly
2 cloves garlic, crushed
8 green onions, sliced thinly
¾ cup (180ml) beef stock
⅓ cup (95g) crunchy peanut butter
¼ cup (60ml) sweet chilli sauce
2 teaspoons lemon juice
400g packet fresh asian-style stir-fry vegetables

1 Place noodles in large heatproof bowl, cover with boiling water, stand until just tender; drain.
2 Heat half the oil in wok; stir-fry pork, in batches, until browned. Heat remaining oil in wok; stir-fry garlic and onion until onion softens.
3 Add stock, peanut butter, sauce and juice. Bring to a boil then reduce heat; simmer, uncovered, 1 minute. Return pork to wok with vegetables and noodles; stir-fry, tossing until hot.

Spicy chicken wings

preparation time **20 minutes** cooking time **20 minutes** serves **4**

1kg chicken wings
1 tablespoon peanut oil
1 clove garlic, crushed
2 tablespoons soy sauce
¼ cup (60ml) hoisin sauce
1 tablespoon sweet chilli sauce
2 teaspoons caster sugar
½ cup (125ml) water
3 green onions, chopped finely

1 Cut chicken wings into pieces at joints.
2 Heat oil in wok; stir-fry garlic until aromatic. Add sauces, sugar and the water; stir over heat 1 minute. Add chicken; cook, covered, about 15 minutes, stirring occasionally, or until chicken is cooked through. Stir in onion.

Thai chicken noodle stir-fry

preparation time **10 minutes** cooking time **15 minutes** serves **4**

180g dried rice noodles
700g chicken breast fillets, sliced thinly
2 teaspoons grated fresh ginger
2 tablespoons peanut oil
1½ cups (120g) bean sprouts
300g baby bok choy, chopped coarsely
⅓ cup (80ml) lime juice
¼ cup (60ml) sweet chilli sauce
2 teaspoons fish sauce
2 tablespoons chopped fresh coriander
⅓ cup torn fresh mint leaves
4 green onions, sliced thinly

1 Place noodles in large heatproof bowl, cover with boiling water, stand 5 minutes or until tender; drain.
2 Meanwhile, combine chicken and ginger in medium bowl. Heat oil in wok or large frying pan; stir-fry chicken mixture, in batches, until cooked through.
3 Return chicken to wok with sprouts, bok choy and combined juice, sauces, coriander and mint; stir until hot. Add onion and noodles; stir-fry until hot.

Mongolian garlic lamb

preparation time **10 minutes** cooking time **15 minutes** serves **4**

700g lamb fillets, sliced thinly
3 cloves garlic, crushed
¼ cup (60ml) soy sauce
⅓ cup (80ml) sweet sherry
1 tablespoon cornflour
2 tablespoons vegetable oil
1 tablespoon brown sugar
1 teaspoon sesame oil
8 green onions, sliced thinly

1 Combine lamb, garlic, half the sauce, half the sherry and cornflour in large bowl; mix well.
2 Heat oil in wok; stir-fry lamb mixture, in batches, until browned all over.
3 Return lamb mixture to wok. Add remaining sauce, remaining sherry, sugar and sesame oil; stir-fry until sauce boils and thickens slightly. Remove from heat; stir in onion.

Spicy pork spare ribs

preparation time **10 minutes** cooking time **30 minutes** serves **4**

1.5kg pork spare ribs, chopped
1 tablespoon peanut oil
¼ cup (60ml) chinese barbecue sauce
2 tablespoons soy sauce
2 tablespoons sweet chilli sauce
2 cloves garlic, crushed
2 teaspoons grated fresh ginger
¼ cup (90g) honey
⅓ cup (75g) firmly packed brown sugar
¼ cup (60ml) dry sherry

1 Cook spare ribs in large saucepan of boiling water, uncovered, about 10 minutes or until just cooked; drain, pat dry on absorbent paper.
2 Heat oil in wok; stir-fry spare ribs, in batches, until browned all over and cooked as desired. Drain spare ribs on absorbent paper.

3 Drain oil from wok. Add remaining ingredients to wok; bring to a boil. Add spare ribs; stir-fry about 10 minutes, tossing until pork is well coated in thickened sauce.

Beef with oyster sauce and mushrooms

preparation time **15 minutes** cooking time **15 minutes** serves **4**

2 tablespoons peanut oil
600g beef strips
1 medium red capsicum (200g), sliced thinly
350g broccoli, cut into florets
2 cloves garlic, crushed
2 teaspoons cornflour
¼ cup (60ml) water
1 tablespoon soy sauce
¼ cup (60ml) oyster sauce
150g snow peas, halved lengthways
150g oyster mushrooms

1 Heat half the oil in wok; stir-fry beef, in batches, until browned all over.
2 Heat remaining oil in wok; stir-fry capsicum, broccoli and garlic until vegetables are just tender. Add combined cornflour, water and sauces to wok; bring to a boil.
3 Return beef to wok, add snow peas and mushrooms; stir-fry until hot.

Singapore chilli crab

preparation time **45 minutes** (plus standing time) cooking time **20 minutes**
serves **4**

2 whole uncooked mud crabs (1.5kg)
2 tablespoons peanut oil
1 fresh long red chilli, chopped finely
2 cloves garlic, crushed
2 teaspons finely grated fresh ginger
⅓ cup (80ml) chinese cooking wine
400g can crushed tomatoes
1 cup (250ml) water
1 tablespoon brown sugar
2 lebanese cucumbers (260g), halved lengthways, sliced thinly
3 green onions, sliced thinly
¼ cup loosely packed fresh coriander leaves
2 fresh long red chillies, sliced thinly

1 Place crabs in large container filled with ice and water; stand about 1 hour.
Remove the v-shaped flaps on undersides of crabs. Remove top shell and
grey fibrous tissue; wash crabs. Crack nippers slightly; cut each crab into six.
2 Heat oil in wok; stir-fry chopped chilli, garlic and ginger until fragrant. Add
wine; cook until liquid has reduced by half. Add undrained tomatoes, the
water and sugar; bring to a boil.
3 Add crab to wok, reduce heat; simmer, covered, about 15 minutes or until
crab changes in colour. Stir in cucumber.
4 Serve crab sprinkled with combined onion, coriander and chilli.

Chicken and mixed mushroom stir-fry

preparation time **15 minutes** cooking time **10 minutes** serves **4**

600g hokkien noodles
1 tablespoon peanut oil
750g chicken strips
600g mixed mushrooms, halved
3 green onions, chopped finely
2 tablespoons mild chilli sauce
½ cup (125ml) oyster sauce

1 Place noodles in medium heatproof bowl; cover with boiling water, separate with fork, drain.
2 Heat half the oil in wo; stir-fry chicken, in batches, until cooked as desired.
3 Heat remaining oil in wok; stir-fry mushrooms, in batches, until browned. Return chicken and mushrooms to wok with noodles, onion and sauces; stir-fry until hot.

Spinach and beef stir-fry

preparation time **10 minutes** cooking time **10 minutes** serves **4**

2 tablespoons peanut oil
700g beef strips
2 cloves garlic, crushed
250g broccolini, chopped coarsely
300g enoki mushrooms
250g baby spinach leaves
¼ cup (60ml) beef stock
¼ cup (60ml) oyster sauce

1 Heat half the oil in wok; stir-fry beef, in batches, until browned all over.
2 Heat remaining oil in wok; stir-fry garlic and broccolini until just tender.
3 Return beef to wok with mushrooms, spinach, stock and sauce; stir-fry until spinach is just wilted.

Cajun chicken with tomato salsa

preparation time **20 minutes** cooking time **10 minutes** serves **4**

750g chicken breast fillets, sliced thinly
¼ cup cajun seasoning
2 teaspoons grated lime rind
2 trimmed corn cobs (500g)
2 tablespoons olive oil
1 small red onion (100g), cut into thin wedges

Tomato salsa
2 small egg tomatoes (120g), chopped finely
2 green onions, sliced thinly
2 teaspoons lime juice
2 teaspoons balsamic vinegar

1 Combine ingredients for tomato salsa in small bowl; mix well.

2 Combine chicken, seasoning and rind in large bowl; mix well. Cut kernels from corn.

3 Heat half the oil in wok; stir-fry chicken mixture, in batches, until cooked as desired.

4 Heat remaining oil in wok; stir-fry corn and onion until onion is soft.

5 Return chicken to wok; stir-fry until hot. Serve chicken mixture topped with tomato salsa.

Pork burgers

preparation time **15 minutes** cooking time **15 minutes** serves **6**

500g minced pork
1 cup (70g) stale breadcrumbs
1 egg, beaten lightly
1 medium brown onion (150g), chopped finely
2 cloves garlic, crushed
2 tablespoons finely chopped fresh mint
2 tablespoons finely chopped fresh coriander
2 teaspoons worcestershire sauce
1 tablespoon tomato sauce
1 loaf pide, cut into 6 pieces
½ cup (130g) prepared hummus
80g prepared tabbouleh
6 small pieces char-grilled capsicum (80g)

1 Combine pork, breadcrumbs, egg, onion, garlic, herbs and sauces in large bowl. Using hands, shape mixture into six patties. Pan-fry patties, in batches, until browned both sides and cooked through.
2 Split pide pieces in half; toast under preheated grill until lightly browned.
3 Spread bases with hummus; top with patties, tabbouleh and capsicum, then with remaining bread halves.

Mussel broth with black bean sauce

preparation time **20 minutes** cooking time **20 minutes** serves **4**

1kg black mussels
1 cup (250ml) water
⅓ cup (80ml) black bean sauce
2 fresh long red chillies, sliced thinly
4 green onions, sliced thinly

1 Scrub mussels; remove beards. Place the water, black bean sauce and chilli in wok or large saucepan; bring to a boil.
2 Add mussels; cook, covered, about 3 minutes or until mussels open (discard any that remain closed). Sprinkle with green onion.

Sausages with pea and bacon mash

preparation time **5 minutes** cooking time **20 minutes** serves **4**

3 bacon rashers (210g), chopped
1 tablespoon olive oil
2 medium brown onions (300g), sliced thinly
8 thick beef sausages (640g)
1kg potatoes, peeled, quartered
1 cup (250ml) milk, warmed
40g butter
½ cup (60g) frozen peas

1 Cook bacon in lightly oiled frying pan until crisp; remove from pan.
2 Heat oil in same pan, add onions and sausages; cook, uncovered, until onions are soft and sausages are cooked through.
3 Meanwhile, boil, steam or microwave potatoes until soft; drain. Mash potatoes with milk and butter.
4 Boil, steam or microwave peas until just tender; drain. Add peas and bacon to mash. Serve mash topped with sausages and onion.

Chicken chow mein

preparation time **15 minutes** cooking time **15 minutes** serves **4**

1 tablespoon peanut oil
500g chicken thigh fillets, sliced thinly
2 medium brown onions (300g), sliced thinly
2 cloves garlic, crushed
1 tablespoon grated fresh ginger
2 trimmed stalks celery (150g), sliced thinly
1 medium red capsicum (200g), sliced thinly
2 teaspoons cornflour
½ cup (125ml) chicken stock
¼ cup (60ml) light soy sauce
5 green onions, sliced thickly
1 cup (80g) bean sprouts
2 cups (160g) finely shredded chinese cabbage

1 Heat half the oil in wok; stir-fry chicken, in batches, until browned and cooked through.
2 Heat remaining oil in wok; stir-fry brown onion, garlic and ginger until fragrant. Add celery and capsicum; stir-fry until vegetables are just tender.
3 Blend cornflour with stock and sauce in small jug. Return chicken to wok with cornflour mixture; stir-fry until sauce boils and thickens. Add green onion sprouts and cabbage; stir-fry until hot.

Pork schnitzels in lemon and parsley

preparation time **10 minutes** cooking time **20 minutes** serves **4**

2 cups (140g) coarse stale breadcrumbs
2 tablespoons finely grated lemon rind
2 tablespoons finely chopped fresh flat-leaf parsley
4 x 150g pork leg steaks (schnitzels)
⅓ cup (50g) plain flour
1 egg, beaten lightly
2 tablespoons milk
Vegetable oil for shallow-frying

1 Combine breadcrumbs, rind and parsley in a medium bowl.
2 Toss pork in flour, shake away excess.
3 Dip pork in combined egg and milk, then in breadcrumb mixture; press on lightly. Heat oil in large, frying pan; cook schnitzels until browned on both sides and cooked as desired. Drain on absorbent paper. Season with freshly ground black pepper.

serving suggestion Serve with lemon wedges and steamed green beans.

Salmon patties

preparation time **20 minutes** cooking time **25 minutes** serves **4**

4 medium potatoes (800g), chopped coarsely
415g can red salmon, drained, flaked
1 tablespoon lemon juice
4 green onions, chopped coarsely
½ cup (75g) plain flour
2 eggs, beaten lightly
1 cup (100g) packaged breadcrumbs
Vegetable oil, for shallow-frying

1 Boil, steam or microwave potato until tender; drain. Mash potato in medium bowl until smooth; cool 5 minutes. Add salmon, juice and onion; stir until well combined.

2 Using hands, shape salmon mixture into eight patties. Coat each patty with flour, shaking off excess; dip patties in egg then coat with breadcrumbs.

3 Heat oil in large frying pan; cook patties, in batches, until browned both sides.

Pepper-crusted swordfish

preparation time **10 minutes** cooking time **10 minutes** serves **4**

1 teaspoon ground white pepper
2 teaspoons cracked black pepper
⅓ cup (35g) packaged breadcrumbs
4 x 200g swordfish fillets

1 Combine peppers and breadcrumbs in small bowl. Press pepper mixture onto one side of each fish fillet.

2 Cook fish, crumbed-side down, in heated oiled large non-stick frying pan until browned lightly and crisp; turn, cook as desired.

serving suggestion Serve fish with steamed potatoes and green beans.

Fish with fennel salad

preparation time **15 minutes** cooking time **20 minutes** serves **4**

4 fish fillets (750g)
¼ cup (35g) plain flour
¼ cup (60ml) olive oil

Fennel salad
3 baby fennel bulbs (300g), sliced thinly
1 tablespoon chopped fennel tips
¾ cup firmly packed flat-leaf parsley leaves
2 small zucchini (180g), grated coarsely
1 teaspoon grated lemon rind
1½ tablespoons lemon juice
2 tablespoons olive oil
1 teaspoon wholegrain mustard
1 clove garlic, crushed

1 Make fennel salad.
2 Toss fish in flour, shake off excess. Heat oil in large frying pan; cook fish, in batches, until browned on both sides and cooked as desired.
3 Serve fish with fennel salad.

Fennel salad Combine fennel, fennel tips, parsley and zucchini in large bowl. Combine rind, juice, oil, mustard and garlic in screw-top jar; shake well. Add dressing to fennel mixture; toss well.

Pork and chinese broccoli stir-fry

preparation time **10 minutes** cooking time **10 minutes** serves **4**

500g fresh singapore noodles
2 tablespoons peanut oil
750g pork strips
1 large brown onion (200g), sliced
1 clove garlic, crushed
1kg chinese broccoli, chopped coarsely
⅓ cup (80ml) oyster sauce
1 tablespoon soy sauce

1 Place noodles in large heatproof bowl; cover with boiling water, separate with fork. Drain.
2 Heat half the oil in wok; stir-fry pork, in batches, until browned and cooked as desired.
3 Heat remaining oil in wok; stir-fry onion and garlic until onion softens. Return pork to wok with broccoli, combined sauces and noodles; stir-fry until broccoli is just wilted.

Veal campagnola

preparation time **10 minutes** cooking time **10 minutes** serves **4**

4 large veal steaks (500g)
¼ cup (35g) plain flour
30g butter
2 cups (500ml) bottled tomato pasta sauce
3 cups (200g) thawed, drained frozen spinach
2 cups (200g) grated mozzarella

1 Place veal between pieces of plastic wrap; pound until each piece is of the same thickness. Discard plastic wrap. Toss veal in flour; shake off excess flour.
2 Heat butter in large frying pan; cook veal until cooked as desired. Drain on absorbent paper.
3 Add pasta sauce to same pan, bring to a boil; place veal, in single layer, on top of boiling sauce. Spread quarter of spinach on top of each piece of veal, top with cheese. Cover; simmer mixture about 1 minute or until cheese melts.

Chicken with parsley and lemon

preparation time **15 minutes** cooking time **20 minutes** serves **4**

8 chicken thigh fillets (1kg)
1/3 cup (50g) plain flour
1 tablespoon olive oil
20g butter
1 cup coarsely chopped fresh flat-leaf parsley
2 tablespoons lemon juice
350g baby green beans

Polenta
3 cups (750ml) hot water
1 cup (250ml) chicken stock
1 cup (170g) instant polenta
20g butter
1/2 cup (40g) grated parmesan

1 Make polenta.
2 Meanwhile, toss chicken in flour; shake away excess flour. Heat oil and butter in large frying pan; add chicken, cook until browned on both sides and cooked through. Add parsley and lemon, stir to coat chicken.
3 Boil, steam or microwave beans until just tender; drain.
4 Serve chicken with polenta and beans.

Polenta Combine the water and stock in large saucepan. Bring to the boil then reduce heat to a simmer; gradually whisk in polenta and cook, uncovered, stirring frequently, about 10 minutes or until mixture is thick and soft. Stir in butter and parmesan.

Pork with maple mustard sauce

preparation time **10 minutes** cooking time **15 minutes** serves **4**

4 pork midloin butterflied steaks (800g)
2 tablespoons wholegrain mustard
¼ cup (60ml) maple syrup
1 tablespoon finely chopped fresh flat-leaf parsley
1 tablespoon olive oil
½ cup (125ml) dry white wine

1 Place pork in shallow dish, pour over combined mustard, syrup and parsley; stand 10 minutes. Drain pork, reserving marinade.
2 Heat oil in large frying pan, add pork; cook until browned both sides and cooked as desired. Remove pork from pan; cover to keep warm.
3 Combine reserved marinade and wine in pan. Bring to a boil then reduce heat; simmer, uncovered, until sauce thickens slightly. Serve sauce over pork.

Garlic chicken stir-fry with bok choy

preparation time **10 minutes** cooking time **10 minutes** serves **4**

700g chicken breast fillets, sliced thinly
½ cup (75g) plain flour
2 tablespoons peanut oil
6 cloves garlic, crushed
1 medium red capsicum (200g), sliced thinly
6 green onions, sliced thinly
½ cup (125ml) chicken stock
2 tablespoons light soy sauce
500g bok choy, chopped coarsely

1 Coat chicken in flour; shake off excess.
2 Heat oil in wok or large frying pan; stir-fry chicken, in batches, until browned and cooked as desired.
3 Add garlic, capsicum and onion to wok; stir-fry until capsicum is tender.
4 Return chicken to wok with stock and sauce; stir-fry until sauce boils and thickens slightly. Just before serving, add bok choy; stir-fry until bok choy wilts.

Lemon and anchovy chicken with garlic pumpkin

preparation time **15 minutes** cooking time **15 minutes** serves **4**

800g piece butternut pumpkin, peeled
2 tablespoons olive oil
4 cloves garlic, sliced thinly
½ cup (125ml) chicken stock
12 fresh sage leaves
4 single chicken breast fillets (680g)
40g butter
3 anchovy fillets, drained, chopped finely
1 tablespoon lemon juice

1 Chop pumpkin into 1.5cm pieces. Heat half the oil in large saucepan, add pumpkin and garlic; cook, stirring, until pumpkin begins to brown. Add 2 tablespoons of stock; cover, steam 5 minutes or until pumpkin is just tender. Stir in sage.

2 Meanwhile, cut chicken in half horizontally to give eight thin pieces. Melt half of butter and remaining oil in large frying pan; add chicken, cook, uncovered, until browned on both sides and cooked as desired. Remove chicken from pan; keep warm.

3 Add remaining butter to pan with anchovy; cook, stirring, until butter melts.

4 Add juice and remaining stock; simmer, uncovered, 1 minute or until reduced slightly.

5 Serve pumpkin topped with chicken and sauce.

serving suggestion Serve with rocket or a green salad.

Fish burger

preparation time **20 minutes** cooking time **10 minutes** serves **4**

600g boneless white fish fillets, chopped
1 egg
1 teaspoon ground cumin
1 teaspoon ground coriander
1 loaf turkish bread
2 lebanese cucumbers (260g)
¾ cup (210g) plain yogurt
1 tablespoon finely chopped fresh mint

1 Blend or process fish, egg and spices until smooth. Using hands, shape mixture into four patties. Cook patties in large heated oiled non-stick frying pan until browned both sides and cooked as desired.
2 Cut bread into four even pieces; slice horizontally through centre of each piece. Toast pieces, cut-side up, under heated grill.
3 Using vegetable peeler, slice cucumber into thin strips.
4 Combine yogurt and mint in small bowl.
5 Top bread bases with fish patties, cucumber and yogurt mixture, then remaining bread.

Beef burritos

preparation time **20 minutes** cooking time **35 minutes** serves **4**

4 x 25cm-round wheat flour tortillas
1 cup (125g) grated cheddar
1 teaspoon hot paprika
¾ cup (180g) sour cream
1 tablespoon chopped fresh coriander

Bean and beef filling
1 tablespoon olive oil
500g beef mince
1 medium brown onion (150g), chopped finely
1 clove garlic, crushed
400g can tomatoes
35g packet taco seasoning mix
½ cup (125ml) water
300g can kidney beans, rinsed, drained

1 Preheat oven to moderately hot.
2 Make bean and beef filling. Divide warm bean and beef filling among tortillas, roll; secure with toothpicks.
3 Place filled tortillas on oiled oven tray; sprinkle with cheese and paprika. Bake in moderately hot oven about 10 minutes or until hot.
4 Remove toothpicks; serve burritos topped with sour cream and coriander.

Bean and beef filling Heat oil in medium frying pan; cook beef, stirring, until browned. Add onion and garlic; cook, stirring, until onion is soft. Stir in undrained crushed tomatoes and remaining ingredients; simmer, uncovered, about 15 minutes or until mixture is thickened.

Chilli con carne

preparation time **25 minutes**
cooking time **1 hour 10 minutes** (plus cooling time) serves **4**

1 tablespoon olive oil
600g beef mince
1 medium brown onion (150g), chopped coarsely
2 cloves garlic, crushed
1 teaspoon ground cumin
1 teaspoon ground coriander
¼ teaspoon cayenne pepper
1 teaspoon sweet paprika
420g can kidney beans, rinsed, drained
400g can tomatoes
1 tablespoon tomato paste
1 cup (250ml) beef stock
2 tablespoons chopped fresh coriander
⅓ cup (65g) finely chopped, bottled jalapeño chillies

1 Heat oil in large saucepan; cook mince, onion and garlic, stirring, until onion is soft. Add spices; cook, stirring, until fragrant. Add beans, undrained crushed tomatoes, paste and stock. Bring to a boil then reduce heat; simmer, covered, 1 hour.
2 Just before serving, stir in coriander and chilli.

serving suggestion Serve chilli con carne with boiled rice.

tip Freeze leftover chilli con carne in single portions for up to two months.

Wiener schnitzel with lemon spaetzle

preparation time **20 minutes** (plus refrigeration time)
cooking time **20 minutes** serves **4**

½ cup (75g) plain flour
3 eggs, beaten lightly
2 tablespoons milk
2 cups (140g) stale breadcrumbs
¾ cup (75g) packaged breadcrumbs
½ cup (40g) finely grated parmesan
8 veal schnitzels (800g)
Vegetable oil, for shallow-frying

Lemon spaetzle
2 cups (300g) plain flour
4 eggs, beaten lightly
½ cup (125ml) water
2 teaspoons finely grated lemon rind
40g butter, chopped

1 Whisk flour, egg and milk in medium shallow bowl; combine breadcrumbs and cheese in another medium shallow bowl. Coat schnitzels, one at a time, in flour mixture then in breadcrumb mixture. Place, in single layer, on tray. Cover; refrigerate 15 minutes.
2 Make lemon spaetzle.
3 Heat oil in large frying pan; cook schnitzels, in batches, until browned both sides and cooked as desired.
4 Serve schnitzel with lemon spaetzle.

Lemon spaetzle Place flour in large bowl, make well in centre. Gradually add egg and the water, stirring, until batter is smooth. Stir in rind. Pour half the batter into metal colander set over large saucepan of boiling water; using wooden spoon, push batter through holes of colander, remove colander. When water returns to a boil, boil, uncovered, about 2 minutes or until spaetzle float to surface. Use slotted spoon to remove spaetzle; drain, place in large bowl. Add half the butter; toss spaetzle gently until butter melts. Keep warm; repeat with remaining batter and butter.

Chicken schnitzel burgers

preparation time **10 minutes** cooking time **20 minutes** serves **4**

4 chicken breast fillets (680g)
¼ cup (35g) plain flour
2 eggs, beaten lightly
1 tablespoon milk
½ cup (80g) corn flake crumbs
½ cup (50g) packaged breadcrumbs
2 medium tomatoes (380g), seeded, chopped finely
1 medium avocado (250g), chopped finely
2 teaspoons lemon juice
1 long loaf turkish bread
½ cup (150g) mayonnaise
1 small white onion (80g), chopped finely
1 tablespoon sweet fruit chutney
40g baby rocket leaves

1 Preheat oven to hot.
2 Using meat mallet, gently pound chicken between sheets of plastic wrap until 1cm thick.
3 Combine flour, egg and milk in medium bowl; combine corn flakes and breadcrumbs in another medium bowl. Coat chicken, one piece at a time, first in flour mixture then in breadcrumb mixture.
4 Place chicken, in single layer, on oiled oven tray; roast, uncovered, in hot oven, about 20 minutes or until chicken is lightly browned all over and cooked as desired.
5 Meanwhile, combine tomato, avocado and juice in small bowl. Quarter pide; split pieces horizontally, toast one side lightly. Whisk mayonnaise, onion and chutney in separate small bowl until well combined.
6 To serve, sandwich rocket, schnitzel, tomato mixture and mayonnaise mixture between two pieces of turkish bread.

Chicken enchiladas with corn salsa

preparation time **30 minutes** cooking time **35 minutes** serves **4**

1 large red onion (300g), chopped finely
2 tablespoons vegetable oil
2 cloves garlic, crushed
1 tablespoon tomato paste
¼ cup (45g) drained bottled jalapeño chillies, chopped coarsely
400g can tomatoes
1 cup (250ml) chicken stock
500g chicken breast fillets, sliced thinly
10 corn tortillas
2 cups (250g) coarsely grated cheddar
½ cup (120g) sour cream

Corn salsa
1 small red capsicum (150g), chopped finely
310g can corn kernels, drained
1 tablespoon lime juice
1 cup loosely packed, coarsely chopped fresh coriander

1 Reserve quarter of onion for corn salsa. Preheat oven to moderate.
2 Heat oil in large frying pan; cook remaining onion with garlic, stirring, until onion softens. Add tomato paste, chilli, undrained crushed tomatoes, stock and chicken. Bring to a boil then reduce heat; simmer, uncovered, until chicken is cooked through. Remove chicken from pan; cover to keep warm.
3 Soften tortillas in oven or microwave oven, according to manufacturer's instructions. Dip tortillas, one at a time, in tomato mixture in pan; place on board. Divide chicken and half the cheese among tortillas, placing along edge; roll tortilla to enclose filling. Place enchiladas, seam-side down, in large oiled 3-litre (12-cup) shallow ovenproof dish; enchiladas should fit snugly, without overcrowding.
4 Pour remaining mixture over enchiladas; top with sour cream, sprinkle with remaining cheese. Bake, uncovered, in moderate oven about 15 minutes or until hot.
5 Meanwhile, make corn salsa. Divide enchiladas among serving plates; serve with corn salsa.

Corn salsa Place reserved onion in small bowl with capsicum, corn, juice and coriander; toss to combine.

Lamb rissoles with potato crush and rosemary gravy

preparation time **20 minutes** cooking time **35 minutes** serves **4**

500g lamb mince
1 large brown onion (200g), grated coarsely
1 clove garlic, crushed
1 egg
½ cup (35g) fresh breadcrumbs
1 tablespoon olive oil
500g baby new potatoes
20g butter
1 tablespoon plain flour
1 cup (250ml) beef stock
1 tablespoon fresh rosemary leaves
250g cherry tomatoes

1 Using hands, combine lamb, onion, garlic, egg and breadcrumbs in medium bowl. Shape lamb mixture into eight patties.
2 Heat oil in large frying pan; cook rissoles both sides, four at a time, about 15 minutes or until browned and cooked as desired. Drain on absorbent paper; cover with foil to keep warm. Reserve pan with rissole drippings.
3 Meanwhile, boil, steam or microwave potatoes until tender; drain. Crush potatoes in medium bowl with potato masher; stir in butter.
4 Cook flour in rissole pan, stirring, until mixture browns and bubbles. Gradually stir in stock; stir until gravy boils and thickens. Strain gravy; stir in rosemary leaves.
5 Meanwhile, cook tomatoes, stirring, in heated small frying pan about 2 minutes or until split and just softened.
6 Divide potatoes among serving plates, top with rissoles, rosemary gravy and tomatoes.

Chicken tandoori pockets with raita

preparation time **10 minutes**   cooking time **10 minutes**   makes **8**

1 tablespoon lime juice
⅓ cup (100g) tandoori paste
¼ cup (70g) plain yogurt
400g chicken tenderloins
8 large wheat flour tortillas
60g snow pea tendrils

Raita
1 cup (280g) plain yogurt
1 lebanese cucumber (130g), halved, seeded, chopped finely
1 tablespoon finely chopped fresh mint

1 Combine juice, paste and yogurt in medium bowl; add chicken, toss to coat chicken in marinade.
2 Cook chicken in heated, lightly oiled large frying pan until cooked through. Stand 5 minutes; slice thickly.
3 Meanwhile, heat tortillas according to manufacturer's instructions.
4 Combine ingredients for raita in small bowl.
5 Place equal amounts of chicken, snow pea tendrils and raita on quarter section of each tortilla; fold tortilla in half, then in half again to enclose filling and form triangle-shaped pockets.

Crab cakes

preparation time **30 minutes** cooking time **15 minutes** serves **4**

2 green onions, chopped finely
1 trimmed celery stalk (100g), chopped finely
500g crab meat
2 egg whites, beaten lightly
1 tablespoon finely chopped fresh dill
1 tablespoon worcestershire sauce
1 cup (70g) stale breadcrumbs

Soy and honey sauce
½ cup (125ml) soy sauce
2 tablespoons honey

1 Cook onion and celery in lightly oiled, large frying pan until onion is soft.
2 Combine onion mixture with remaining ingredients in large bowl. Using hands, shape mixture into 12 cakes.
3 Cook crab cakes, in batches, in same pan until browned both sides and cooked as desired.
4 Combine ingredients for soy and honey sauce in small bowl.
5 Serve crab cakes with soy and honey sauce.

serving suggestion Serve crab cakes with a mixed green salad.

Sausages with caramelised onions, roasted kipflers and mushrooms

preparation time **10 minutes**   cooking time **25 minutes**   serves **4**

750g kipfler potatoes
¼ cup coarsely chopped fresh chives
200g swiss brown mushrooms, sliced thickly
8 thick beef sausages (640g)
1 tablespoon olive oil
2 large red onions (600g), sliced thinly
1 tablespoon balsamic vinegar
1 tablespoon brown sugar

1 Boil, steam or microwave potatoes until just tender; drain. Cook potatoes in lightly oiled, large frying pan, uncovered, until crisp. Remove from heat; sprinkle with chives. Cover to keep warm.

2 Cook mushrooms and sausages in same pan, uncovered, until mushrooms are browned and sausages are cooked through.

3 Meanwhile, heat oil in medium saucepan; cook onion, stirring, until soft. Add vinegar and sugar; cook, stirring, until onion is caramelised.

4 Divide potatoes, sausages and mushrooms among serving plates; top with onion mixture.

ONE-POT WONDERS

Sausage and bean hot pot

preparation time **10 minutes** cooking time **25 minutes** serves **4**

1 teaspoon vegetable oil
500g thin beef sausages
1 medium brown onion (150g), sliced thinly
2 tablespoons plain flour
1 cup (250ml) beef stock
415g can baked beans in tomato sauce
2 tablespoons tomato paste
400g can tomatoes
1 teaspoon cracked black pepper
2 tablespoons chopped fresh flat-leaf parsley

1 Heat oil in large frying pan; cook sausages, uncovered, until well browned. Drain on absorbent paper; slice thickly.
2 Cook onion in same pan, stirring, until onion softens. Add flour; cook, stirring, until mixture bubbles and thickens. Gradually add stock; cook, stirring, until sauce boils and thickens.
3 Return sausages to pan. Add undrained beans, paste, undrained crushed tomatoes, pepper and half of the parsley; cook, stirring, until hot. Serve sprinkled with remaining parsley.

tip Freeze leftover stew in single portions for up to two months.

Curried chicken and zucchini soup

preparation time **15 minutes**   cooking time **25 minutes**   serves **4**

1 tablespoon peanut oil
1 medium brown onion (150g), chopped finely
1 clove garlic, crushed
1 teaspoon curry powder
½ cup (100g) white long-grain rice
340g chicken breast fillets, sliced thinly
2 cups (500ml) water
1 litre (4 cups) chicken stock
4 medium zucchini (480g), grated coarsely

1 Heat oil in large saucepan; cook onion and garlic, stirring, until onion softens. Add curry powder; cook, stirring, until mixture is fragrant.
2 Add rice and chicken; cook, stirring, 2 minutes. Add the water and stock. Bring to a boil then reduce heat; simmer, covered, 10 minutes. Add zucchini; cook, stirring, about 5 minutes or until chicken is cooked through.

tip Freeze leftover soup in single portions for up to two months.

Lancashire hot pot

preparation time **15 minutes**   cooking time **2 hours**   serves **4**

8 lamb neck chops (1kg)
3 medium brown onions (450g), sliced thinly
3 large potatoes (900g), sliced thinly
4 bacon rashers (285g), chopped finely
1¾ cups (430ml) beef stock
30g butter, chopped coarsely

1 Preheat oven to moderately slow.
2 Trim fat from chops; place chops in 3-litre (12-cup) ovenproof casserole dish. Top with layer of onion, potato and bacon. Repeat layering, ending with potatoes. Pour over stock; top with butter.
3 Cook, covered, in moderately slow oven 1 hour. Remove cover; cook about 1 hour or until chops are tender.

Corn and bacon chowder

preparation time **15 minutes** cooking time **20 minutes** serves **4**

40g butter
1 medium brown onion (150g), chopped finely
1 clove garlic, crushed
2 bacon rashers (140g), chopped coarsely
¼ cup (35g) plain flour
2 medium potatoes (400g), chopped coarsely
2 cups (500ml) chicken stock
1 litre (4 cups) milk
2 cups (320g) frozen corn kernels
½ cup (125ml) cream
2 tablespoons finely chopped fresh chives

1 Heat butter in large saucepan; cook onion, garlic and bacon, stirring, until onion softens.
2 Stir in flour; cook, stirring, 1 minute. Stir in potato, stock and half the milk; simmer, covered, about 15 minutes or until potato is soft.
3 Add corn, remaining milk and cream; cook, stirring, until hot. Stir in chives.

tip Freeze leftover soup in single portions for up to two months.

Balinese lamb chops

preparation time **15 minutes** cooking time **15 minutes** serves **4**

1 tablespoon peanut oil
12 lamb loin chops (1.2kg), trimmed
2 small brown onions (160g), sliced thinly
½ cup (130g) crunchy peanut butter
¼ cup (60ml) sweet chilli sauce
2 tablespoons lemon juice
⅔ cup (160ml) coconut milk
¾ cup (180ml) water
2 tablespoons coarsely chopped fresh coriander

1 Heat oil in large frying pan; cook lamb, uncovered, until browned and cooked as desired. Remove lamb from pan; drain excess fat from pan.
2 Add onion to pan; cook, stirring, until browned. Add peanut butter,

sauce, juice, and combined coconut milk and water; cook, stirring, until sauce thickens slightly.

3 Return lamb to pan, coat with sauce.

4 Serve sprinkled with coriander.

Winter vegetable soup with couscous

preparation time **20 minutes** cooking time **30 minutes** serves **4**

1 tablespoon olive oil
2 medium brown onions (300g), chopped coarsely
3 trimmed celery stalks (300g), chopped coarsely
1 clove garlic, crushed
1 teaspoon sweet paprika
3 medium potatoes (600g), chopped coarsely
2 large parsnips (700g), chopped coarsely
2 large carrots (360g), chopped coarsely
1 ½ cups (375ml) chicken stock
1.25 litres (5 cups) water
½ cup (100g) couscous
2 tablespoons coarsely chopped fresh flat-leaf parsley

1 Heat oil in large saucepan; cook onion, celery, garlic and paprika, stirring, until onion softens.

2 Add potato, parsnip, carrot, stock and the water. Bring to a boil then reduce heat; simmer, covered, about 15 minutes or until vegetables are tender.

3 Stir in couscous and parsley; cook, uncovered, 2 minutes or until couscous is just tender.

Japanese-style chicken and egg on rice

preparation time **20 minutes** cooking time **10 minutes** serves **4**

²⁄₃ cup (160ml) chicken stock
¼ cup (60ml) soy sauce
2 tablespoons mirin
1 teaspoon white sugar
500g chicken breast fillets, sliced thinly
1 small brown onion (80g), sliced thinly
2 baby eggplant (120g), sliced thinly
1 medium red capsicum (200g), sliced thinly
4 eggs, beaten lightly
4 cups cooked sushi rice
4 green onions, sliced thinly

1 Combine stock, soy sauce, mirin and sugar in large frying pan; bring to boil.
2 Add chicken, onion, eggplant and capsicum; cook, covered, about 5 minutes or until chicken is just cooked through.
3 Pour egg over chicken mixture; cook, covered, over low heat about 2 minutes or until egg is just set.
4 Divide rice among serving bowls; top with chicken mixture, sprinkle with green onions.

tip Substitute sherry or sweet white wine for mirin, if you prefer.

Beef and vegetables with beer

preparation time **15 minutes** cooking time **1 hour 30 minutes** serves **6**

1½ tablespoons vegetable oil
1.5kg rolled roast of beef brisket
2 large carrots (360g), chopped coarsely
2 large parsnips (360g), chopped coarsely
6 baby onions (150g)
6 baby new potatoes (240g)
2 x 375ml cans beer

1 Preheat oven to moderately hot.

2 Heat oil in large baking dish; cook beef until browned. Remove from dish.

3 Add vegetables to dish; cook, stirring, until browned all over.

4 Return beef to dish; add beer. Cook, covered, in moderately hot oven 1 hour. Remove vegetables; cover to keep warm.

5 Turn beef; cook, uncovered, about 15 minutes or until beef is cooked as desired. Remove beef from dish; wrap in foil.

6 Place baking dish over heat; simmer, uncovered, until liquid reduces to about 1 cup (250ml).

7 Serve sliced beef with vegetables and sauce.

Chunky vegetable and pasta soup

preparation time **15 minutes** cooking time **20 minutes** serves **6**

1 tablespoon olive oil
2 medium brown onions (300g), chopped finely
2 cloves garlic, crushed
4 trimmed celery stalks (400g), chopped finely
2 medium carrots (240g), chopped finely
400g can tomato puree
⅓ cup (90g) tomato paste
400g can red kidney beans, rinsed, drained
3 litres (12 cups) chicken stock
500g penne
¼ cup finely chopped fresh flat-leaf parsley

1 Heat oil in large saucepan, add onion, garlic, celery and carrot; cook, stirring, until onion softens.

2 Add tomato puree, paste, beans and stock; bring to a boil. Add pasta; boil, uncovered, until pasta is tender. Serve sprinkled with parsley.

tip Freeze leftover soup in single portions for up to two months.

Chicken cacciatore

preparation time **30 minutes** (plus standing time) cooking time **40 minutes**
serves **4**

2 tablespoons olive oil
1.5kg chicken pieces
1 medium brown onion (150g), chopped finely
1 clove garlic, crushed
½ cup (125ml) dry white wine
½ cup (125ml) chicken stock
400g can tomatoes
1 tablespoon tomato paste
1 teaspoon chopped fresh basil
¼ cup (60ml) milk
60g seeded black olives, halved
1 tablespoon chopped fresh flat-leaf parsley

1 Heat oil in large frying pan; cook chicken, uncovered, until browned both
sides. Remove from pan.
2 Pour off most pan juices, leaving about 1 tablespoon in pan. Add onion
and garlic to pan; cook, stirring, until onion is soft. Add wine, bring to a boil;
boil until reduced by half. Add stock; stir over high heat 2 minutes. Push
tomatoes with their liquid through sieve. Add tomatoes to pan with paste
and basil; cook 1 minute.
3 Return chicken to pan. Bring to a boil, reduce heat; simmer, covered, about
20 minutes or until chicken is cooked through.

tip Freeze leftover casserole in single portions for up to two months.

Coq au vin

preparation time **30 minutes**   cooking time **55 minutes**   serves **4**

800g spring onions
6 bacon rashers (420g)
¼ cup (60ml) olive oil
300g button mushrooms
2 cloves garlic, crushed
8 chicken thigh fillets (880g)
¼ cup (35g) plain flour
2 cups (500ml) dry red wine
1½ cups (375ml) chicken stock
2 tablespoons tomato paste
3 bay leaves
4 sprigs fresh thyme

1 Trim green ends from onions, leaving about 4cm of stem attached; trim roots. Remove rind from bacon, cut bacon into 3cm pieces. Heat 1 tablespoon of the oil in large frying pan; cook onion, stirring, until browned all over, remove from pan. Add bacon, mushrooms and garlic to same pan; cook, stirring, until bacon is crisp, remove from pan.
2 Toss chicken in flour; shake off excess. Heat remaining oil in same pan. Cook chicken, in batches, until browned; drain on absorbent paper.
3 Return chicken to pan with wine, stock, paste, bay leaves, thyme, onion, and bacon and mushroom mixture. Bring to a boil then reduce heat; simmer, uncovered, about 35 minutes or until chicken is tender and sauce has thickened slightly. Remove bay leaves before serving.

tip Freeze leftover casserole in single portions for up to two months.

Chicken sausages with beans

preparation time **15 minutes** cooking time **35 minutes** serves **6**

1 tablespoon vegetable oil
800g chicken sausages
2 medium brown onions (300g), sliced thinly
3 cloves garlic, crushed
4 bacon rashers (285g), chopped finely
415g can baked beans in tomato sauce
400g can tomatoes
150g char-grilled capsicum, chopped coarsley
¼ cup (60ml) worcestershire sauce

1 Heat oil in large saucepan; cook sausages until browned. Remove from pan; cut sausages in half.
2 Add onion to pan with garlic and bacon; cook, stirring, until onion is soft and bacon is browned lightly.
3 Add beans, undrained crushed tomatoes, capsicum, sauce and sausage; simmer, covered, 20 minutes.

Chicken and noodles in broth

preparation time **15 minutes** cooking time **20 minutes** serves **4**

3 cups (750ml) chicken stock
3 cups (750ml) boiling water
2cm piece fresh ginger (10g), grated
2 cloves garlic, crushed
2 tablespoons soy sauce
2 fresh red thai chillies, sliced thinly
4 single chicken breast fillets (680g)
450g hokkien noodles
250g asparagus, quartered lengthways
4 green onions, sliced thinly

1 Combine stock, the water, ginger, garlic, sauce and chilli in medium saucepan, cover; bring to a boil.
2 Add chicken; reduce heat, simmer, covered, about 10 minutes or until chicken is just cooked through. Remove chicken from stock mixture.

3 Return stock mixture to a boil; add noodles, using a fork to break up noodles. Add asparagus; simmer, uncovered, until just tender.
4 Meanwhile, slice chicken thickly. Divide noodles and stock mixture among serving bowls. Top with chicken, asparagus and onion.

serving suggestion Serve broth with extra soy sauce and chilli.

Minestrone with meatballs

preparation time **40 minutes** cooking time **35 minutes** serves **4**

400g pork mince
1 teaspoon sweet paprika
1 egg, beaten lightly
1 medium brown onion (150g), chopped finely
¼ cup (70g) tomato paste
2 tablespoons olive oil
2 cloves garlic, crushed
2 medium carrots (240g), diced into 1cm pieces
1 trimmed celery stalk (100g), diced into 1cm pieces
2 x 400g cans diced tomatoes
2 cups (500ml) chicken stock
2 cups (500ml) water
2 large zucchini (300g), diced into 1cm pieces
400g can borlotti beans, rinsed, drained
½ cup (110g) risoni

1 Combine mince, paprika, egg, half the onion and 1 tablespoon of tomato paste in medium bowl. Roll level tablespoons of mixture into balls.
2 Heat oil in large saucepan; cook meatballs, in batches, until browned. Cook garlic and remaining onion in same pan, stirring, until onion softens. Add carrot and celery; cook, stirring, until vegetables are just tender.
3 Add remaining paste to pan; cook, stirring, 1 minute. Add undrained tomatoes, stock and the water; bring to a boil.
4 Add zucchini, beans, risoni and meatballs; return to a boil then reduce heat; simmer, covered, about 15 minutes or until meatballs are cooked through.

Chicken with red beans
preparation time **15 minutes** cooking time **35 minutes** serves **6**

1 tablespoon vegetable oil
1 medium brown onion (150g), chopped finely
2 medium red capsicums (400g), chopped finely
2 cloves garlic, crushed
½ teaspoon chilli powder
1 teaspoon ground cumin
750g minced chicken
2 x 215g cans red kidney beans, rinsed, drained
425g can tomatoes
2 tablespoons tomato paste

1 Heat oil in large saucepan; cook onion, capsicum and garlic, stirring, until onion is soft.
2 Stir in spices; cook, stirring, until fragrant.
3 Add chicken; cook, stirring, until browned all over and cooked as desired.
4 Add beans, undrained crushed tomatoes and paste; cook, covered, about 15 minutes or until thickened slightly.

Apples, pork and prunes
preparation time **25 minutes** cooking time **1 hour 30** minutes serves **4**

2 tablespoons vegetable oil
2 small leeks (400g), sliced thinly
4 forequarter pork chops (1.75kg)
Plain flour
1 litre (4 cups) chicken stock
½ cup (100g) white long-grain rice
4 medium apples (600g), sliced thickly
1 cup (170g) seeded prunes
2 tablespoons coarsely chopped fresh sage

1 Preheat oven to moderate.
2 Heat one-third of the oil in 2.5-litre (10-cup) flameproof casserole dish; cook leek, stirring, until soft. Remove from dish.
3 Trim fat and bone from chops; cut pork into 5cm pieces. Toss pork in flour; shake away excess flour.

4 Heat remaining oil in dish; cook pork, stirring, until browned all over and cooked as desired. Add leek and stock to dish; cook, covered, in moderate oven 45 minutes.

5 Remove dish from oven; skim off any fat. Stir in rice, apple, prunes and half the sage; cook, covered, in oven, a further 20 minutes or until pork is tender.

6 Serve sprinkled with remaining sage.

Chilli tomato chicken

preparation time **15 minutes** cooking time **1 hour** serves **6**

12 chicken legs (1.5kg)
Plain flour
2 tablespoons olive oil
1 medium red onion (150g), sliced thinly
2 cloves garlic, crushed
2 fresh red thai chillies, sliced thinly
3 bacon rashers (220g), chopped coarsely
3 medium tomatoes (390g), peeled, chopped coarsely
1½ cups (375ml) chicken stock
¼ cup finely chopped fresh basil
¼ cup (70g) tomato paste
½ cup (80g) seeded black olives

1 Toss chicken in flour; shake away excess flour. Heat oil in large saucepan; cook chicken, in batches, until browned all over and cooked as desired. Remove from pan.

2 Add onion, garlic, chilli and bacon to pan; cook, stirring, until onion is soft. Stir in tomato, stock, basil, paste and olives.

3 Add chicken, simmer, uncovered, 45 minutes or until chicken is tender.

tip Freeze leftover chicken in single portions for up to two months.

MICROWAVE MEALS

Creamy mushroom fish

preparation time **10 minutes** cooking time **15 minutes** serves **4**

40g butter
1 medium brown onion (150g), chopped
2 teaspoons chopped fresh thyme
250g button mushrooms, sliced
4 boneless white fish fillets (800g)
2 tablespoons dry white wine
¼ cup (60ml) fish stock
3 teaspoons cornflour
⅓ cup (80ml) cream

1 Combine butter, onion and thyme in large shallow microwave-safe dish; cook, uncovered, on HIGH (100%) 4 minutes, stirring once during cooking. Place mushrooms in same dish; top with fish, folding thin ends under. Pour over wine and stock; cook, covered, on HIGH (100%) about 5 minutes or until fish is just cooked through. Remove fish from dish; cover to keep warm.
2 Reserve 1 cup (250ml) liquid in dish, stir in blended cornflour and cream; cook, uncovered, on HIGH (100%) about 4 minutes or until sauce boils and thickens slightly, stirring once during cooking. Serve sauce over fish.

Chilli and ginger beef

preparation time **15 minutes** cooking time **15 minutes** serves **4**

1 tablespoon peanut oil
2 small leeks, sliced
1 teaspoon grated fresh ginger
1 clove garlic, crushed
2 small fresh red chillies, chopped
500g beef strips
1 tablespoon dark soy sauce
1 tablespoon oyster sauce
2 teaspoons cornflour
2 tablespoons water

1 Combine oil with leeks, ginger, garlic and chillies in a large shallow microwave-safe dish; cook, covered, on HIGH (100%) 5 minutes. Add beef and sauces; cook, covered, on HIGH (100%) about 5 minutes or until tender. Stir in blended cornflour and water; cook, covered, on HIGH (100%) about 5 minutes or until mixture boils and thickens, stirring occasionally.

Saucy chicken in yogurt

preparation time **10 minutes** cooking time **15 minutes** serves **4**

750g chicken tenderloins
2 cups (500ml) satay sauce
2 large brown onions (400g), cut into wedges
250g cherry tomatoes, halved
⅓ cup shredded fresh basil
200ml plain yogurt
2 tablespoons sweet chilli sauce

1 Combine chicken, half the satay sauce and onion in large microwave-safe bowl; cook, uncovered, on HIGH (100%) 10 minutes, stirring twice during cooking. Add remaining satay sauce; cook, covered, on HIGH (100%) about 2 minutes or until chicken is cooked through.
2 Add tomatoes and basil; cook, uncovered, on HIGH (100%) 2 minutes. Serve drizzled with combined yogurt and chilli sauce.

Spicy indian-style fish

preparation time **10 minutes** cooking time **25 minutes** serves **4**

20g butter
1 large brown onion (200g), sliced
4 cloves garlic, crushed
1 tablespoon grated fresh ginger
2 teaspoons garam masala
2 x 400g cans crushed tomatoes
½ cup (125ml) cream
1 tablespoon lemon juice
750g thick boneless white fish fillets, chopped coarsely
2 tablespoons chopped fresh coriander

1 Combine butter and onion in large shallow microwave-safe dish; cook, uncovered, on HIGH (100%) about 8 minutes or until onion is browned lightly, stirring three times during cooking. Add garlic, ginger and spice; cook, uncovered, on HIGH (100%) 30 seconds. Add tomatoes, cream and juice; cook, uncovered, on HIGH (100%) 7 minutes, stirring once.
2 Add fish, in single layer; cook, uncovered, on HIGH (100%) about 8 minutes or until fish is cooked through. Just before serving, sprinkle with coriander.

Mushroom risotto

preparation time **10 minutes** cooking time **30 minutes** serves **4**

40g butter
1 medium brown onion (150g), chopped
2 cloves garlic, crushed
2½ cups (400g) arborio rice
500g mixed mushrooms, quartered
2 cups (625ml) chicken stock
1¾ cups (430ml) boiling water
2 green onions, sliced thinly
¼ cup (20g) finely grated parmesan

1 Place butter, onion and garlic in large microwave-safe bowl; cook, uncovered, on HIGH (100%) 2 minutes or until onion softens. Add rice and mushrooms; stir well. Cook, covered, on HIGH (100%) 3 minutes.

2 Add stock and the water; stir well. Cook, covered, on HIGH (100%) about 20 minutes, stirring every 5 minutes or until rice is just soft. Stir in green onions and cheese.

Asparagus and chicken risotto

preparation time **10 minutes** cooking time **15 minutes** serves **4**

You will need one large barbecued chicken for this recipe.

300g asparagus, chopped
2 tablespoons olive oil
1 cup (300g) arborio rice
1 clove garlic, crushed
1 litre (4 cups) boiling chicken stock
2½ cups (340g) coarsely chopped cooked chicken
¼ cup (20g) coarsely grated parmesan
¼ cup (60ml) cream

1 Place asparagus in large microwave-safe bowl; cook, covered, on HIGH (100%) 1 minute. Rinse asparagus under cold water; drain.
2 Combine oil, rice and garlic in large microwave-safe bowl; cook, covered, on HIGH (100%) 1 minute. Add 2 cups (500ml) boiling stock; cook, covered, on HIGH (100%) 5 minutes. Add remaining boiling stock; cook, covered, on HIGH (100%) 5 minutes, stirring twice during cooking.
3 Gently stir asparagus and remaining ingredients into risotto; cook, covered, on HIGH (100%) 2 minutes. Stand, covered, 5 minutes.

Gnocchi with spinach, tomato and pine nuts

preparation time **5 minutes** cooking time **15 minutes** serves **4**

½ cup (80g) pine nuts
¾ cup (180ml) cream
400g can crushed tomatoes
3 cloves garlic, crushed
½ cup (75g) drained chopped sun-dried tomatoes in oil
½ cup (60g) seeded black olives, sliced
750g packaged potato gnocchi
1.5 litres (6 cups) boiling water
500g spinach, chopped coarsely

1 Place nuts in large shallow microwave-safe dish; cook, uncovered, on HIGH (100%) 6 minutes or until browned lightly, stirring three times during cooking.
2 Combine cream, tomatoes and garlic in large microwave-safe bowl; cook, uncovered, on HIGH (100%) 3 minutes. Add sun-dried tomatoes and olives; cook, uncovered, on HIGH (100%) 2 minutes. Cover to keep warm.
3 Place gnocchi in large microwave-safe bowl, cover with the boiling water; cook, uncovered, on HIGH (100%) 2 minutes. Drain gnocchi, gently toss in large microwave-safe bowl with tomato sauce, nuts and spinach; cook, uncovered, on HIGH (100%) 2 minutes.

Pork steaks in apple sauce

preparation time **10 minutes** cooking time **12 minutes** serves **4**

30g butter
4 green onions, sliced
4 thin pork steaks (400g)
100g baby mushrooms, sliced
2 teaspoons cornflour
¼ cup cream
1½ cups (375ml) apple juice
½ cup water
1 beef stock cube, crumbled

1 Melt butter in a large shallow microwave-safe dish; add onions and pork in single layer, cook, covered, on HIGH (100%) about 8 minutes or until pork is almost tender. Turn steaks once during cooking. Stir in mushrooms; cook, covered, on HIGH (100%) 2 minutes.

2 Blend cornflour with cream; stir in juice, the water and stock cube. Add to pork mixture; cook, covered, on HIGH (100%) about 2 minutes or until mixture boils and thickens, stirring occasionally.

Hearty bean soup

preparation time **15 minutes** cooking time **15 minutes** serves **4**

1 tablespoon olive oil
1 medium brown onion (150g), chopped
1 clove garlic, crushed
300g can butter beans, rinsed, drained
300g can red kidney beans, rinsed, drained
400g can tomatoes
2 tablespoons tomato paste
2 cups (500ml) hot water
1 teaspoon chopped fresh oregano
60g piece spicy salami, chopped
2 tablespoons shredded fresh basil

1 Combine oil, onion and garlic in large microwave-safe bowl; cook, uncovered, on HIGH (100%) 4 minutes, stirring once during cooking. Add beans, undrained crushed tomatoes, paste, the hot water and oregano; cook, covered, on HIGH (100%) 10 minutes.

2 Stir in salami; serve sprinkled with basil.

Chicken, tomato and leek casserole

preparation time **10 minutes** cooking time **20 minutes** serves **4**

30g butter
1 medium leek (350g), sliced
1 clove garlic, crushed
1 ½ cups (375ml) tomato pasta sauce
2 medium zucchini (240g), sliced
¼ cup (60ml) stock
660g chicken thigh fillets, chopped
200g button mushrooms, sliced
1 tablespoon chopped fresh basil leaves

1 Combine butter, leek and garlic in large microwave-safe bowl; cook, uncovered, on HIGH (100%) 4 minutes, stirring once during cooking. Add pasta sauce and zucchini; cook, covered, on HIGH (100%) 4 minutes. Add chicken, mushrooms and basil; cook, covered, on HIGH (100%) about 12 minutes or until chicken is cooked through, stirring twice during cooking.

Chicken burritos

preparation time **5 minutes** cooking time **10 minutes** serves **4**

You will need 1 cooked chicken for this recipe.

2½ cups (425g) finely chopped cooked chicken
3 cups (750ml) bottled salsa
⅓ cup (80ml) water
8 x 20cm wheat flour tortillas
1 cup (100g) shredded lettuce
1 cup (125g) grated cheddar
1 large tomato (250g), chopped finely

1 Combine chicken, salsa and the water in large microwave-safe bowl; cook, covered, on HIGH (100%) 5 minutes, stirring once during cooking.
2 Heat tortillas in microwave, according to manufacturer's instructions.
3 Divide chicken mixture among tortillas; top with lettuce, cheese and tomato. Roll into cigar shapes.

Mince and macaroni casserole

preparation time **10 minutes** cooking time **35 minutes** serves **4**

250g macaroni
1.5 litres (6 cups) boiling water
30g butter
2 medium brown onions (300g), chopped finely
3 cloves garlic, crushed
500g minced beef
⅓ cup (50g) plain flour
2 tablespoons tomato paste
1 teaspoon mild english mustard
3 cups (750ml) milk
1 cup (125g) coarsely grated cheddar
1 cup (100g) coarsely grated mozzarella
¼ cup chopped fresh flat-leaf parsley

1 Spread pasta over base of 3-litre (12-cup) deep microwave-safe dish, cover with the boiling water; cook, uncovered, on HIGH (100%) about 10 minutes or until just tender, stirring twice during cooking. Drain; cover to keep warm.
2 Combine butter, onion and garlic in same dish; cook, uncovered, on HIGH (100%) 5 minutes. Stir in beef; cook, uncovered, on HIGH (100%) 10 minutes, stirring twice during cooking. Stir in flour, paste and mustard; cook, uncovered, on HIGH (100%) 4 minutes. Stir in milk; cook, uncovered, on HIGH (100%) about 6 minutes or until mixture boils and thickens, stirring twice during cooking.
3 Stir in pasta, and half the combined cheeses and parsley. Top with remaining cheese and parsley mixture; cook, uncovered, on HIGH (100%) about 2 minutes or until cheese melts.

Savoury mince with fresh herbs

preparation time **15 minutes** cooking time **35 minutes** serves **2**

1 tablespoon olive oil
2 medium brown onions (300g), chopped
1 large carrot (180g), chopped
3 cloves garlic, crushed
1kg minced beef
4 medium zucchini (480g), chopped
400g can tomatoes
⅔ cup (160ml) tomato paste
2 tablespoons worcestershire sauce
2 beef stock cubes
2 tablespoons fruit chutney
¼ cup chopped fresh oregano
2 tablespoons chopped fresh basil
1 cup (125g) frozen peas, thawed

1 Combine oil, onion, carrot and garlic in large microwave-safe bowl; cook, covered, on HIGH (100%) 10 minutes, stirring once during cooking. Stir in beef; cook, covered, on HIGH (100%) 7 minutes, stirring once during cooking.
2 Add zucchini, undrained crushed tomatoes, paste, sauce, crumbled stock cubes, chutney and herbs; cook, covered, on HIGH (100%) 12 minutes, stirring three times. Stir in peas; cook, covered, on HIGH (100%) 5 minutes.

Mushroom and ham pockets

preparation time **5 minutes** cooking time **2 minutes** serves **4**

2 pocket pittas
1½ cups grated tasty cheese
75g mushrooms, sliced
100g ham, chopped
2 tablespoons tomato paste
2 tablespoons chopped fresh parsley

1 Cut each pitta in half, gently open each half to form a pocket. Combine remaining ingredients in bowl, mix well; spoon mixture into pockets.
2 Place pockets on flat dish covered with absorbent paper. Cook on HIGH (100%) about 2 minutes or until heated through.

Spinach and pumpkin curry

preparation time **15 minutes** cooking time **30 minutes** serves **4**

1 tablespoon flaked almonds
1kg butternut pumpkin
20g unsalted butter
2 medium brown onions (300g), sliced
2 cloves garlic, crushed
1 teaspoon grated fresh ginger
2 small green chillies, sliced thinly
1 teaspoon ground coriander
1 teaspoon ground cumin
300ml cream
250g spinach, chopped coarsely
2 tablespoons chopped fresh coriander

1 Place nuts in small shallow microwave-safe dish; cook, uncovered, on HIGH (100%) about 4 minutes or until nuts are browned lightly, stirring twice.

2 Peel pumpkin, cut into 3cm pieces.

3 Combine butter and onion in large microwave-safe bowl; cook, uncovered, on HIGH (100%) about 10 minutes or until browned lightly, stirring three times during cooking. Add garlic, ginger, chilli and spices; cook, uncovered, on HIGH (100%) 30 seconds. Add pumpkin and cream; cook, covered, on HIGH (100%) about 12 minutes or until pumpkin is just tender, stirring gently twice during cooking. Add spinach and coriander; cook, uncovered, on HIGH (100%) 1 minute. Just before serving, sprinkle with nuts.

Devilled chicken

preparation time **5 minutes** cooking time **15 minutes** serves **4**

20g butter
¼ cup (60ml) tomato sauce
1 tablespoon soy sauce
2 teaspoons worcestershire sauce
2 tablespoons fruit chutney
2 tablespoons brown sugar
1 teaspoon mild curry powder
8 chicken drumsticks (1kg)

1 Place butter in large shallow microwave-safe dish; cook, uncovered, on HIGH (100%) 30 seconds. Add remaining ingredients, coating chicken with curry mixture.

2 Arrange chicken around edge of dish; cook, uncovered, on HIGH (100%) 15 minutes or until chicken is cooked through, brushing with sauce twice during cooking.

Risotto napoletana

preparation time **10 minutes** cooking time **15 minutes** serves **4**

2 tablespoons olive oil
1 large brown onion (200g), chopped
1½ cups (300g) arborio rice
400g can tomatoes
3 cups (750ml) boiling water
100g thin slices spicy salami, chopped coarsely
¼ cup (35g) drained sliced sun-dried tomatoes in oil
½ cup (40g) coarsely grated parmesan

1 Combine oil and onion in large microwave-safe bowl; cook, uncovered, on HIGH (100%) 4 minutes, stirring once during cooking. Stir in rice; cook, uncovered, on HIGH (100%) 1 minute. Add undrained crushed tomatoes and the boiling water; cook, covered, on HIGH (100%) 10 minutes, stirring twice during cooking. Stand, covered, 5 minutes. Stir in remaining ingredients.

Marinated sesame drumsticks

preparation time **5 minutes** cooking time **15 minutes** serves **4**

8 chicken drumsticks (1.2kg)
¼ cup (60ml) soy sauce
2 tablespoons hoisin sauce
1 tablespoon sweet sherry
1 tablespoon honey
1 tablespoon sesame seeds
2 cloves garlic, crushed
2 teaspoons grated fresh ginger

1 Place chicken in large shallow microwave-safe dish; pour over combined remaining ingredients. Cover; stand 10 minutes.
2 Arrange chicken, in single layer, in same dish, with thick ends towards edge of dish; brush with marinade. Cover with absorbent paper; cook on HIGH (100%) about 15 minutes or until chicken is cooked through, brushing with marinade twice during cooking.

Beef and vegetable curry

preparation time **10 minutes** cooking time **40 minutes** serves **4**

1 medium brown onion (150g), chopped
⅔ cup (160ml) mild curry paste
1kg minced beef
400g can tomatoes
1 large kumara (500g), chopped
1 medium (300g) eggplant, chopped
1 cup (250ml) beef stock
1 cup (125g) frozen peas
¼ cup chopped fresh coriander

1 Combine onion and paste in large microwave-safe bowl; cook, covered, on HIGH (100%) 5 minutes, stirring once during cooking. Add beef; cook, covered, on HIGH (100%) 10 minutes, stirring twice during cooking. Add undrained crushed tomatoes, kumara, eggplant and stock; cook, uncovered, on HIGH (100%) 20 minutes, stirring twice during cooking. Add peas; cook, uncovered, on HIGH (100%) 5 minutes. Stir in coriander.

Chinese-style pork spare ribs

preparation time **15 minutes** (plus refrigeration time)
cooking time **20 minutes** serves **4**

1kg pork spare ribs
¼ cup dry sherry
2 tablespoons soy sauce
2 tablespoons tomato sauce
2 tablespoons honey
2 tablespoons lemon juice
2 teaspoons grated fresh ginger
2 cloves garlic, crushed
2 teaspoons cornflour
1 tablespoon water

1 Remove rind and excess fat from ribs; cut ribs into 3cm lengths.
2 Combine sherry, sauces, honey, juice, ginger and garlic in large bowl. Add pork; mix well. Cover; refrigerate 3 hours or overnight.
3 Drain pork, reserve marinade. Place pork pieces on rack in single layer over shallow dish. Cook, covered, on HIGH (100%) about 15 minutes or until pork is tender; turning pork occasionally. Blend cornflour and water; add to reserved marinade in bowl, cook, covered, on HIGH (100%) about 5 minutes or until mixture boils and thickens, stirring occasionally. Serve over spare ribs.

Fish cutlets in tomato sauce

preparation time **5 minutes** cooking time **15 minutes** serves **4**

400g can tomato puree
1 medium brown onion (150g), chopped finely
1 tablespoon chopped fresh oregano
2 teaspoons chopped fresh thyme
1 clove garlic, crushed
2 chicken stock cubes
4 white fish cutlets (1kg)

1 Combine puree, onion, herbs, garlic and crumbled stock cubes in large microwave-safe bowl; cook, covered, on HIGH (100%) 5 minutes, stirring once during cooking.

2 Place fish, in single layer, in large shallow microwave-safe dish; cook, covered, on HIGH (100%) 5 minutes. Pour tomato mixture over fish; cook, covered, on HIGH (100%) about 5 minutes or until fish is cooked through.

Mexican chilli beef

preparation time **10 minutes** cooking time **40 minutes** serves **4**

1 tablespoon olive oil
1 medium brown onion (150g), chopped
2 cloves garlic, crushed
1kg minced beef
1 long red chilli, chopped finely
400g can crushed tomatoes
1 cup (250ml) beef stock
¾ cup (180ml) tomato paste
425g can mexican-style baked beans
2 tablespoons chopped fresh parsley

1 Combine oil, onion and garlic in large microwave-safe bowl; cook, uncovered, on HIGH (100%) 4 minutes, stirring once during cooking.

2 Stir in beef; cook, uncovered, on HIGH (100%) 10 minutes, stirring twice. Add chilli, undrained crushed tomatoes, stock and paste. Cook, uncovered, on HIGH (100%) about 25 minutes or until thick, stirring twice.

3 Stir in beans; cook, uncovered, on HIGH (100%) 2 minutes. Stir in parsley.

15-MINUTE MEALS

Teriyaki pork stir-fry

preparation time **5 minutes** cooking time **10 minutes** serves **4**

750g pork fillets, sliced thinly
6 green onions, chopped finely
1 clove garlic, crushed
3 baby bok choy (450g), chopped coarsely
⅓ cup (80ml) teriyaki marinade

1 Cook pork, in batches, in heated oiled wok, until browned all over and cooked as desired; remove from wok.
2 Cook onion and garlic in same wok, stirring, until fragrant. Return pork to wok with bok choy; cook, stirring, until bok choy is wilted.
3 Add teriyaki marinade; cook until hot.

Beef steaks with mustard butter

preparation time **5 minutes** cooking time **10 minutes** serves **4**

8 beef thin minute steaks (600g)
500g baby new potatoes, halved
200g green beans, trimmed
80g butter, softened
1 tablespoon horseradish cream
1 tablespoon wholegrain mustard

1 Cook steak on a heated oiled grill plate (or grill or barbecue) until browned and cooked as desired. Remove from grill and cover to keep warm.
2 Meanwhile, boil or steam potatoes until almost tender. Add beans, cook further 2 minutes or until potatoes and beans are just tender. Drain well.
3 Place butter, horseradish and mustard in small bowl. Beat with wooden spoon until combined. Toss 1 tablespoon of butter mixture through vegetables.
4 Serve potatoes, beans and steak with remaining mustard butter.

Sausages with lentil and vegetable sauce

preparation time **5 minutes** cooking time **10 minutes** serves **2**

4 flavoured beef sausages, chopped coarsely
1 small brown onion (80g), chopped finely
1 clove garlic, crushed
2 bacon rashers, chopped
1 medium zucchini (120g), sliced
1½ cups (375ml) tomato pasta sauce
200g canned brown lentils, rinsed, drained

1 Cook sausages, onion, garlic and bacon in heated oiled medium frying pan until sausages are browned all over.
2 Add remaining ingredients; bring to the boil, stirring until hot.

Salmon with lime and chilli sauce

preparation time **5 minutes** cooking time **10 minutes** serves **2**

1 clove garlic, crushed
1 teaspoon grated lime rind
1 teaspoon grated fresh ginger
2 salmon fillets (400g)
20g butter
1 tablespoon peanut oil
4 baby bok choy; halved
¼ cup (60ml) sweet chilli sauce
2 tablespoons lime juice
1 tablespoon finely chopped fresh coriander

1 Rub half combined garlic, rind and ginger on flesh side of salmon.
2 Heat butter and oil in large frying pan; cook salmon, uncovered, until browned both sides and cooked as desired.
3 Add bok choy to same pan with remaining garlic mixture, chilli sauce and juice; stir until bok choy is tender.
4 Sprinkle salmon with coriander and serve with bok choy mixture.

Fish with wasabi mayonnaise

preparation time **5 minutes** cooking time **10 minutes** serves **4**

1 tablespoon peanut oil
4 firm white fish fillets (600g)
⅓ cup (80ml) mayonnaise
1-2 tablespoons wasabi paste
2 green onions, chopped finely
2 tablespoons coarsely chopped fresh coriander
2 tablespoons lime juice

1 Heat oil in large frying pan; cook fish until cooked as desired.
2 Combine mayonnaise, wasabi to taste, onion, coriander and juice in a small bowl.
3 Serve fish with wasabi mayonnaise.

tip Wasabi, Japanese horseradish, is available as a paste in tubes from some supermarkets, fishmongers and Asian food stores.

Spinach, capsicum and fetta pizza

preparation time **10 minutes** cooking time **8 minutes** serves **4**

4 large pittas
½ cup (125ml) tomato pasta sauce
2 cups (250g) grated pizza cheese
75g baby spinach leaves
1 medium red capsicum (200g), sliced thinly
100g fetta, crumbled

1 Preheat oven to very hot.
2 Place pittas on oven trays, spread with sauce.
3 Sprinkle half of cheese over pittas; top with spinach, capsicum and fetta, sprinkle with remaining cheese.
4 Bake in very hot oven about 8 minutes or until browned.

Lamb fillets with greek salad and tzatziki

preparation time **10 minutes** cooking time **5 minutes** serves **2**

¼ cup (60ml) lemon juice
¼ cup (60ml) olive oil
2 teaspoons chopped fresh oregano
1 clove garlic, crushed
250g lamb fillets
4 medium egg tomatoes (360g) , chopped coarsely
2 lebanese cucumbers (260g), chopped
½ medium red onion (75g), sliced
1 large green capsicum (350g), chopped
½ cup (80g) kalamata olives
150g fetta, chopped
⅔ cup (180g) tzatziki

1 Combine juice, oil and oregano in small jug; reserve half of mixture. Add garlic to one half.
2 Cook lamb on heated oiled grill plate (or grill or barbecue), brushing with garlic mixture.
3 Combine reserved juice mixture with tomato, cucumber, onion, capsicum, olives and fetta. Serve lamb with salad and tzatziki.

Red curry pork with basil

preparation time **5 minutes** cooking time **10 minutes** serves **4**

1 tablespoon peanut oil
8 pork thin steaks (650g)
2 tablespoons red curry paste
¾ cup (180ml) chicken stock
140ml can coconut cream
¼ cup shredded fresh basil
200g char-grilled capsicum, chopped coarsely

1 Heat oil in large non-stick frying pan. Cook pork until browned both sides and cooked as desired. Remove from pan; cover to keep warm.
2 Add paste to same pan; cook, stirring, until fragrant. Add stock; bring to a boil. Stir in coconut cream, basil and capsicum until hot. Serve pork with sauce.

Pork and corn salsa
tortilla wraps

preparation time **5 minutes** cooking time **10 minutes** serves **4**

600g pork fillet, sliced thinly
2 tablespoons vegetable oil
35g packet taco seasoning mix
16 corn tortillas
310g can corn kernels, drained
3 medium tomatoes (350g), chopped coarsely
1 small red onion (100g), chopped finely
½ cup coarsely chopped fresh coriander
1 butter lettuce, torn
½ cup (120g) light sour cream

1 Combine pork, oil and seasoning mix in medium bowl; toss to coat pork.
2 Warm tortillas according to manufacturer's instructions.
3 Cook pork on heated oiled grill plate (or grill or barbecue) until pork is browned and tender.
4 Combine corn, tomato, onion and coriander in a medium bowl.
5 Serve pork wrapped in tortillas with corn salsa, lettuce and sour cream.

Lamb with red lentil salad

preparation time **5 minutes** cooking time **10 minutes** serves **2**

½ **cup (100g) red lentils**
400g lamb eye of loin (backstraps)
125g cherry tomatoes
1 trimmed celery stalk (100g), chopped finely
¼ **cup lightly packed fresh coriander leaves**
50g baby rocket leaves

Dressing
2 tablespoons lemon juice
1 tablespoon olive oil
½ **teaspoon ground cumin**

1 Rinse lentils under cold water; drain. Place lentils in medium saucepan, cover with cold water. Bring lentils to the boil then reduce heat; simmer, uncovered, about 5 minutes or until just tender. Drain; rinse under cold water, drain well.
2 Meanwhile, cook lamb on heated, oiled grill plate (or grill or barbecue) until cooked as desired.
3 Place ingredients for dressing in screw-top jar; shake well.
4 Combine lentils with tomato, celery, coriander and dressing in large bowl. Season with salt and freshly ground black pepper.
5 Serve lamb with lentil salad and rocket.

Chicken, basil and cabbage salad

preparation time **10 minutes** serves **4**

You will need one large barbecued chicken for this recipe.

3 cups (480g) shredded cooked chicken
4 cups (320g) finely shredded chinese cabbage
4 green onions, sliced thinly
¼ cup chopped fresh basil

Dressing
1 clove garlic, crushed
¼ cup (60ml) peanut oil
¼ cup (60ml) lime juice
2 tablespoons fish sauce
1 tablespoon white sugar

1 Place chicken, cabbage, onion and basil in large bowl.
2 Place ingredients for dressing in screw-top jar; shake well. Drizzle over salad; toss gently to combine.

Salami and vegetable pasta

preparation time **5 minutes** cooking time **10 minutes** serves **2**

200g spiral pasta
1 tablespoon olive oil
1 small brown onion (80g), chopped
1 small red capsicum (100g), chopped
2 baby eggplants (120g), sliced thickly
100g sliced salami
1½ cup (375ml) tomato pasta sauce
2 tablespoons chopped fresh flat-leaf parsley
¼ cup (20g) parmesan flakes

1 Cook pasta in large saucepan of boiling water, uncovered, until tender; drain.
2 Meanwhile, heat oil in large frying pan. Add onion, capsicum, eggplant and salami; cook, stirring, until vegetables are tender.
3 Add sauce and parsley, stir until hot.
4 Combine pasta and vegetable mixture; serve sprinkled with parmesan.

Tandoori chicken salad

preparation time **5 minutes** cooking time **10 minutes** serves **4**

1 ¼ cups (340g) plain yogurt
1 ½ tablespoons tandoori paste
750g chicken tenderloins
¼ cup (60ml) mint sauce
250g mesclun
4 large egg tomatoes (360g), chopped
2 lebanese cucumbers (260g), chopped

1 Combine ½ cup (140g) yogurt and paste in large bowl, add chicken; stir until combined.
2 Cook chicken, in batches, on heated oiled grill plate (or grill or barbecue) until cooked as desired.
3 Meanwhile, combine remaining yogurt and sauce in small bowl.
4 Divide mesclun among serving plates, top with tomato, cucumber and chicken. Serve drizzled with yogurt mint sauce.

Creamy pesto chicken with gnocchi

preparation time **5 minutes** cooking time **10 minutes** serves **4**

You will need one large barbecued chicken for this recipe.

500g fresh gnocchi
1 tablespoon olive oil
2 cloves garlic, crushed
½ cup (125ml) dry white wine
¼ cup (60g) basil pesto
300ml cream
3 cups (400g) coarsely chopped cooked chicken

1 Cook gnocchi in large saucepan of boiling water, uncovered, about 5 minutes or until gnocchi rise to surface and are just tender; drain.
2 Meanwhile, heat oil in large saucepan; cook garlic, stirring, until fragrant. Add wine, pesto and cream; bring to a boil then reduce heat; simmer, uncovered, 3 minutes.
3 Add chicken and gnocchi; stir until hot.

Fish with antipasto salad

preparation time **5 minutes** cooking time **10 minutes** serves **4**

2 tablespoons olive oil
4 x 200g white fish cutlets
500g jars antipasto vegetables, drained
½ cup fresh flat-leaf parsley leaves
1 large red onion (300g), sliced thinly
2 tablespoons lemon juice

1 Heat oil in large frying pan, add fish; cook until browned on both sides and cooked through.
2 Meanwhile, combine antipasto vegetables with parsley, onion and juice in medium bowl.
3 Serve fish with antipasto mixture.

Penne with tomato salsa and tuna

preparation time **5 minutes** cooking time **10 minutes** serves **4**

375g penne
3 medium tomatoes (570g), seeded, chopped finely
1 medium red onion (170g), chopped finely
2 cloves garlic, crushed
¼ cup firmly packed torn fresh basil leaves
500g can tuna in brine, drained, flaked
¼ cup (60ml) balsamic vinegar

1 Cook pasta in large saucepan of boiling water, uncovered, until just tender; drain, keep warm.
2 Combine tomato, onion, garlic, basil, tuna, pasta and vinegar in large bowl; toss to combine.

Asian-style chicken burgers

preparation time **5 minutes** cooking time **10 minutes** serves **4**

500g chicken tenderloins
1 tablespoon kecap manis
4 hamburger buns
75g snow pea sprouts
1 lebanese cucumber (130g), sliced thinly lengthways
¼ cup (70g) crunchy peanut butter
1 tablespoon sweet chilli sauce
2 tablespoons coconut milk

1 Combine chicken and kecap manis in medium bowl. Cook chicken on heated oiled grill plate (or grill or barbecue) until browned all over and cooked through.
2 Split buns in half; toast buns. Top base of buns with sprouts, chicken and cucumber; spoon over combined remaining ingredients.

Peanut pork schnitzels

preparation time **5 minutes** cooking time **10 minutes** serves **4**

2 tablespoons smooth peanut butter
2 tablespoons plain yogurt
2 teaspoons lemon juice
1 clove garlic, crushed
2 teaspoons honey
1 teaspoon ground cumin
4 pork leg schnitzels (500g), halved

1 Combine peanut butter with yogurt, juice, garlic, honey and cumin in small bowl; mix well.
2 Brush pork with peanut butter mixture; cook pork on heated oiled grill plate (or grill or barbecue) until cooked as desired.

Thai chicken salad

preparation time **10 minutes** cooking time **5 minutes** serves **4**

You will need one large barbecued chicken for this recipe.

350g yellow string beans, trimmed, halved
2 tablespoons lime juice
1 clove garlic, crushed
1 tablespoon peanut oil
½ cup finely chopped fresh mint
2 teaspoons sweet chilli sauce
1 tablespoon fish sauce
3 cups (480g) shredded cooked chicken
1 cup coarsely chopped fresh coriander
250g cherry tomatoes, halved
1 small fresh red thai chilli, chopped finely

1 Boil, steam or microwave beans until almost tender. Rinse under cold running water; drain.
2 Meanwhile, combine juice, garlic, oil, mint and sauces in large bowl. Add beans, chicken, ¾ cup coriander and tomato; toss gently to combine.
3 Top salad with remaining coriander and chilli just before serving.

Spiced fish with cucumber yogurt sauce

preparation time **5 minutes** cooking time **10 minutes** serves **6**

6 x 200g white fish fillets
2 teaspoons ground cumin
2 teaspoons ground coriander
2 teaspoons finely grated lemon rind
2 teaspoons olive oil

Cucumber yogurt sauce
2 lebanese cucumbers (260g), seeded, chopped finely
1 ½ cups (420g) plain yogurt
1 ½ tablespoons lemon juice

1 Combine fish in large bowl with remaining ingredients. Cook fish in heated oiled large non-stick frying pan, in batches, until browned both sides and cooked through.
2 Combine ingredients for cucumber yogurt sauce in small bowl.
3 Serve fish with cucumber yogurt sauce.

Fresh tomato and chilli pasta

preparation time **5 minutes** cooking time **10 minutes** serves **4**

500g penne
⅓ cup (80ml) olive oil
2 teaspoons bottled crushed garlic
2 teaspoons bottled chopped chilli
4 medium ripe tomatoes (800g), chopped
1 cup chopped fresh flat-leaf parsley
½ cup (40g) parmesan flakes

1 Cook pasta in large saucepan of boiling water, uncovered, until tender; drain.
2 Meanwhile, heat oil in large frying pan, add garlic and chilli; cook, stirring, about 1 minute or until fragrant. Add tomato and parsley; remove from heat.
3 Add sauce to pasta; toss gently. Serve topped with parmesan.

Greek chicken salad

preparation time **5 minutes** cooking time **10 minutes** serves **4**

You will need one large barbecued chicken for this recipe.

375g small shell pasta
3 cups (480g) shredded cooked chicken
1 medium red onion (170g), sliced thinly
500g cherry tomatoes, quartered
2 lebanese cucumbers (260g), chopped coarsely
1 large green capsicum (350g), chopped coarsely
1 cup (120g) seeded kalamata olives
200g fetta, chopped coarsely
¼ cup coarsely chopped fresh oregano
¼ cup (60ml) olive oil
¼ cup (60ml) lemon juice

1 Cook pasta in large pan of boiling water, uncovered, until just tender; drain. Rinse under cold water; drain.
2 Place pasta in large bowl with chicken, onion, tomato, cucumber, capsicum, olives, cheese, oregano and combined oil and juice; toss gently to combine.

Tomato pesto tortellini

preparation time **5 minutes** cooking time **10 minutes** serves **6**

1kg spinach and ricotta tortellini
⅓ cup (90g) sun-dried tomato pesto
300ml cream
2 tablespoons shredded fresh basil
½ cup (40g) finely grated parmesan

1 Cook pasta in large saucepan of boiling water, uncovered, until tender; drain.
2 Meanwhile, combine pesto, cream and basil in large frying pan. Bring to a boil then reduce heat; simmer, uncovered, 5 minutes.
3 Add tortellini to sauce; toss to combine. Serve topped with cheese.

Lime and coriander octopus

preparation time **5 minutes** cooking time **10 minutes** serves **2**

600g cleaned baby octopus, halved
1 tablespoon sweet chilli sauce
2 tablespoons lime juice
1 clove garlic, crushed
2 tablespoons coarsely chopped fresh coriander

1 Combine ingredients in a large bowl.
2 Cook octopus on heated oiled grill plate (or grill or barbecue), uncovered, until cooked as desired.

tip Ask your fishmonger to remove head and beak from octopus; this is called cleaned octopus.

Tomato, fetta and spinach galettes

preparation time **5 minutes** cooking time **10 minutes** serves **2**

125g frozen spinach, thawed
1 sheet ready-rolled puff pastry
2 tablespoons bottled pesto
100g soft fetta, crumbled
125g cherry tomatoes, halved
2 tablespoons coarsely grated parmesan

1 Preheat oven to very hot.
2 Drain spinach. Using hands, squeeze excess liquid from spinach; chop roughly.
3 Place pastry on oiled oven tray. Fold pastry edges inward to form 1cm border. Spread pesto over pastry base. Top with spinach, crumbled cheese and tomato; sprinkle with grated cheese. Cook in very hot oven about 10 minutes or until crisp and browned lightly.

MEALS FROM THE LARDER

Tuna pasta bake

preparation time **15 minutes** cooking time **40 minutes** serves **4**

200g small pasta shells
½ small brown onion (40g), chopped coarsely
2 bay leaves
6 black peppercorns
3 cups (750ml) milk
60g butter
2 tablespoons plain flour
1 tablespoon wholegrain mustard
400g can tuna, drained
1 cup (125g) coarsely grated cheddar
1 cup (70g) stale breadcrumbs

1 Preheat oven to moderate.
2 Cook pasta in large saucepan of boiling water, uncovered, until just tender; drain.
3 Combine onion, leaves, peppercorns and milk in medium pan; bring to a boil. Remove from heat; cover, stand 5 minutes. Strain into medium bowl; discard vegetables and spices.
4 Heat butter in large pan. Add flour; cook, stirring, until mixture thickens and bubbles. Gradually stir in infused milk; stir until sauce boils and thickens. Stir mustard into sauce. Combine pasta and tuna with sauce; mix well.
5 Place mixture in oiled deep 2-litre (8-cup capacity) ovenproof dish; sprinkle with combined cheese and breadcrumbs. Bake, uncovered, in moderate oven about 25 minutes or until browned lightly and heated through.

Bean and potato bake

preparation time **10 minutes** cooking time **25 minutes** serves **2**

4 small potatoes (480g), sliced thinly
2 green onions, sliced thinly
½ x 220g can mexican chilli beans
½ cup (125ml) milk
¼ cup (20g) finely grated parmesan

1 Preheat oven to moderate.
2 Layer potato, onion and beans in two lightly oiled 1-cup (250ml) ovenproof dishes. Pour milk over vegetables; sprinkle with cheese.
3 Bake, uncovered, in moderate oven about 25 minutes or until vegetables are soft.

Baked pasta with mushrooms

preparation time **15 minutes** cooking time **35 minutes** serves **4**

500g penne
2 tablespoons olive oil
500g mixed mushrooms, sliced thinly
750g tomato pasta sauce
2 cups (250g) grated pizza cheese

1 Preheat oven to moderate. Oil deep 3-litre (12-cup) ovenproof dish.
2 Cook pasta in large saucepan of boiling water, uncovered, until just tender; drain. Do not rinse.
3 Heat oil in large frying pan; cook mushrooms, stirring, until tender and browned lightly. Place half of the pasta over base of prepared dish. Top with half of the pasta sauce and half of the mushrooms and cheese. Repeat layers with remaining pasta, pasta sauce, mushrooms and cheese. Bake, uncovered, in moderate oven about 25 minutes or until browned lightly and heated through.

Indian rice

preparation time **5 minutes** cooking time **20 minutes** serves **4**

2 teaspoons peanut oil
1 medium brown onion (150g), chopped finely
1 clove garlic, crushed
½ teaspoon ground turmeric
1 teaspoon ground coriander
1 teaspoon ground cumin
1 teaspoon garam masala
1½ cups (300g) white long-grain rice
3 cups (750ml) chicken stock

1 Heat oil in medium heavy-base saucepan; cook onion and garlic, stirring, until onion is soft. Add spices; cook, stirring, until fragrant.
2 Stir in rice, then stock. Bring to a boil then reduce heat; simmer, covered, 12 minutes. Remove from heat; stand, covered, 10 minutes.

Bean nachos

preparation time **10 minutes** cooking time **10 minutes** serves **4**

Mexican-style beans are a mildly spiced, canned combination of red kidney or pinto beans, capsicum and tomato.

420g can mexican-style beans, drained
215g can red kidney beans, rinsed, drained, mashed
2 tablespoons tomato paste
1 tablespoon water
230g plain corn chips
1½ cups (185g) coarsely grated cheddar
½ cup (120g) sour cream
1 tablespoon coarsely chopped fresh coriander

1 Preheat oven to moderately hot. Heat combined beans, paste and the water, stirring, in large non-stick frying pan. Cover; keep warm.
2 Place corn chips in large ovenproof dish; sprinkle with cheese. Bake in moderately hot oven 5 minutes or until cheese melts.
3 Top corn chips with bean mixture and sour cream; sprinkle with coriander.

serving suggestion Serve nachos with ready-made or fresh guacamole.

Pasta with currants and pine nuts

preparation time **10 minutes**   cooking time **15 minutes**   serves **4**

2 tablespoons olive oil
2 cloves garlic, crushed
2 medium brown onions (300g), chopped finely
2 teaspoons ground cumin
2 teaspoons ground coriander
1 teaspoon garam masala
310g can chickpeas, rinsed, drained
⅓ cup drained sun-dried tomatoes, chopped coarsely
⅓ cup (50g) dried currants
⅓ cup (80ml) olive oil, extra
500g penne
⅓ cup (50g) toasted pine nuts
¼ cup shredded fresh basil

1 Heat oil in large frying pan, add garlic and onion; cook, stirring, until onion is soft. Add spices; cook, stirring, until fragrant. Add chickpeas, tomato, currants and extra oil; stir until combined and heated through.
2 Add pasta to large pan of boiling water; boil, uncovered, until just tender. Drain. Combine chickpea mixture and pasta in bowl; sprinkle with nuts and basil.

Smoked fish kedgeree

preparation time **5 minutes**   cooking time **15 minutes**   serves **2**

1 cup (200g) white long-grain rice
400g frozen smoked cod fish steaks, thawed
60g butter
⅓ cup coarsely chopped fresh flat-leaf parsley
1 tablespoon lemon juice
2 hard-boiled eggs, peeled, chopped

1 Cook rice in large saucepan of boiling water, uncovered, until tender; drain.
2 Meanwhile, poach fish in large frying pan of shallow boiling water until tender; drain, flake fish.
3 Melt butter in large saucepan; stir in rice, parsley and juice. Gently stir in fish and egg; cook, uncovered, over low heat until heated through.

Tuna with shells, capers, olives and green beans

preparation time **10 minutes** cooking time **10 minutes** serves **4**

375g small pasta shells
2 cups (220g) frozen chopped green beans
2 x 200g cans smoked tuna slices in oil, drained
150g seeded black olives, halved
1 medium red capsicum (200g), sliced thinly
¼ cup (60ml) olive oil
¼ cup (60ml) white wine vinegar
2 tablespoons drained capers, chopped
1 clove garlic, crushed

1 Cook pasta in large saucepan of boiling water, uncovered, until just tender; drain. Rinse under cold water; drain.
2 Meanwhile, boil, steam or microwave beans until just tender; rinse under cold water; drain.
3 Place pasta and beans in large bowl with tuna, olives, capsicum and combined remaining ingredients; toss gently to combine.

Almond coriander couscous

preparation time **5 minutes** cooking time **5 minutes** serves **1**

¼ cup (125ml) chicken stock
¼ cup (100g) couscous
5g butter
2 tablespoons toasted slivered almonds
2 tablespoons coarsely chopped fresh coriander

1 Bring stock to a boil in medium saucepan; stir in couscous and butter. Remove pan from heat; stand, covered, about 5 minutes or until all stock is absorbed, fluffing with fork occasionally.
2 Gently toss almonds and coriander through couscous.

Vegetable pesto tartlets

preparation time **10 minutes** cooking time **15 minutes** serves **4**

2 sheets ready-rolled puff pastry, thawed
½ cup (130g) sun-dried tomato pesto
280g jar antipasto char-grilled vegetables
150g fetta, crumbled

1 Preheat oven to very hot.
2 Cut pastry sheets in half. Place pastry pieces on two oven trays. Fold pastry edges in to make 1cm border. Spread pesto over centre of pastry.
3 Drain vegetables; pat dry with absorbent paper. Cut vegetables into strips. Arrange vegetables on pastry pieces; sprinkle with cheese.
4 Bake, uncovered, in very hot oven about 15 minutes or until pastry is puffed and browned.

Soy beans and rice

preparation time **10 minutes** cooking time **30 minutes** serves **4**

1 tablespoon olive oil
1 clove garlic, crushed
1 large brown onion (200g), chopped finely
1 tablespoon grated lemon rind
1 cup (200g) white long-grain rice, rinsed, drained
400g can soy beans, rinsed, drained
2 cups (500ml) chicken stock
50g butter
1 teaspoon ground cinnamon
1 cup (150g) dried apricots, halved
1 cup (170g) seeded prunes, halved
⅓ cup (80ml) lemon juice

1 Heat oil in large saucepan; cook garlic, onion and rind, stirring, until onion is soft. Add rice, beans and stock. Bring to boil then reduce heat; simmer, covered, about 20 minutes or until rice is tender.
2 Meanwhile, melt butter in medium pan; cook cinnamon, apricots, prunes and juice, stirring, until apricots are browned lightly. Serve beans and rice topped with fruit, drizzled with pan juices.

Deli pasta salad

preparation time **10 minutes** cooking time **15 minutes** serves **4**

500g large spiral pasta
150g bottled char-grilled eggplant, drained, chopped coarsely
150g bottled char-grilled capsicum, drained, chopped coarsely
1 cup (150g) drained sun-dried tomatoes
⅓ cup small fresh basil leaves

Pesto dressing
1 cup (250ml) bottled italian dressing
2 tablespoons basil pesto

1 Cook pasta in large saucepan of boiling water, uncovered, until just tender. Drain pasta, rinse under cold water.
2 Combine ingredients for pesto dressing in small bowl.
3 Combine pasta with remaining ingredients and dressing in large bowl.

Italian baked beans

preparation time **10 minutes** cooking time **20 minutes** serves **1**

1 tablespoon olive oil
1 small brown onion (80g), sliced thickly
1 clove garlic, crushed
1 cup (250ml) crushed tomatoes
1 cup (250ml) water
300g can red kidney beans, rinsed, drained
1 cup (70g) stale breadcrumbs
2 tablespoons finely grated parmesan

1 Heat oil in large frying pan; cook onion and garlic, stirring, until soft. Add tomatoes, the water and beans, bring to boil; stir in basil.
2 Transfer bean mixture to small ovenproof dish. Sprinkle with combined breadcrumbs and cheese; cook under preheated grill until lightly browned.

Fettuccine with char-grilled vegetables

preparation time **5 minutes** cooking time **15 minutes** serves **2**

250g fettuccine
280g jar antipasto char-grilled vegetables
100g baby spinach leaves
½ cup (40g) parmesan flakes

1 Cook pasta in large saucepan of boiling water, uncovered, until tender; drain.
2 Meanwhile, drain vegetables; reserve ¼ cup (60ml) of oil. Chop vegetables coarsely. In same pan, cook vegetables and reserved oil until hot.
3 Toss pasta with vegetable mixture, spinach and half the cheese. To serve, top with remaining cheese.

Sweet corn soup

preparation time **10 minutes** cooking time **20 minutes** serves **4**

1 tablespoon olive oil
1 medium white onion (150g), chopped
1 teaspoon bottled crushed garlic
1 litre (4 cups) chicken stock
2 cups (320g) frozen corn kernels
130g can creamed corn
1 medium potato (200g), chopped coarsely
¼ cup (60ml) cream

1 Heat oil in large saucepan, add onion and garlic; cook, stirring, until onion is soft.
2 Add stock, 1 cup of corn kernels, creamed corn and potato. Bring to a boil then reduce heat; simmer, uncovered, about 15 minutes or until potato is tender.
3 Blend or process soup, in batches, until smooth. Return soup to pan; stir in remaining corn kernels and cream. Stir over low heat until corn is tender.

SNACKS

Pizza supreme jaffles

preparation time **10 minutes** cooking time **10 minutes** serves **4**

1 tablespoon olive oil
2 cloves garlic, crushed
1 small red onion (100g), sliced thinly
1 small green capsicum (150g), sliced thinly
50g swiss brown mushrooms, sliced thinly
1 long loaf turkish bread
¼ cup (70g) tomato paste
120g hot salami, sliced thinly
80g marinated artichoke hearts, drained, sliced thinly
100g bocconcini, sliced thickly

1 Heat oil in large frying pan; cook garlic and onion, stirring, until onion softens. Add capsicum and mushrooms; cook, stirring, until mushrooms soften.
2 Preheat sandwich press or jaffle maker. Cut bread crossways into four pieces; split each piece horizontally.
3 Spread paste evenly over four pieces of bread; top with equal amounts of vegetable mixture, salami, artichoke and cheese. Top with remaining bread.
4 Toast jaffles in preheated sandwich press.

tip If you do not have a sandwich press or jaffle maker, you can make these sandwiches in either a frying pan or your oven.

Teriyaki rice paper rolls

preparation time **20 minutes** serves **4**

1 cup (160g) shredded cooked chicken
1 small carrot (70g), grated coarsely
1 small red capsicum (150g), sliced thinly
100g shiitake mushrooms, sliced thinly
50g snow pea tendrils
2 tablespoons coarsely chopped fresh coriander
2 tablespoons teriyaki sauce
1 tablespoon sweet chilli sauce
12 x 22cm rice paper rounds

1 Combine chicken, carrot, capsicum, mushrooms, tendrils, coriander and sauces in large bowl; mix gently.
2 Place one sheet of rice paper in medium bowl of warm water until softened; lift sheet carefully from water, place on board covered with tea towel.
3 Place some of the filling in centre of sheet; fold in sides, roll top to bottom to enclose filling. Repeat with remaining rice paper sheets and filling.

serving suggestion Serve rice paper rolls with sweet chilli sauce.

Mexican beef pizza

preparation time **10 minutes** cooking time **30 minutes** serves **4**

500g minced beef
35g packet taco seasoning mix
1¾ cups (430ml) bottled tomato salsa
2 x 335g prepared pizza bases
2 cups (250g) pizza cheese
⅓ cup (80g) sour cream

1 Preheat oven to very hot.
2 Cook beef in large lightly oiled frying pan, stirring, until browned all over. Add taco seasoning and 1½ cups (375ml) of the salsa; bring to a boil.
3 Place pizza bases on pizza trays, spread with beef mixture; sprinkle with cheese. Bake, uncovered, in very hot oven, about 20 minutes or until pizzas are browned and bases are crisp.
4 Serve pizzas topped with dollops of sour cream and remaining salsa.

Lamb and pesto focaccia

preparation time **5 minutes** cooking time **15 minutes** serves **2**

20cm-square piece focaccia
¼ cup (65g) basil pesto
400g roast lamb, sliced thinly
½ cup (50g) shaved parmesan
¼ cup (35g) drained sliced sun-dried tomatoes

1 Preheat sandwich press.
2 Cut focaccia in half crossways, then in half horizontally. Spread pesto over bases of focaccia, top with lamb, cheese, tomato and remaining focaccia.
3 Place focaccia in sandwich press about 5 minutes or until cheese melts and focaccia is hot. Slice diagonally to serve.

Sumac-spiced potato wedges

preparation time **10 minutes** cooking time **25 minutes** serves **1**

Sumac is a reddish-purple ground spice made from the berries of a wild shrub grown in Lebanon. It is available from Middle Eastern food stores and delicatessens.

2 medium potatoes (400g)
2 teaspoons vegetable oil
½ teaspoon sumac
pinch chilli powder

1 Preheat oven to very hot. Line baking tray with baking paper.
2 Cut unpeeled potatoes into wedges. Combine oil, sumac and chilli in large bowl; add potato wedges, combine well.
3 Place wedges, skin-side down, on tray; bake in very hot oven for 25 minutes or until tender and golden brown.

serving suggestion Serve wedges with sour cream.

Chicken nachos

preparation time **15 minutes** cooking time **10 minutes** serves **4**

1 tablespoon vegetable oil
1 medium brown onion (150g), chopped finely
425g can mexican-style beans, drained
3 cups (480g) shredded cooked chicken
390g jar mild nachos topping sauce
230g packet corn chips
2 cups (220g) grated pizza cheese
1 medium avocado (250g), mashed coarsely
²/₃ cup (160g) sour cream

1 Heat oil in medium frying pan; cook onion, stirring, until softened. Stir in beans, chicken and sauce. Bring to a boil then reduce heat; simmer, uncovered, about 3 minutes or until mixture thickens slightly.
2 Meanwhile, divide corn chips among four microwave-safe serving dishes; top each with cheese. Microwave, one plate at a time, uncovered, on HIGH (100%) about 1 minute or until cheese has melted.
3 Top plates of corn chips and cheese with equal amounts of chicken mixture, avocado and sour cream.

Fried bocconcini

preparation time **20 minutes** cooking time **10 minutes** serves **4**

10 bocconcini (100g)
¼ cup (25g) packaged breadcrumbs
2 tablespoons finely grated parmesan
2 teaspoons finely chopped fresh basil
Plain flour
1 egg, beaten lightly
Vegetable oil, for deep-frying

1 Dry bocconcini on absorbent paper. Combine breadcrumbs, cheese and basil in bowl; mix well.
2 Toss bocconcini in flour, shake off excess flour. Dip in egg, then press breadcrumb mixture on firmly. Repeat egg and breadcrumbing process.
3 Deep-fry bocconcini in hot hoil in large frying pan, in batches, until browned. Drain on absorbent paper.

Grilled open sandwiches

Each of these recipes takes about **15 minutes** to prepare and makes **2** open sandwiches.

Ham, cheese and tomato melt

Preheat grill. Spread 2 teaspoons tomato chutney on each of two slices of white bread; top each slice of bread with half a slice of ham, a quarter of a thinly sliced tomato, and one slice of swiss cheese. Place under grill 5 minutes or until cheese melts.

Pesto chicken on pitta

Preheat grill. Spread 2 tablespoons pesto over two pocket pitta bread; top with ½ cup (80g) coarsely chopped barbecued chicken meat and ¼ cup (25g) coarsely grated pizza cheese. Place pittas under grill 5 minutes or until cheese melts.

Turkey baguette

Preheat grill. Slice 10cm piece french bread stick in half horizontally; top each half with one slice of smoked turkey breast, a quarter of a thinly sliced green capsicum, and one slice of edam cheese. Place under grill 5 minutes or until cheese melts.

Tuna salad on focaccia

Preheat grill. Combine half of a drained 185g can tuna in brine, 2 tablespoons mayonnaise, half of a finely chopped small red onion, and 2 tablespoons finely chopped fresh flat-leaf parsley in small bowl. Cut one garlic focaccia roll in half horizontally; spread tuna mixture over two halves, top each half with one slice of tasty cheese. Place under grill 5 minutes or until cheese melts.

Cheesy chips topped with bacon and sour cream

preparation time **10 minutes** cooking time **25 minutes** serves **1**

250g frozen potato chips
2 bacon rashers (180g), sliced thinly
2 tablespoons sour cream
2 teaspoons finely chopped fresh chives
2 tablespoons coarsely grated cheddar

1 Preheat oven to moderately hot. Lightly grease oven tray.
2 Place chips, in single layer, on prepared tray. Cook, uncovered, in moderately hot oven 20 minutes. Add bacon to tray; cook with chips another 5 minutes or until chips are browned lightly and bacon is crisp.
3 Combine sour cream and chives in small bowl. Place chips on ovenproof serving plate. Sprinkle with bacon and cheese; cook, uncovered, in moderately hot oven about 5 minutes or until cheese melts.
4 Serve chips topped with sour cream mixture.

Parmesan walnut wafers

preparation time **15 minutes** cooking time **8 minutes** serves **2**

1 cup (80g) finely grated parmesan
2 tablespoons finely chopped walnuts
2 teaspoons finely chopped fresh thyme

1 Preheat oven to hot.
2 Combine cheese and nuts in medium bowl; drop rounded teaspoons of mixture on oven tray lined with baking paper, sprinkle with thyme. Cook in hot oven about 8 minutes or until browned lightly; stand until set.

Dips

Each of these dips takes **10 minutes** to prepare and makes about **2 cups**.

Sweet chilli cream cheese

Beat 250g softened packaged cream cheese, ½ cup (120g) sour cream and ½ cup (125ml) sweet chilli sauce in small bowl with electric mixer until smooth. Stir in ¼ cup coarsely chopped fresh coriander.

Salmon and gherkin

Discard skin and bones from two 210g cans drained pink salmon. Blend or process salmon with 250g softened packaged cream cheese and ¼ cup (60ml) lemon juice. Stir in 1 tablespoon coarsely chopped fresh dill and one finely chopped gherkin.

Spinach and water chestnut

Boil, steam or microwave 50g baby spinach leaves until wilted; drain. Chop spinach finely; combine in medium bowl with 230g can drained finely chopped water chestnuts, one finely chopped small red capsicum, ²/₃ cup (160g) sour cream, ¹/₃ cup (100g) whole-egg mayonnaise and one crushed clove garlic.

Tzatziki

Combine one seeded coarsely grated lebanese cucumber with 500g greek-style yogurt, 1 teaspoon ground cumin and 2 tablespoons coarsely chopped fresh mint in small bowl.

Beef and bean tacos

preparation time **10 minutes** cooking time **15 minutes** serves **2**

1 clove garlic, crushed
80g lean beef mince
½ teaspoon chilli powder
220g can kidney beans, rinsed, drained
2 tablespoons tomato paste
½ cup (125ml) water
2 medium tomatoes (380g), chopped finely
4 taco shells
¼ small iceberg lettuce, shredded finely
2 tablespoons mild chilli sauce

1 Preheat oven to moderate.
2 Heat large lightly oiled non-stick frying pan; cook garlic and beef, stirring, until beef is browned. Add chilli, beans, paste, the water and half of tomato; cook, covered, over low heat about 15 minutes or until mixture thickens slightly.
3 Meanwhile, toast taco shells, upside-down and uncovered, on oven tray in moderate oven for 5 minutes.
4 Just before serving, fill taco shells with beef mixture, lettuce, remaining tomato and chilli sauce.

Grilled fetta

preparation time **5 minutes** cooking time **5 minutes** serves **2**

150g fetta, halved
1 tablespoon olive oil
½ teaspoon chilli flakes
½ teaspoon dried oregano leaves

1 Place fetta on large sheet of foil; place on oven tray.
2 Combine oil, chilli and oregano in small bowl; drizzle over cheese. Grill about 5 minutes or until browned lightly. Stand 5 minutes; slice thickly.

serving suggestion Serve fetta with crusty bread.

Potato wedges with sloppy joe topping

preparation time **10 minutes** cooking time **30 minutes** serves **2**

2 medium potatoes (400g)
1 tablespoon olive oil
1 clove garlic, crushed
1 small brown onion (80g), chopped finely
1 small green capsicum (150g), chopped finely
350g beef mince
1 tablespoon mild american mustard
1 tablespoon cider vinegar
¼ cup (60ml) tomato sauce
¼ cup (30g) coarsely grated cheddar

1 Preheat oven to hot.
2 Cut each potato into eight wedges; place in large shallow baking dish, drizzle with half of the oil.
3 Roast, uncovered, in hot oven about 30 minutes or until wedges are tender.
4 Meanwhile, heat remaining oil in large frying pan; cook garlic, onion and capsicum, stirring, until vegetables soften. Add mince; cook, stirring, until changed in colour. Stir in mustard, vinegar and sauce. Bring to a boil then reduce heat; cook, stirring, until sloppy joe is cooked and slightly thickened.
5 Serve wedges topped with sloppy joe mixture; sprinkle with cheese.

tips Leftover sloppy joe topping can be stored in freezer for up to two months. Make sloppy joe jaffles by toasting mixture between bread with grated cheese.

Chicken chilli pizza

preparation time **10 minutes**   cooking time **20 minutes**   serves **4**

4 x 125g pizza bases
2 tablespoons tomato paste
1 tablespoon barbecue sauce
1 ½ teaspoons bottled crushed chilli
1 clove garlic, crushed
1 cup (170g) coarsely chopped cooked chicken
100g button mushrooms, sliced thickly
1 small tomato (130g), halved, sliced thinly
1 ½ cups (150g) coarsely grated pizza cheese

1 Preheat oven to hot.
2 Place pizza bases on oven tray. Combine paste, sauce, chilli and garlic in small bowl; spread evenly over bases. Divide chicken, mushrooms, tomato and cheese among bases.
3 Cook, uncovered, in hot oven about 20 minutes or until bases are crisp.

Greek wraps

preparation time **10 minutes** serves **4**

You will need one large barbecue chicken for this recipe.

80g baby spinach leaves
140g fetta, crumbled
2½ cups (425g) coarsely chopped cooked chicken
200g tzatziki
4 pieces lavash bread

1 Combine spinach, cheese, chicken and tzatziki in large bowl.
2 Place a quarter of the mixture along short side of one piece of lavash; roll to enclose filling. Repeat with remaining mixture and bread. Use toothpicks to secure wraps, if necessary.

Prosciutto and cheese croissants

preparation time **10 minutes** cooking time **10 minutes** serves **4**

4 croissants
2 teaspoons olive oil
8 slices prosciutto (120g)
½ cup (50g) coarsely grated parmesan
100g semi-dried tomatoes, drained, sliced thinly
30g baby rocket leaves

1 Preheat oven to moderately slow.
2 Split croissants in half horizontally, without separating; place on oven tray. Heat, uncovered, in moderately slow oven about 5 minutes.
3 Meanwhile, heat oil in small frying pan; cook prosciutto about 5 minutes or until crisp. Drain on absorbent paper.
4 Place equal amounts of cheese inside croissants; cook, uncovered, in moderately slow oven about 5 minutes or until cheese melts. Fill croissants with prosciutto, tomato and rocket.

Deep-fried onion rings

preparation time **20 minutes** cooking time **20 minutes** serves **6**

½ cup (75g) plain flour
½ cup (75g) cornflour
1 egg, beaten lightly
¾ cup (180ml) water
1½ cups (150g) packaged breadcrumbs
2 large white onions (400g), sliced thickly
Vegetable oil, for deep-frying

Sweet chilli dipping sauce
½ cup (120g) sour cream
¼ cup (60ml) sweet chilli sauce
2 tablespoons cream

1 Whisk flour, cornflour, egg and the water in medium bowl until smooth. Place breadcrumbs in small bowl.
2 Separate onion slices into rings. Dip rings, one at a time, in batter, then in breadcrumbs to coat; place, in single layer, on tray until all rings are coated.
3 Heat oil in large frying pan; deep-fry rings, in batches, until golden brown. Drain on absorbent paper.
4 Make sweet chilli dipping sauce; serve with hot onion rings.

Sweet chilli dipping sauce Place sour cream, sauce and cream in small bowl; mix well.

Honey-vindaloo glazed chicken wings

preparation time **15 minutes** cooking time (plus refrigeration time) **40 minutes** serves **4**

24 chicken wings (approximately 2kg)
⅓ cup (115g) honey
2 tablespoons vindaloo curry paste
⅓ cup (80ml) soy sauce
2 tablespoons peanut oil

1 Cut chicken wings into three pieces at joints; discard wing tips.
2 Combine remaining ingredients in large bowl with chicken; toss to coat chicken in marinade. Cover; refrigerate 30 minutes.
3 Preheat oven to hot. Place undrained chicken on oiled oven rack over baking dish; roast, uncovered, in hot oven about 40 minutes or cooked as desired, turning once during cooking.

Quesadilla wedges

preparation time **5 minutes** cooking time **5 minutes** serves **2**

20g baby spinach leaves
50g sliced salami
50g char-grilled capsicum
¼ cup (25g) grated mozzarella
4 large burrito tortillas
2 teaspoons olive oil

1 Sandwich spinach, salami, capsicum and cheese between tortillas; brush tortillas with oil.
2 Cook quesadilla on heated, oiled grill plate (or grill or barbecue) until hot; cut into wedges.

Bruschetta with eggplant and olive topping

preparation time **15 minutes** cooking time **10 minutes** serves **4**

¼ cup olive oil
1 small onion (80g), chopped finely
2 cloves garlic, crushed
1 celery stalk (75g), chopped finely
150g char-grilled eggplant, chopped finely
150g char-grilled capsicum, chopped finely
¼ cup (40g) seeded black olives, chopped coarsely
1 tablespoon drained baby capers
¼ cup shredded fresh basil
350g loaf ciabatta

1 Heat 1 tablespoon of oil in medium frying pan; cook onion, garlic and celery, stirring, until soft. Transfer to medium bowl.
2 Add eggplant, capsicum, olives, capers and basil to onion mixture; mix well.
3 Cut bread on slight angle into eight slices. Brush one side of bread slices with remaining oil, grill on both sides until toasted.
4 Top toast with eggplant mixture.

tip Ciabatta can be replaced with one baguette.

EASY
DINNER PARTIES

Formal dinner party

This menu will serve **4 people**.

Margarita

preparation time **5 minutes**

180ml tequila
120ml fresh lime juice
120ml cointreau
2 cups ice cubes

1 Combine all ingredients in a cocktail shaker. Shake vigorously; strain into a salt-rimmed glass.

Mustard beef canapés

preparation time **10 minutes**   cooking time **5 minutes**

1 tablespoon wholegrain mustard
1 tablespoon horseradish cream
2 x 175g new york cut steaks
2 teaspoons olive oil
2 tablespoons sour cream
18 baby spinach leaves

Crostini
1 small french bread stick
Olive-oil spray

1 Combine half the mustard and half the horseradish in small bowl; spread over steaks. Refrigerate, covered, until required.
2 Meanwhile, make crostini, as instructed on following page.

3 Heat oil in large frying pan; cook steaks, uncovered, until cooked as desired. Cover; stand 5 minutes, then slice thinly.
4 Combine remaining mustard and remaining horseradish with sour cream in small bowl. Top crostini with spinach, steak slices and sour cream mixture.

Crostini Preheat oven to moderately slow. Discard ends of bread; cut into 1cm slices. Place slices, in single layer, on oven tray; spray with oil. Toast, both sides, in moderately slow oven.

Onion soup with gruyère croûtons

preparation time **30 minutes** cooking time **50 minutes**

50g butter
4 large brown onions (800g), halved, sliced thinly
¾ cup (180ml) dry white wine
3 cups (750ml) water
1 litre (4 cups) beef stock
1 bay leaf
1 tablespoon plain flour
1 teaspoon fresh thyme leaves
1 small french bread stick
1 cup (125g) finely grated gruyère

1 Melt butter in large saucepan; cook onion, stirring occasionally, over medium heat, about 30 minutes or until caramelised.
2 Meanwhile, bring wine to a boil in medium saucepan; boil 1 minute. Stir in the water, stock and bay leaf; return to a boil. Remove from heat.
3 Stir flour into onion mixture; cook, stirring, until mixture bubbles and thickens. Gradually add hot stock mixture, stirring, until mixture boils and thickens slightly. Reduce heat; simmer soup, uncovered, stirring occasionally, 20 minutes. Discard bay leaf; stir in thyme.
4 Meanwhile, preheat grill. Cut bread into 1.5cm slices; discard end pieces. Toast slices on one side under grill. Turn, then top each with 1 tablespoon of the cheese; grill croûtons until cheese melts.
5 Divide soup among serving bowls; top with croûtons, sprinkle with remaining cheese.

Slow-roasted lamb shanks with tomato and olives

preparation time **15 minutes** cooking time **2 hours 25 minutes**

8 french-trimmed lamb shanks (2kg)
¼ cup (35g) plain flour
1 tablespoon olive oil
1 clove garlic, crushed
¾ cup (180ml) dry white wine
¾ cup (180ml) beef stock
2 x 400g cans chopped tomatoes
6 anchovy fillets, drained, chopped coarsely
1 sprig fresh basil
1 cup (150g) seeded kalamata olives
1 tablespoon balsamic vinegar
½ cup loosely packed small fresh basil leaves

1 Preheat oven to moderate.
2 Toss lamb in flour; shake away excess flour. Heat oil in 3-litre (12-cup) flameproof casserole dish; cook lamb, in batches, until browned all over.
3 Add garlic and wine to same dish; bring to a boil. Add stock, undrained tomatoes, anchovies and basil sprig; stir to combine.
4 Return lamb to dish; bring to a boil. Remove from heat. Cover with lid or tightly with foil; cook in moderate oven 2 hours or until lamb is tender, turning lamb halfway through cooking. Remove lamb from dish; cover to keep warm.
5 Add olives and vinegar to dish; simmer, uncovered, over medium heat about 5 minutes or until thickened slightly. Remove basil sprig.
6 Sprinkle basil leaves over lamb and sauce.

serving suggestion Serve lamb shanks with risoni.

Gourmet chocolate tart

preparation time **40 minutes** (plus refrigeration time)
cooking time **30 minutes**

1½ cups (240g) plain flour
½ cup (110g) caster sugar
140g cold butter, chopped
1 egg, beaten lightly

Filling
2 eggs
2 egg yolks
¼ cup (55g) caster sugar
250g dark eating chocolate, melted
200g butter, melted

1 Blend or process flour, sugar and butter until crumbly; add egg, process until ingredients just come together. Knead dough on floured surface until smooth. Wrap in plastic wrap; refrigerate 30 minutes.

2 Grease 24cm-round loose-based flan tin. Roll dough between sheets of baking paper until large enough to line prepared tin. Lift dough into tin; press into side, trim edge, prick base all over with fork. Cover; refrigerate 30 minutes.

3 Preheat oven to moderately hot. Place tin on oven tray; cover dough with baking paper, fill with dried beans or rice. Bake in moderately hot oven 10 minutes. Remove paper and beans; bake, uncovered, a further 5 minutes or until tart shell browns lightly. Cool to room temperature.

4 Reduce oven temperature to moderate.

5 Meanwhile, make filling; pour into shell. Bake tart, uncovered, in moderate oven 10 minutes or until filling is set; cool 10 minutes. Refrigerate 1 hour.

Filling Whisk eggs, yolks and sugar in medium heatproof bowl over medium saucepan of simmering water, about 15 minutes or until light and fluffy. Gently whisk chocolate and butter into egg mixture.

tip A pre-made frozen unbaked tart shell can be used in this recipe.

serving suggestion Serve chocolate tart dusted with cocoa powder.

Finger food party

This menu will serve up to **16 people**.

Party punch

preparation time **5 minutes** (plus refrigeration time)

3 x 750ml bottles chilled medium-dry white wine
2 tablespoons dark rum
⅔ cup (160ml) peach schnapps
⅓ cup (80ml) triple sec
3 cups (750ml) apple and mandarin juice
3 star fruit (450g), sliced thickly
4 small peaches (460g), sliced thickly

1 Combine wine, rum, schnapps, triple sec and juice in large bowl. Stir in fruit. Refrigerate, covered, 1 hour before serving.

Blt on mini toasts

preparation time **20 minutes** cooking time **5 minutes**

4 bacon rashers (280g)
1 packet (100g) mini toasts
6 butter lettuce leaves
¼ cup (75g) mayonnaise
200g grape tomatoes, halved

1 Remove rind from bacon; cut each rasher into pieces slightly smaller than mini toasts. Heat large frying pan; cook bacon, stirring, until browned and crisp. Drain on absorbent paper.
2 Cut lettuce into pieces slightly larger than mini toasts.
3 Divide mayonnaise among mini toasts; top each with lettuce, bacon and tomato. Serve at room temperature.

Curry puffs

preparation time **40 minutes** cooking time **25 minutes**

1 tablespoon vegetable oil
2 green onions, chopped finely
1 clove garlic, crushed
2 teaspoons curry powder
300g beef mince
2 teaspoons lemon juice
⅓ cup (110g) mango chutney
4 sheets ready-rolled puff pastry
1 egg, beaten lightly

1 Heat oil in medium saucepan; cook onion and garlic, stirring, until onion softens. Add curry powder; cook, stirring, until fragrant. Add beef; cook, stirring, until beef is browned and cooked as desired. Remove from heat; stir in juice and chutney.
2 Using rolling pin, roll each pastry sheet into 30cm square. Using 8cm-round cutter, cut eight rounds from each pastry sheet.
3 Preheat oven to moderately hot. Lightly oil two oven trays.
4 Place one heaped teaspoon of the beef mixture on one round; brush edges with a little egg, fold over to enclose filling. Press edges with fork to seal; repeat with remaining beef mixture and pastry.
5 Place curry puffs on prepared oven trays; brush with remaining egg. Bake, uncovered, in moderately hot oven about 15 minutes or until browned lightly.

serving suggestion Serve curry puffs hot, with mango chutney.

Chile con queso

preparation time **10 minutes** cooking time **10 minutes**

2 teaspoons vegetable oil
½ small green capsicum (75g), chopped finely
½ small brown onion (40g), chopped finely
1 tablespoon drained bottled jalapeño chillies, chopped finely
1 clove garlic, crushed
½ x 400g can undrained chopped peeled tomatoes
250g cream cheese, softened

1 Heat oil in medium saucepan; cook capsicum, onion, chilli and garlic, stirring, until onion softens. Add tomato; cook, stirring, 2 minutes.
2 Add cheese; whisk until cheese melts and dip is smooth.
3 Serve hot with bowl of crispy corn chips.

Mini pizzas

preparation time **20 minutes** cooking time **10 minutes**

335g (30cm) ready-made pizza base
2 tablespoons tomato paste
100g shaved leg ham
2 tablespoons mascarpone cheese
2 teaspoons finely chopped fresh chives

1 Preheat oven to moderately hot.
2 Using 4.5cm-round cutter, cut rounds from pizza base.
3 Place rounds on oven trays. Divide paste evenly over rounds; top with ham, cheese and chives. Bake, uncovered, in moderately hot oven about 5 minutes or until pizzas are heated through. Serve hot.

Honey soy wings

preparation time **10 minutes** cooking time **30 minutes**

16 small chicken wings (1.3kg)
⅓ cup (115g) honey
½ cup (125ml) salt-reduced soy sauce
3 cloves garlic, crushed
1 tablespoon grated fresh ginger

1 Preheat oven to hot.
2 Cut wings into three pieces at joints; discard tips. Combine chicken with remaining ingredients in large bowl; toss to coat chicken all over.
3 Place chicken, in single layer, in large shallow baking dish; brush any remaining marinade over chicken. Bake, uncovered, in hot oven, turning occasionally, about 30 minutes or until chicken is browned and cooked through.

Thai banquet

This menu will serve **8 people**.

Caipiroska

preparation time **10 minutes**

Cut six limes into eight wedges each. Using muddler (or end of rolling pin), crush half the wedges, 1 tablespoon white sugar, 50ml sugar syrup (see p362) and 10 x 5cm pieces of watermelon in large jug. Combine watermelon mixture in cocktail shaker with 200ml vodka, 100ml watermelon liqueur and 1 cup ice cubes. Shake vigorously; pour into glass with crushed ice; do not strain.

Chicken green curry

preparation time **20 minutes**   cooking time **20 minutes**

¼ cup (75g) green curry paste
2 x 400ml cans coconut milk
2 fresh kaffir lime leaves, torn
1kg chicken thigh fillets
2 tablespoons peanut oil
2 tablespoons fish sauce
2 tablespoons lime juice
1 tablespoon grated palm sugar
150g green beans, halved
1 small zucchini (150g), cut into 5cm pieces
⅓ cup loosely packed fresh thai basil leaves
¼ cup coarsely chopped fresh coriander

1 Stir curry paste in large saucepan over heat until fragrant. Add coconut milk and lime leaves. Bring to a boil then reduce heat; simmer, stirring, 5 minutes.
2 Meanwhile, quarter chicken pieces. Heat oil in large frying pan; cook chicken, in batches, until just browned. Drain on absorbent paper.
3 Add chicken to curry mixture with sauce, juice and sugar; simmer, covered, about 5 minutes or until chicken is cooked through. Add beans, zucchini, basil and coriander; cook, stirring, until zucchini is just tender.

Yellow coconut rice

preparation time **5 minutes** (plus standing time) cooking time **15 minutes**

1 ¾ cups (350g) white long-grain rice
1 ¼ cups (310ml) water
400ml can coconut cream
½ teaspoon salt
1 teaspoon white sugar
1 teaspoon ground turmeric

1 Soak rice in large bowl of cold water for 30 minutes. Pour rice into strainer; rinse under cold water until water runs clear. Drain.
2 Place rice and remaining ingredients in large heavy-base saucepan; cover, bring to boil, stirring occasionally. Reduce heat; simmer, covered, 15 minutes or until rice is tender. Remove from heat; stand, covered, 5 minutes.

Beef massaman curry

preparation time **20 minutes** cooking time **2 hours**

1kg beef skirt steak, cut into 3cm pieces
2 x 400ml cans coconut milk
1 ½ cups (375ml) beef stock
5 cardamom pods, bruised
2 star anise
1 tablespoon grated palm sugar
2 tablespoons fish sauce
1 tablespoon tamarind concentrate
2 tablespoons massaman curry paste
2 teaspoons tamarind concentrate, extra
½ cup (125ml) beef stock, extra
8 baby brown onions (300g), halved
1 medium kumara (400g), chopped coarsely
¼ cup (35g) coarsely chopped unsalted toasted peanuts
2 green onions, sliced thinly

1 Place beef, half the coconut milk, stock, cardamom, star anise, sugar, sauce and tamarind in large saucepan. Bring to a boil then reduce heat; simmer, uncovered, about 1 hour 30 minutes or until beef is almost tender.

2 Strain beef over large bowl; reserve spicy beef sauce, discard cardamom and star anise.

3 Place curry paste in same cleaned pan; stir over heat until fragrant. Add remaining coconut milk, extra tamarind and stock; bring to a boil, stir about 1 minute or until mixture is smooth. Add beef, brown onion, kumara and 1 cup of reserved sauce; cook, uncovered, 30 minutes.

4 Place curry in serving bowl; sprinkle with peanuts and green onion.

Vegetarian pad thai

preparation time **20 minutes** (plus standing time) cooking time **10 minutes**

200g rice stick noodles
2 cloves garlic, quartered
2 fresh red thai chillies, chopped coarsely
¼ cup (60ml) peanut oil
2 eggs, beaten lightly
1 cup (90g) fried onion
125g fried tofu, cut into small pieces
¼ cup (35g) coarsely chopped toasted unsalted peanuts
3 cups (240g) bean sprouts
6 green onions, sliced thinly
2 tablespoons soy sauce
1 tablespoon lime juice
2 tablespoons coarsely chopped fresh coriander

1 Place noodles in large heatproof bowl; cover with boiling water, stand until noodles just soften, drain.

2 Meanwhile, using mortar and pestle, crush garlic and chilli until mixture forms paste.

3 Heat 2 teaspoons of oil in wok; pour in egg, swirl to make thin omelette. Cook, uncovered, until egg is just set. Remove from wok; roll omelette, cut into thin strips.

4 Heat remaining oil in wok; stir-fry paste and fried onion until fragrant. Add tofu; stir-fry 1 minute. Add half the nuts, half the sprouts and half the green onion; stir-fry until sprouts are just wilted. Add noodles, sauce and juice; stir-fry, tossing gently to combine. Remove from heat; toss remaining nuts, sprouts and green onion with omelette strips and coriander through pad thai.

Romantic dinner for two

Champagne cocktail

preparation time **5 minutes**

5cm strip orange rind
2 sugar cubes
10 drops angostura bitters
1 ⅓ cup (310ml) chilled champagne

1 Slice rind thinly. Place sugar cube in champagne glass; top with bitters then champagne. Garnish with rind.

Salade composé

preparation time **15 minutes** cooking time **20 minutes**

½ small french bread stick
1 clove garlic, crushed
2 tablespoons olive oil
3 bacon rashers (210g), rind removed, sliced thickly
50g mesclun
2 medium egg tomatoes (150g), sliced thinly
2 hard-boiled eggs, halved lengthways

Red wine vinaigrette
2 tablespoons red wine vinegar
1 teaspoon dijon mustard
2 tablespoons extra virgin olive oil

1 Cut bread into 1cm slices. Brush both sides with combined garlic and oil; toast under preheated grill.
2 Cook bacon in small frying pan until crisp; drain on absorbent paper.
3 Meanwhile, place ingredients for red wine vinaigrette in screw-top jar; shake well.
4 Layer bread and bacon in large bowl with mesclun and tomato, top with egg; drizzle with vinaigrette.

Prawn and fennel risotto

preparation time **30 minutes** cooking time **45 minutes**

300g uncooked small prawns
2 cups (500ml) fish stock
1 cup (250ml) water
2 tablespoons olive oil
1 small fennel bulb (200g), sliced thinly
1 small brown onion (80g), chopped finely
1 clove garlic, crushed
1 cup (200g) arborio rice
¼ cup (60ml) dry white wine
30g butter
2 tablespoons chopped fennel-frond tips

1 Shell and devein prawns, leaving tails intact. Place stock, and the water in large saucepan. Bring to a boil then reduce heat; simmer, covered.
2 Meanwhile, heat oil in large saucepan; add fennel, cook, stirring, until tender. Remove fennel from pan with slotted spoon. Add prawns to same pan; cook, stirring, until prawns just change colour. Remove from pan with slotted spoon. Add onion and garlic to same pan; cook, stirring, until onion is soft.
3 Add rice to pan; stir about 1 minute or until rice is well coated. Stir in ½ cup (125ml) hot stock; cook, stirring, over medium heat until liquid is absorbed. Continue adding stock in ½-cup batches, stirring after each addition until absorbed. Cooking time should be about 25 minutes.
4 Return fennel to pan with prawns and chilli; cook, stirring until hot; stir in butter and fennel tips.

White chocolate fondue

preparation time **10 minutes** cooking time **5 minutes**

100g white eating chocolate, chopped coarsely
¼ cup (60ml) cream
1 tablespoon coconut-flavoured liqueur

1 Combine chocolate and cream in small saucepan, stir over low heat until smooth; stir in liqueur. Transfer fondue to serving bowl; place bowl in centre of dining table; serve with a platter of fresh fruit and marshmallows.

tip Serve fondue with fruits such as strawberries, banana and pineapple.

DESSERTS

Choc chip nougat frozen parfait with caramel sauce

preparation time **25 minutes** (plus refrigeration time)
cooking time **10 minutes** serves **8**

2 cups (400g) ricotta
1²⁄₃ cups (370g) caster sugar
2 cups (500ml) whipping cream
150g almond nougat, chopped
50g chopped dark eating chocolate

1 Line 9cm x 21cm loaf pan with strip of foil or baking paper to cover the base and extend over two long sides.
2 Process ricotta and ²⁄₃ cup (150g) of the sugar until smooth. Beat 1¹⁄₃ cups (330ml) of the cream in small bowl with electric mixer until soft peaks form. Combine ricotta mixture, nougat and chocolate in large bowl; fold in cream.
3 Spoon mixture into prepared pan, cover and freeze overnight or until firm.
4 Meanwhile, to make caramel sauce, combine the remaining 1 cup (220g) of sugar with ½ cup (125ml) of water in small pan; stir over low heat until sugar is dissolved. Boil, uncovered, without stirring, until a caramel colour.
5 Remove pan from heat, allow bubbles to subside. Carefully add remaining ²⁄₃ cup (160ml) of cream and stir over low heat to dissolve toffee. Cool.
6 Turn out parfait; slice. Allow parfait to soften slightly before serving with caramel sauce.

Pear and caramel puddings

preparation time **15 minutes** cooking time **30 minutes** serves **4**

415g can pear halves in natural juice
100g butter, softened
¾ cup (150g) firmly packed brown sugar
2 eggs
1¼ cups (185g) self-raising flour
¼ teaspoon mixed spice
¼ cup (30g) chopped walnuts

1 Preheat oven to moderate. Grease 4 x 1-cup (250ml) ovenproof dishes.
2 Drain pears over bowl; reserve four pear halves for pudding tops, chop remaining pears coarsely and place in prepared dishes.
3 Beat butter, sugar, eggs, flour, spice and reserved juice in medium bowl with electric mixer on low speed until combined. Increase speed to medium; beat until mixture is just smooth. Spread mixture over chopped pears in dishes. Place one pear half on surface of each pudding; sprinkle with walnuts.
4 Place dishes on oven tray and bake in moderate oven about 30 minutes or until cooked through.

Creamed rice

preparation time **10 minutes** cooking time **25 minutes** serves **4**

3 cups (750ml) milk
2 cups (600g) white medium-grain rice
2 tablespoons caster sugar
1 teaspoon vanilla essence
½ teaspoon ground nutmeg
570g canned plums, drained, seeded, halved

1 Combine milk and rice in medium saucepan. Bring to a boil then reduce heat; simmer 15 minutes.
2 Add sugar; return to the boil then reduce heat, simmer, stirring, about 10 minutes or until rice is tender. Stir in essence. (If rice is too thick, add a little extra milk.)
3 Serve rice sprinkled with nutmeg and topped with plums.

Caramelised apple tarts

preparation time **15 minutes** cooking time **20 minutes** serves **4**

1 sheet ready-rolled puff pastry
1 egg yolk, beaten lightly
1 tablespoon milk
1 tablespoon caster sugar
2 large (400g) apples
60g butter, softened
⅓ cup (75g) firmly packed brown sugar
½ teaspoon ground cinnamon

1 Preheat oven to hot.
2 Score puff pastry sheet lightly using top of sharp knife. Brush pastry with combined yolk and milk; sprinkle with caster sugar. Cut into four squares. Place on greased oven tray.
3 Using mandolin or sharp knife, cut unpeeled apples crossways into 5mm-thick slices. Place sliced apples, overlapping if necessary, over base of large baking dish; dot with butter, sprinkle with sugar and cinnamon.
4 Bake pastry and apple in hot oven about 10 minutes or until pastry is puffed and browned. Remove pastry from the oven. Turn apples over and bake further 10 minutes or until soft and browned.
5 Top pastry squares with apples; drizzle with caramel mixture in dish.

serving suggestion Serve apple tarts with yogurt or ice-cream.

Sour cherry baked custards

preparation time **10 minutes** cooking time **25 minutes** serves **4**

1 cup (170g) drained morello cherries
3 eggs
1 teaspoon vanilla extract
½ cup (110g) caster sugar
2 cups (500ml) hot milk
2 teaspoons custard powder
1 tablespoon cold milk
½ teaspoon ground nutmeg or cinnamon

1 Preheat oven to moderately slow.

2 Pat cherries dry, divide among four ¾-cup (180ml) ovenproof dishes.

3 Whisk eggs, extract and sugar together in medium bowl. Gradually whisk hot milk into egg mixture.

4 Combine custard powder and cold milk in small bowl, stir until smooth; whisk into egg mixture.

5 Pour mixture over cherries in dishes. Bake in moderately slow oven about 25 minutes or until just set (a small sharp knife inserted into centre of custard comes out clean). Sprinkle with nutmeg, serve warm or cooled.

tip Sour or morello cherries are available in jars; you can substitute any canned fruit of your choice.

Summer berry clafoutis

preparation time **15 minutes** cooking time **35 minutes** serves **4**

500g mixed berries
3 eggs
⅓ cup (75g) caster sugar
1 teaspoon vanilla essence
⅓ cup (50g) plain flour
1 tablespoon self-raising flour
¾ cup (180ml) low-fat milk

1 Preheat oven to moderate.

2 Lightly grease four 1¾-cup (430ml) shallow ovenproof dishes; place on oven tray. Divide berries among dishes.

3 Whisk eggs, sugar and essence in medium bowl until frothy; whisk in sifted flours and milk until combined. Pour mixture, over back of spoon, into dishes.

4 Bake, uncovered, in moderate oven about 35 minutes or until set.

serving suggestion Serve clafoutis warm, dusted with sifted icing sugar.

Lemon delicious

preparation time **20 minutes** cooking time **45 minutes** serves **4**

3 eggs
½ cup (110g) caster sugar
1 cup (250ml) milk
1 tablespoon self-raising flour
½ cup (125ml) lemon juice

1 Preheat oven to moderate.
2 Separate eggs; place whites and yolks in two separate small bowls. Add sugar to yolks in small bowl; beat using electric mixer until thick and creamy. Gradually beat in milk on low speed, then flour and juice. Pour into large bowl.
3 Using electric mixer, beat egg whites in small bowl until soft peaks form; fold into yolk mixture in two batches. Use plastic spatula for this; do not stir or beat, as you will deflate mixture. Mixture appears curdled at this stage.
4 Pour mixture into deep 1-litre (4-cup) ovenproof dish. Place dish in baking dish; add enough boiling water to baking dish to come halfway up side of ovenproof dish. Bake in moderate oven 45 minutes or until firm to touch.

serving suggestion Serve lemon delicious sprinkled with icing sugar.

Orange soufflés

preparation time **15 minutes** cooking time **20 minutes** serves **4**

1 tablespoon caster sugar
30g butter
1½ tablespoons plain flour
½ cup (125ml) low-fat milk
2 teaspoons finely grated orange rind
2 tablespoons orange juice
¼ cup (55g) caster sugar, extra
3 yolks
2 egg whites

1 Preheat oven to moderately hot. Grease four ¾-cup (180ml) soufflé dishes; sprinkle bases and sides with sugar, shake off excess. Place on oven tray.
2 Heat butter in medium pan, stir in flour; cook, stirring, until mixture

thickens and bubbles. Gradually stir in combined milk, rind, juice and extra sugar; stir until mixture boils and thickens.

3 Pour mixture into medium bowl, stir in yolks. Beat egg whites in small bowl with electric mixer until soft peaks form; fold gently into orange mixture, in two batches.

4 Spoon into prepared dishes; level tops. Bake in moderately hot oven about 20 minutes or until soufflés are puffed. Serve immediately.

Caramel self-saucing pudding

preparation time **15 minutes** cooking time **40 minutes** serves **6**

1 cup (150g) self-raising flour
¾ cup (165g) firmly packed brown sugar
20g butter, melted
½ cup (125ml) milk
4 fresh dates (75g), seeded, chopped finely

Caramel sauce
¾ cup (165g) firmly packed brown sugar
2 cups (500ml) boiling water
60g butter, chopped

1 Preheat oven to moderate. Grease 2-litre (8-cup) shallow ovenproof dish.

2 Combine flour, sugar, butter, milk and dates in large bowl; mix well. Spread mixture into prepared dish.

3 Make caramel sauce.

4 Pour sauce slowly over back of spoon over batter in dish. Bake in moderate oven about 40 minutes or until firm in centre.

Caramel sauce Combine all ingredients in medium heatproof jug; stir until sugar is dissolved and butter melted.

serving suggestion Serve pudding immediately, with cream or ice-cream.

Plum and apple cobbler

preparation time **10 minutes** cooking time **30 minutes** serves **6**

570g can dark plums in syrup
1 medium apple (150g), sliced
½ teaspoon finely grated orange rind
2 tablespoons caster sugar
½ cup (75g) self-raising flour
¼ cup (35g) plain flour
2 tablespoons brown sugar
20g butter, chopped
1 egg, lightly beaten
2 tablespoons low-fat milk

1 Preheat oven to moderate.
2 Drain plums; reserve 2 tablespoons syrup. Halve plums, remove stones. Combine apple, rind, caster sugar and syrup in medium pan. Bring to boil then reduce heat; simmer, covered, 8 minutes, stirring occasionally. Stir in plums, spoon into 1.5-litre (6-cup) ovenproof dish.
3 Sift flours into medium bowl, stir in brown sugar; rub in butter. Stir in egg and milk. Drop heaped tablespoons of mixture around edge of dish. Bake, uncovered, in moderate oven 30 minutes.

Banana tarte tatin

preparation time **10 minutes** cooking time **18 minutes** serves **6**

50g butter, chopped
⅓ cup (75g) firmly packed brown sugar
¼ cup (60ml) cream
¼ teaspoon ground cinnamon
3 medium bananas (600g), sliced thinly
1 sheet frozen puff pastry, thawed
1 egg, beaten lightly

1 Preheat oven to hot.
2 Combine butter, sugar, cream and cinnamon in small saucepan; stir over low heat until sugar dissolves. Bring to the boil then reduce heat, simmer, uncovered, 2 minutes.

3 Pour caramel sauce into base of 23cm pie dish; arrange banana slices over base of dish.
4 Trim corners from pastry sheet to form 24cm circle. Place pastry sheet over bananas, ease pastry into side of dish. Brush pastry with egg; cook in hot oven about 15 minutes or until pastry is browned. Invert tarte.

serving suggestion Serve tarte tatin with cream or ice-cream.

Lemon tart

preparation time **20 minutes** (plus refrigeration time)
cooking time **1 hour 10 minutes** (plus cooling time) serves **8**

1¼ cups (185g) plain flour
⅓ cup (55g) icing sugar
¼ cup (30g) almond meal
125g cold butter, chopped
1 egg yolk

Lemon filling
1 tablespoon finely grated lemon rind
½ cup (125ml) lemon juice
5 eggs
¾ cup (165g) caster sugar
300ml cream

1 Process flour, icing sugar, almond meal and butter until combined. Add yolk; process until ingredients just come together. Knead dough on floured surface until smooth. Cover; refrigerate 30 minutes.
2 Preheat oven to moderately hot. Grease 24cm loose-base flan tin.
3 Roll pastry between sheets of baking paper until large enough to line prepared tin. Ease pastry into tin; trim edges. Cover; refrigerate 30 minutes.
4 Cover pastry with baking paper, fill with dried beans or rice; place tin on oven tray. Bake in moderately hot oven 10 minutes. Remove paper and beans; bake about 10 minutes or until tart shell browns lightly. Remove from oven; reduce temperature to moderately slow. Refrigerate cooled shell until cold.
5 Make lemon filling; pour into shell. Bake, uncovered, in moderately slow oven 40 minutes or until filling just sets. Stand 10 minutes; refrigerate until cold.

Lemon filling Whisk ingredients in medium bowl. Stand 5 minutes; strain.

Summer berry sundae

preparation time **5 minutes** cooking time **15 minutes** serves **4**

¼ cup (55g) caster sugar
500g mixed fresh berries
1 tablespoon orange juice
1 litre vanilla ice-cream
⅔ cup (100g) toasted macadamias, chopped

1 Combine sugar and berries in medium saucepan; stir over low heat, without boiling, until sugar dissolves.
2 Bring to a boil then reduce heat; simmer, uncovered, about 5 minutes or until berries are soft. Stir in juice and cool, if desired.
3 To serve, layer scoops of ice-cream, berry mixture and nuts in four tall serving glasses.

Waffles and ice-cream à la suzette

preparation time **10 minutes** cooking time **10 minutes** serves **4**

125g butter
½ cup (110g) caster sugar
2 teaspoons finely grated orange rind
1 tablespoon orange juice
¼ cup (60ml) cointreau
8 belgian-style waffles
200ml vanilla ice-cream

1 Melt butter in small heavy-base saucepan; add sugar, rind, juice and liqueur. Stir over low heat, without boiling, until sugar dissolves. Bring to a boil then reduce heat; simmer, uncovered, without stirring, about 1 minute or until sauce thickens slightly.
2 Warm waffles according to manufacturer's instructions. Divide half of waffles among serving plates; top with ice-cream, remaining waffles and suzette sauce.

Mango and raspberry jelly

preparation time **20 minutes** (plus refrigeration time) serves **4**

400g can sliced mango
85g packet mango jelly crystals
2 cups (500ml) boiling water
150g raspberries
135g packet raspberry jelly crystals
1 cup (250ml) cold water
300ml whipping cream

1 Drain mango in sieve over small bowl; reserve liquid. Measure ¼ cup mango slices and reserve. Divide remaining mango slices among four 1-cup (250ml) glasses.
2 Combine mango jelly crystals with 1 cup of the boiling water in small bowl, stirring, until jelly dissolves; stir in reserved mango liquid. Divide evenly among glasses over mango, cover; refrigerate about 2 hours or until jelly sets.
3 Divide raspberries among glasses over jelly. Combine raspberry jelly crystals and remaining cup of the boiling water in small bowl, stirring, until jelly dissolves; stir in the cold water. Divide evenly among glasses over raspberries, cover; refrigerate about 2 hours or until jelly sets.
4 Beat cream in small bowl with electric mixer until soft peaks form. Using rubber spatula, spread equally among glasses; top with reserved mango.

Melon and pineapple with honey lime syrup

preparation time **10 minutes** cooking time **5 minutes** serves **1**

1 tablespoon honey
1 tablespoon lime juice
100g fresh pineapple pieces
100g fresh honeydew melon pieces
2 tablespoons honey-flavoured yogurt

1 Combine honey and juice in small saucepan; bring to a boil then reduce heat; simmer, uncovered, 5 minutes.
2 Pour honey mixture over fruit in large bowl and mix gently.
3 Serve fruit mixture with yogurt.

Ice-cream with three toppings

Each of these recipes makes enough to top **four 250ml bowls of ice-cream**.

Pistachio praline

preparation time **5 minutes** (plus standing time) cooking time **10 minutes**

Preheat oven to hot. Sprinkle ¼ cup (55g) sugar evenly over oven tray lined with baking paper; place in hot oven about 8 minutes or until sugar just becomes a light golden-brown toffee. Remove from oven; place on heat-resistant surface. Sprinkle 1 tablespoon toasted coarsely chopped shelled pistachios over hot toffee; cool completely, break praline into bits. Blend or process until it resembles breadcrumbs.

Rocky road topping

preparation time **5 minutes**

Combine two coarsely chopped 55g snickers bars in medium bowl with 50g baby marshmallows and 2 tablespoons crushed toasted peanuts. Spoon over ice-cream; drizzle with ¼ cup (60ml) bottled chocolate topping.

Mixed berry sauce

preparation time **5 minutes** cooking time **4 minutes**

Heat ½ cup (125ml) cream and ¼ cup (55g) firmly packed brown sugar in medium saucepan, stirring, until sugar dissolves. Add 1 cup (150g) frozen mixed berries; cook, stirring, 2 minutes; cool.

Rhubarb fool

preparation time **20 minutes** (plus refrigeration time)
cooking time **10 minutes** serves **4**

2 cups (250g) coarsely chopped rhubarb
¼ cup (55g) caster sugar
½ cup (125ml) water
½ teaspoon ground cinnamon
¾ cup (180ml) whipping cream
1 tablespoon icing sugar
1 cup (250ml) prepared vanilla custard

1 Combine rhubarb in medium saucepan with caster sugar, the water and cinnamon. Bring to a boil then reduce heat; simmer, uncovered, stirring occasionally, about 10 minutes or until rhubarb is tender. Transfer to large bowl. Cover; refrigerate 1 hour.
2 Beat cream and icing sugar in small bowl with electric mixer until soft peaks form. Stir custard into rhubarb mixture; fold whipped cream mixture into rhubarb mixture. Divide mixture among four ⅔-cup (160ml) serving glasses. Refrigerate, covered, 1 hour before serving.

Chocolate mousse

preparation time **15 minutes** (plus refrigeration time)
cooking time **5 minutes** (plus cooling time) serves **4**

200g dark eating chocolate
300ml whipping cream
3 eggs, separated
2 tablespoons caster sugar

1 Chop chocolate coarsely; combine it with half the cream in large heatproof bowl. Place bowl over saucepan of simmering water; stir until chocolate has melted. Cool chocolate mixture 5 minutes; stir in yolks, one at a time.
2 Beat egg whites in small bowl on highest speed with electric mixer until soft peaks form; add sugar, beat until dissolved. Gently fold whites, in two batches, into chocolate mixture; pour mixture into four ⅔-cup (160ml) serving glasses. Refrigerate 3 hours or overnight.
3 Whip remaining cream until soft peaks form. Top each mousse with cream.

Grilled bananas with malibu syrup

preparation time **10 minutes** cooking time **5 minutes** serves **4**

4 large ripe bananas (920g)
⅓ cup (80ml) maple syrup
2 tablespoons malibu
¼ cup (15g) shredded coconut, toasted

1 Split bananas lengthways. Combine maple syrup and liqueur; brush about a quarter of mixture over cut-sides of bananas.
2 Cook bananas, cut-side down, on heated lightly greased grill plate (or grill or barbecue) until lightly browned and hot.
3 Serve bananas while hot, drizzled with warmed remaining syrup and toasted coconut.

Chocolate cream rice

preparation time **10 minutes** (plus refrigeration time) cooking time **1 hour**
serves **4**

1 litre (4 cups) milk
½ cup (100g) firmly packed brown sugar
⅔ cup (130g) white short-grain rice
100g dark eating chocolate, chopped
300ml whipping cream
30g dark chocolate, grated

1 Combine milk and sugar in medium, heavy-base saucepan, stir over heat until sugar is dissolved. Bring to a boil, stir in rice. Reduce heat; simmer, covered, about 50 minutes or until almost all the milk has been absorbed, stirring several times during cooking. Remove from heat, add chopped chocolate, stir until chocolate melts; cool to room temperature.
2 Beat cream in small bowl with electric mixer until soft peaks form, fold half the cream into rice mixture. Spoon mixture into four serving dishes; refrigerate 1 hour. Decorate with remaining cream and grated chocolate.

Bread and butter pudding

preparation time **20 minutes** (plus standing time) cooking time **50 minutes**
serves **4**

6 thin slices white bread
40g butter, softened
4 eggs
⅓ cup (75g) caster sugar
3½ cups (875ml) milk
1 teaspoon vanilla essence
½ cup (80g) sultanas
Ground cinnamon

1 Trim crusts from bread, butter each slice; cut each slice into four triangles.
Arrange two rows of triangles, butter-side up, overlapping slightly, along base
of shallow 2-litre (8-cup) ovenproof dish. Centre another row of triangles over
first two rows, with triangles facing in opposite direction to first two layers.
2 Whisk eggs, sugar, milk and essence together in bowl.
3 Preheat oven to moderately slow. Pour half the custard mixture over bread;
stand 10 minutes.
4 Whisk remaining custard mixture again, add sultanas; pour into dish.
Sprinkle with cinnamon. Stand dish in larger baking dish, with enough boiling
water to come halfway up side of dish.
5 Bake, uncovered, in moderately slow oven about 50 minutes or until
custard is set.

Baked chocolate custard

preparation time **10 minutes** cooking time **50 minutes** serves **4**

3 eggs
¼ cup (25g) cocoa powder
⅓ cup (75g) caster sugar
2 cups (500ml) milk

1 Preheat oven to moderate.
2 Whisk eggs, sifted cocoa and sugar in large bowl until combined. Heat milk in small saucepan; gradually whisk into egg mixture. Pour into four ¾-cup (180ml) ovenproof dishes.
3 Stand dishes in baking dish with enough hot water to come halfway up sides of ovenproof dishes. Bake in moderate oven 25 minutes. Reduce heat to moderately slow, bake about 20 minutes or until just set.

serving suggestion Serve custard dusted with sifted icing sugar.

Rhubarb galette

preparation time **10 minutes** cooking time **20 minutes** serves **4**

30g butter, melted
2½ cups (275g) coarsely chopped rhubarb
⅓ cup (75g) firmly packed brown sugar
1 teaspoon finely grated orange rind
1 sheet ready-rolled puff pastry
2 tablespoons almond meal

1 Preheat oven to hot. Line oven tray with baking paper.
2 Combine 20g of butter, rhubarb, sugar and rind in medium bowl.
3 Cut 24cm round from pastry, place on prepared tray; sprinkle almond meal evenly over pastry. Spread rhubarb mixture over pastry, leaving 4cm border. Fold 2cm of pastry edge up and around filling. Brush edge with remaining butter.
4 Bake galette, uncovered, in hot oven about 20 minutes or until browned.

Tiramisu trifle

preparation time **20 minutes** (plus refrigeration time) serves **4**

1 tablespoon dried coffee powder
½ **cup (125ml) boiling water**
2 tablespoons sambuca
125g sponge fingers
¾ **cup (180ml) cream**
⅓ **cup (55g) icing sugar**
2 **cups (500g) mascarpone**
⅓ **cup (80ml) marsala**
2 teaspoons cocoa powder

1 Combine coffee and the water in small heatproof bowl, stir until coffee dissolves; stir in liqueur. Cut biscuits in half crossways.
2 Beat cream, icing sugar and mascarpone with electric mixer in small bowl until soft peaks form; fold in marsala.
3 Dip half the biscuits in coffee mixture; divide among four 1½-cup (375ml) serving glasses. Divide half the mascarpone mixture among glasses; dip remaining biscuits in coffee mixture, divide among glasses, top with remaining mascarpone mixture.
4 Dust tiramisu trifles with sifted cocoa; refrigerate until chilled.

tip To reduce cost of recipe, replace mascarpone with 375g cream cheese.

EASY CAKES AND BREADS

Caramel mud cake

preparation time **30 minutes** cooking time **2 hours 10 minutes** serves **12**

250g unsalted butter, chopped
200g white eating chocolate, chopped coarsely
2¼ cups (450g) firmly packed brown sugar
1½ cups (375ml) water
2 cups (300g) plain flour
⅔ cup (100g) self-raising flour
3 eggs, beaten lightly

Caramel frosting
125g butter, chopped
1 cup (200g) firmly packed brown sugar
⅓ cup (80ml) milk
1½ cups (240g) icing sugar

1 Preheat oven to slow. Grease deep 22cm round-cake pan; line base and side with baking paper, extending paper 5cm above edge of pan.
2 Combine butter, chocolate, sugar and the water in medium saucepan; stir, over low heat, until mixture is smooth. Transfer mixture to large bowl; cool 15 minutes. Whisk in flours, then egg.
3 Pour mixture into prepared pan; bake in slow oven about 2 hours. Stand in pan 10 minutes; turn onto wire rack to cool.
4 Make caramel frosting. Place cake, top up, on serving plate; spread cold cake with frosting.

Caramel frosting Melt butter in small saucepan. Stir in brown sugar and milk. Bring to a boil then reduce heat; simmer, uncovered, 3 minutes. Cool. Gradually stir in icing sugar until frosting is of spreadable consistency.

Lime syrup coconut muffins

preparation time **20 minutes** cooking time **25 minutes** makes **12**

2½ cups (375g) self-raising flour
1 cup (90g) desiccated coconut
1 cup (220g) caster sugar
1 tablespoon finely grated lime rind
1 cup (250ml) buttermilk
125g butter, melted
2 eggs

Lime syrup
½ cup (110g) caster sugar
¼ cup (60ml) water
2 teaspoons finely grated lime rind
⅓ cup (80ml) lime juice

1 Preheat oven to moderately hot. Grease 12-hole (⅓-cup/80ml) muffin pan.
2 Combine flour, coconut and sugar in large bowl; stir in combined remaining ingredients. Spoon mixture into prepared pan; bake in moderately hot oven about 20 minutes.
3 Make lime syrup.
4 Transfer muffins to wire rack over tray; pour hot lime syrup over hot muffins. Drain syrup from tray and pour over muffins again.

Lime syrup Combine ingredients in small saucepan; stir over heat, without boiling, until sugar dissolves. Simmer, uncovered, without stirring, 2 minutes.

Choc brownie muffins

preparation time **10 minutes** cooking time **20 minutes** makes **12**

2 cups (300g) self-raising flour
⅓ cup (35g) cocoa powder
⅓ cup (75g) caster sugar
60g butter, melted
½ cup (95g) chocolate chips
½ cup (75g) chopped pistachios
½ cup (125ml) chocolate hazelnut spread
1 egg, lightly beaten
¾ cup (180ml) milk
½ cup (125ml) sour cream

1 Preheat oven to moderately hot. Grease 12-hole (⅓-cup/80ml) muffin pan.
2 Sift dry ingredients into large bowl; stir in remaining ingredients.
3 Spoon mixture into prepared pan. Bake in moderately hot oven 20 minutes.

Orange syrup cake

preparation time **25 minutes** cooking time **1 hour 10 minutes** serves **12**

1 large orange (300g)
2 cups (500ml) water
3 cups (660g) caster sugar
⅔ cup (160ml) brandy
250g unsalted butter, softened
4 eggs
1½ cups (225g) self-raising flour
2 tablespoons cornflour

1 Preheat oven to moderately slow. Grease deep 22cm-round cake pan; line base and side with baking paper.
2 Peel orange. Chop both peel and flesh of orange finely; discard seeds.
3 Stir flesh and peel in medium saucepan with the water, 2 cups of sugar and brandy, over medium heat, until sugar dissolves. Bring to a boil then reduce heat; simmer, uncovered, about 15 minutes or until orange skin is tender. Strain syrup into jug; reserve orange solids separately.
4 Beat butter and remaining sugar in small bowl with electric mixer until

light and fluffy. Add eggs, one at a time, beating until just combined between additions. Transfer mixture to large bowl.

5 Stir in combined sifted flour and cornflour, and reserved orange solids. Pour mixture into prepared pan; bake, uncovered, in moderately slow oven about 50 minutes.

6 Meanwhile, simmer reserved syrup in small saucepan, uncovered, until thickened slightly.

7 Stand cake in pan 5 minutes; turn, top up, onto wire rack set over tray. Pour hot syrup over hot cake; serve warm.

Apricot loaf

preparation time **15 minutes** (plus cooling time)
cooking time **1 hour 20 minutes** serves **8**

200g dried apricots, chopped coarsely
½ cup (125ml) apricot nectar
½ cup (110g) caster sugar
½ cup (110g) firmly packed brown sugar
250g butter, chopped
3 eggs, beaten lightly
1 cup (150g) plain flour
¾ cup (110g) self-raising flour

1 Preheat oven to slow. Grease 14cm x 21cm loaf pan; line base and sides with baking paper, bringing paper 2cm above sides of pan.

2 Place apricots, nectar and sugars in medium saucepan. Bring to a boil then simmer, covered, 5 minutes, stirring occasionally. Remove from heat; add butter, stir until melted. Transfer mixture to large bowl; cover, cool to room temperature.

3 Stir egg and sifted flours into apricot mixture and spread into prepared pan.

4 Bake cake in slow oven about 1¼ hours. Cover hot cake tightly with foil; cool in pan.

tips Cake can be made two days ahead; keep, covered, in airtight container. Cake suitable to freeze for up to three months.

Jam roll

preparation time **20 minutes** cooking time **8 minutes** serves **10**

3 eggs, separated
½ cup (110g) caster sugar
¾ cup (110g) self-raising flour
2 tablespoons hot milk
¼ cup (110g) caster sugar, extra
½ cup (160g) jam, warmed

1 Peheat oven to moderately hot. Grease 25cm x 30cm swiss roll pan; line base and short sides with baking paper, extending paper 5cm above sides, grease paper.

2 Beat egg whites in small bowl with electric mixer until soft peaks form; add sugar, 1 tablespoon at a time, beating until dissolved between additions.

3 With motor operating, add yolks, one at a time, beating until mixture is pale and thick; this will take about 10 minutes.

4 Sift flour three times onto baking paper.

5 Pour hot milk down side of bowl; add triple-sifted flour. Working quickly, use plastic spatula to fold milk and flour through egg mixture. Pour mixture into prepared pan, gently spreading mixture evenly into corners.

6 Bake cake in moderately hot oven about 8 minutes or until top of cake feels soft and springy when touched lightly with fingertips.

7 Meanwhile, place piece of baking paper cut to same size as cake on board or bench; sprinkle evenly with extra sugar. When cooked, immediately turn cake onto sugared paper, quickly peeling away the lining paper. Working fast, use serrated knife to cut away crisp edges from all sides of cake.

8 Using hands, gently roll cake loosely from one of the short sides; unroll, spread evenly with jam.

9 Roll cake again, from same short side, by lifting paper and using it to guide roll into shape. Place on wire rack to cool.

serving suggestion If preferred, jam roll can be served immediately, while still warm, with cream.

Mississippi mud cake

preparation time **10 minutes** (plus cooling time)
cooking time **1 hour 30 minutes** serves **12**

250g butter, chopped
150g dark eating chocolate, chopped
2 cups (440g) white sugar
1 cup (250ml) hot water
⅓ cup (80ml) whisky
1 tablespoon instant coffee powder
1½ cups (225g) plain flour
¼ cup (35g) self-raising flour
¼ cup (25g) cocoa powder
2 eggs, beaten lightly

1 Preheat oven to moderately slow. Grease 23cm-square slab pan, line base with baking paper; grease paper.
2 Combine butter, chocolate, sugar, the water, whisky and coffee in medium saucepan; stir over low heat until chocolate is melted and mixture is smooth, cool to lukewarm.
3 Stir in sifted flours and cocoa, then egg. Pour into prepared pan. Bake in moderately slow oven about 1¼ hours. Stand 10 minutes before turning onto wire rack to cool.

tip Store cake, covered, in the refrigerator for up to five days.

Simple chocolate cake

preparation time **15 minutes** cooking time **50 minutes** serves **10**

1 cup (250ml) water
1½ cups (330g) caster sugar
125g butter
2 tablespoons cocoa powder
½ teaspoon bicarbonate of soda
1½ cups (225g) self-raising flour
2 eggs

1 Grease deep 19cm-square cake pan, line base with baking paper.
2 Combine the water, sugar, butter, cocoa and soda in medium pan;
stir over heat, without boiling, until sugar dissolves. Bring to boil, then
reduce heat; simmer, uncovered, 5 minutes. Transfer mixture to large bowl;
cool 10 minutes.
3 Add flour and eggs to mixture; beat with electric mixer, on low speed,
until smooth. Pour mixture into prepared pan. Bake in moderate oven about
40 minutes. Stand cake in pan 10 minutes; turn onto wire rack to cool.

serving suggestion Serve chocolate cake dusted with cocoa powder.

Cinnamon teacake

preparation time **15 minutes** cooking time **30 minutes** serves **10**

60g butter, softened
1 teaspoon vanilla extract
⅔ cup (150g) caster sugar
1 egg
1 cup (150g) self-raising flour
⅓ cup (80ml) milk
10g butter, extra, melted
1 teaspoon ground cinnamon
1 tablespoon caster sugar, extra

1 Preheat oven to moderate. Grease deep 20cm-round cake pan; line base
with baking paper.
2 Beat softened butter, extract, sugar and egg in small bowl with electric
mixer for 5–10 minutes or until very light and fluffy.

3 Using wooden spoon, gently stir in sifted flour and milk. Spread mixture into prepared pan.
4 Bake cake in moderate oven about 30 minutes. Stand cake 5 minutes before turning, top up, onto wire rack; brush top with melted butter, sprinkle with combined cinnamon and extra sugar.

Upside-down toffee banana cake

preparation time **15 minutes** cooking time **55 minutes** serves **8**

You need two large overripe bananas (460g) to make 1 cup mashed banana.

1 cup (220g) caster sugar
1 cup (250ml) water
2 medium bananas (400g), sliced thinly
2 eggs, beaten lightly
²⁄₃ cup (160ml) vegetable oil
³⁄₄ cup (165g) firmly packed brown sugar
1 teaspoon vanilla extract
²⁄₃ cup (100g) plain flour
¹⁄₃ cup (50g) wholemeal self-raising flour
2 teaspoons mixed spice
1 teaspoon bicarbonate of soda
1 cup mashed banana

1 Preheat oven to moderate. Grease deep 22cm-round cake pan; line base with baking paper.
2 Stir caster sugar and the water in medium saucepan over heat, without boiling, until sugar dissolves; bring to a boil. Boil, uncovered, without stirring, about 10 minutes or until caramel in colour. Pour toffee into prepared pan; top with sliced banana.
3 Combine egg, oil, brown sugar and extract in medium bowl. Stir in sifted dry ingredients, then mashed banana; pour mixture into prepared pan. Bake, uncovered, in moderate oven about 40 minutes. Turn onto wire rack, peel off baking paper; turn cake, top up.

serving suggestion Serve cake warm or at room temperature with thick cream, if desired.

Pizza

preparation time **45 minutes** (plus standing time) cooking time **20 minutes**
makes **2 pizzas**

2 teaspoons (7g) dried yeast
1 teaspoon white sugar
½ teaspoon salt
¾ cup (180ml) warm water
2½ cups (375g) plain flour
2 tablespoons olive oil

1 Combine yeast, sugar, salt and the warm water in small bowl, cover; stand
in warm place about 20 minutes or until mixture is frothy.
2 Combine flour and oil in large bowl; stir in yeast mixture, mix to a soft
dough. Knead dough on floured surface about 5 minutes or until smooth and
elastic. Place dough in large oiled bowl, cover; stand in warm place about
1 hour or until dough doubles in size.
3 Meanwhile, preheat oven to very hot.
4 Turn dough onto floured surface; knead until smooth. Divide dough in half;
using rolling pin, flatten dough and roll each half out to a 32cm round.
5 Carefully lift each round onto oiled pizza pan or oven tray; cover each with
one of the toppings shown here. Bake, uncovered, in very hot oven 20 minutes.

Toppings
Supreme

This topping makes enough to cover **one pizza base.**

Using pastry brush, brush 1 teaspoon olive oil over pizza base. Place
2 tablespoons bottled tomato pasta sauce on base, using back of large spoon
to spread sauce all over base. Sprinkle ½ cup (50g) coarsely grated pizza
cheese over sauce; top with 10cm piece (40g) coarsely chopped cabanossi,
four slices (45g) coarsely chopped danish salami, ⅓ cup (65g) thinly sliced
red capsicum and ⅓ cup (30g) thinly sliced mushrooms. Sprinkle another
½ cup (50g) coarsely grated pizza cheese over pizza.

Vegetarian

This topping makes enough to cover **one pizza base.**

Using pastry brush, brush 1 teaspoon olive oil over pizza base. Place
2 tablespoons bottled tomato pasta sauce on base, using back of large spoon

to spread sauce all over base. Sprinkle ½ cup (50g) coarsely grated pizza cheese over sauce; top with ⅔ cup (130g) coarsely chopped drained bottled char-grilled capsicum, 1 tablespoon finely chopped seeded kalamata olives and ½ cup (75g) coarsely chopped semi-dried tomatoes. Sprinkle another ½ cup (50g) coarsely grated pizza cheese over pizza.

Chilli corn bread

preparation time **20 minutes** cooking time **1 hour** (plus cooling time) serves **10**

1 cup (150g) self-raising flour
1 teaspoon salt
1 cup (170g) polenta
½ cup (100g) kibbled rye
1 tablespoon brown sugar
1 teaspoon ground cumin
2 tablespoons chopped fresh flat-leaf parsley
1 teaspoon chopped fresh thyme
½ cup (60g) grated cheddar
310g can creamed corn
⅔ cup (90g) frozen corn kernels, thawed
⅔ cup (160ml) buttermilk
⅓ cup (80ml) milk
2 teaspoons sambal oelek
2 eggs, beaten lightly
50g butter, melted

1 Preheat oven to moderately hot. Oil deep 19cm-square cake pan; line base with baking paper.
2 Sift flour and salt into large bowl; stir in polenta, rye, sugar, cumin, herbs and cheese.
3 Combine remaining ingredients in medium bowl; stir into dry ingredients.
4 Spread mixture into prepared pan, bake in moderately hot oven about 1 hour. Stand, covered, 10 minutes before turning onto wire rack to cool.

tip Store bread in airtight container up to one week.

Onion focaccia

preparation time **25 minutes** (plus standing time) cooking time **25 minutes**
serves **4**

2 cups (300g) plain flour
½ teaspoon sea salt
2 teaspoons (7g) dry yeast
¼ cup (20g) grated parmesan
1 tablespoon chopped fresh rosemary
1 tablespoon chopped fresh sage leaves
2 teaspoons chopped parsley
3 tablespoons olive oil
1 cup (250ml) warm water
1 small brown onion (80g), finely sliced

1 Preheat oven to hot. Oil oven tray.
2 Place flour, salt, yeast, cheese and herbs in large bowl; stir in combined
2 tablespoons of oil and water; mix to a soft dough.
3 Turn dough onto floured surface; knead about 5 minutes or until dough
is smooth and elastic.
4 Place dough on prepared tray, press into 24cm round. Cover dough with
oiled plastic wrap, stand in warm place about 1 hour or until doubled in size.
5 Remove plastic wrap. Sprinkle dough with onion and sea salt, drizzle with
remaining oil; bake in hot oven about 25 minutes. Lift onto wire rack to cool.

Rosemary pumpkin bread

preparation time **20 minutes** cooking time **1 hour 40 minutes** serves **8**

*Polenta, or cornmeal, is a flour-like cereal made from dried maize; it is sold
ground in several different textures and is available at most supermarkets.*

500g pumpkin, diced into 1cm pieces
1 tablespoon vegetable oil
1 tablespoon finely chopped fresh rosemary
1¾ cups (260g) self-raising flour
¾ cup (125g) polenta
½ cup (40g) finely grated parmesan
2 eggs
1¼ cups (300g) sour cream
⅓ cup (55g) pepitas

1 Preheat oven to moderately hot. Oil 14cm x 21cm loaf pan; line base and long sides with baking paper.

2 Place combined pumpkin, oil and half the rosemary, in single layer, on oven tray; roast, uncovered, in moderately hot oven about 20 minutes or until pumpkin is tender. Cool 10 minutes; mash mixture in medium bowl. (Recipe can be made ahead to this stage. Cover; refrigerate overnight.)

3 Reduce oven temperature to moderate. Stir flour, polenta, cheese and remaining rosemary into pumpkin mixture. Whisk eggs and sour cream in medium jug; pour into mixture, stirring until just combined.

4 Spread mixture into prepared pan; top with pepitas, pressing gently into surface. Cover with piece of foil folded with a pleat; bake in moderate oven 1 hour. Remove foil; bake in moderate oven about 20 minutes. Stand in pan 5 minutes; turn onto wire rack to cool.

tip Store bread in airtight container up to one week.

Chapatis

Preparation time **25 minutes** cooking time **15 minutes** makes **14**

Chapatis need to be cooked over a flame to achieve the blistered appearance.

1 cup (150g) white plain flour
1 cup (160g) wholemeal plain flour
1 teaspoon salt
20g unsalted butter
¾ cup (180ml) warm water, approximately

1 Sift flours and salt into large bowl, rub in butter. Add enough of the warm water to mix to a firm dough. Turn dough onto floured surface; knead about 10 minutes, working in about an extra ¼ cup (35g) plain white flour. Cover dough with cloth, stand 1 hour. Divide into 14 portions. Roll portions on floured surface into 20cm rounds; cover with cloth, stand 10 minutes before cooking.

2 Heat griddle or heavy-base frying pan until very hot, cook one round at a time, about 30 seconds on first side or until round just begins to colour; remove from pan.

3 Place uncooked side of chapati directly over medium flame, checking frequently until chapati begins to blister. Repeat with remaining rounds. Wrap cooked chapatis in a cloth to keep warm.

BISCUITS AND SLICES

No-bake chocolate slice

preparation time **20 minutes** (plus refrigeration time) makes about **24**

200g packet white marshmallows
1 tablespoon water
90g butter, chopped
200g dark eating chocolate, chopped coarsely
125g plain sweet biscuits, chopped coarsely
½ cup (125g) halved glacé cherries
½ cup (75g) toasted hazelnuts
½ cup (50g) walnuts
200g dark eating chocolate, melted, extra
60g butter, melted, extra

1 Grease two 8cm x 25cm bar pans; line base and two long sides with baking paper, extending 2cm over edge.
2 Combine marshmallows, the water and butter in medium saucepan. Stir constantly over low heat until marshmallows are melted. Remove saucepan from heat. Add chocolate; stir until melted.
3 Add biscuits, cherries and nuts to marshmallow mixture; stir gently until ingredients are combined. Spread mixture evenly into prepared pans (do not crush biscuits). Cover; refrigerate 1 hour.
4 Combine extra chocolate and extra butter; spread mixture evenly over slices. Refrigerate 1 hour or until firm. Remove slices from pans. Peel away paper; cut each slice into 12 pieces.

tips The slices can be made a week ahead and kept, covered, in the refrigerator. Pecans can be used instead of walnuts, if preferred.

Peanut butter choc chunk cookies

preparation time **20 minutes** cooking time **15 minutes** makes about **25**

185g butter, chopped
1 cup (200g) firmly packed brown sugar
½ cup (100g) caster sugar
1½ cups (225g) self-raising flour
½ cup (75g) plain flour
1 cup (150g) coarsely chopped toasted peanuts
2 eggs, beaten lightly
1 cup (280g) crunchy peanut butter
1 cup (200g) dark chocolate chips

1 Preheat oven to moderate.
2 Melt butter; cool. Meanwhile, combine sugars, sifted flours and peanuts in large bowl. Add combined butter, egg and peanut butter; mix to soft dough. Stir in chocolate chips.
3 Place 2 level tablespoons of biscuit dough about 6cm apart on oven trays lined with baking paper. Bake in moderate oven about 15 minutes or until browned lightly. For chewier cookies, bake few minutes less; for crisp cookies, bake few minutes longer. Cool on trays.

Butterscotch buttons

preparation time **15 minutes** cooking time **20 minutes** makes about **60**

125g butter
1 teaspoon vanilla essence
½ cup (100g) firmly packed brown sugar
1 tablespoon golden syrup
1¼ cups (185g) self-raising flour

1 Preheat oven to slow.
2 Beat butter, essence, sugar and golden syrup in small bowl with electric mixer until light and fluffy; stir in sifted flour. Roll level teaspoons of mixture into balls, place about 5cm apart on greased oven trays, flatten slightly with fork.
3 Bake in slow oven about 20 minutes or until firm. Cool on wire racks.

Coconut macaroons

preparation time **15 minutes** cooking time **45 minutes** makes **18**

1 egg, separated
1 egg yolk
¼ cup (55g) caster sugar
1⅔ cups (120g) shredded coconut

1 Preheat oven to slow.
2 Beat yolks and sugar in small bowl until creamy; stir in coconut.
3 Beat egg white in small bowl until firm peaks form; fold gently into coconut mixture.
4 Drop heaped teaspoons of mixture onto greased oven trays. Bake in slow oven 15 minutes. Reduce heat to very slow; bake further 30 minutes or until macaroons are golden brown; loosen, cool on trays.

tip Store macaroons in an airtight container up to three weeks; macaroons are also suitable to freeze.

Chocolate rum and raisin slice

preparation time **15 minutes** cooking time **30 minutes** (plus cooling time) makes about **15**

125g butter, chopped
200g dark eating chocolate, chopped
½ cup (110g) caster sugar
1 cup (170g) coarsely chopped raisins
2 eggs, beaten lightly
1½ cups (225g) plain flour
1 tablespoon dark rum

1 Preheat oven to moderately slow. Grease 20cm x 30cm lamington pan.
2 Combine butter, chocolate, sugar and raisins in medium saucepan; stir over low heat until chocolate is melted. Cool to room temperature. Stir in remaining ingredients, mix well; spread mixture into prepared pan.
3 Bake in moderately slow oven about 30 minutes or until just firm; cool in pan.

tip This recipe can be made a week ahead; store slices in an airtight container.

Shortbread

preparation time **15 minutes** cooking time **30 minutes** (plus cooling time)
makes **24 wedges**

250g butter, at room temperature
⅓ cup (75g) caster sugar
2 cups (300g) plain flour
½ cup (75g) rice flour or ground rice

1 Preheat oven to slow.
2 Beat butter and sugar in small bowl with electric mixer until combined. Add large spoonfuls of sifted flours to butter mixture, beating after each addition.
3 Press ingredients together gently; knead on floured surface until smooth.
4 Divide dough into two portions; shape portions into 18cm rounds. Place rounds on greased oven trays; mark each round into 12 wedges, prick with fork. Pinch a decorative edge with floured fingers.
5 Bake in slow oven about 30 minutes. Stand 10 minutes before transferring to wire rack to cool. Cut when cold.

tip Shortbread can be made a month ahead and stored in an airtight container; it is also suitable to freeze.

No-bowl choc-bit slice

preparation time **10 minutes** cooking time **30 minutes** makes about **18**

90g butter, melted
1 cup (100g) plain sweet biscuit crumbs
1½ cups (285g) dark choc chips
1 cup (70g) shredded coconut
1 cup (140g) crushed mixed nuts
395g can sweetened condensed milk

1 Preheat oven to moderate. Grease 23cm-square slab pan; line base and sides with baking paper.
2 Pour butter into prepared pan; sprinkle evenly with biscuit crumbs, choc chips, coconut and nuts. Drizzle with condensed milk.
3 Bake in moderate oven about 30 minutes. Cool in pan; cut into slices.

tip The slices can be made a week ahead and kept, covered, in the refrigerator.

Snickerdoodles

preparation time **25 minutes** (plus refrigeration time)
cooking time **15 minutes** makes **50**

250g butter, softened
½ cup (110g) firmly packed brown sugar
1 cup (220g) caster sugar
2 eggs
2¾ cups (410g) plain flour
1 teaspoon bicarbonate of soda
½ teaspoon ground nutmeg
1 tablespoon caster sugar, extra
2 teaspoons ground cinnamon

1 Beat butter and sugars in small bowl with electric mixer until light and fluffy. Add eggs, one at a time, beating until just combined. Transfer to large bowl.
2 Stir combined sifted flour, soda and nutmeg, in two batches, into egg mixture. Cover; refrigerate dough 30 minutes.
3 Meanwhile, preheat oven to moderate.
4 Combine extra caster sugar and cinnamon in small shallow bowl. Roll level tablespoons of dough into balls; roll balls in cinnamon sugar. Place balls on ungreased oven trays, 7cm apart; bake, uncovered, in moderate oven about 12 minutes. Cool biscuits on trays.

tip Store snickerdoodles in an airtight container up to three weeks.

Greek almond biscuits

preparation time **30 minutes** cooking time **15 minutes** makes **25**

3 cups (375g) almond meal
1 cup (220g) caster sugar
3 drops almond essence
3 egg whites, beaten lightly
1 cup (80g) flaked almonds

1 Preheat oven to moderate.
2 Combine almond meal, sugar and essence in large bowl. Add egg white; stir until mixture forms a firm paste.

3 Roll level tablespoons of mixture in almonds; roll into 8cm logs. Press on any remaining almonds. Shape logs to form crescents.
4 Place on oven trays lined with baking paper; bake in moderate oven about 15 minutes or until browned lightly. Cool on trays.

tip Store biscuits in an airtight container up to one week; suitable to freeze up to three months.

Florentines

preparation time **25 minutes** cooking time **10 minutes** (plus cooling time)
makes **18**

¾ cup (120g) sultanas
2 cups (60g) corn flakes
¾ cup (105g) roasted peanuts, chopped
½ cup (125g) chopped red glacé cherries
⅔ cup (160ml) sweetened condensed milk
150g dark eating chocolate, melted

1 Preheat oven to moderate.
2 Combine sultanas, corn flakes, peanuts, cherries and milk in bowl; mix well.
3 Place 1½-tablespoon portions of mixture about 5cm apart on oven trays lined with baking paper; bake in moderate oven about 10 minutes or until lightly browned. Cool on trays.
4 Spread base of each biscuit with chocolate. Make wavy lines in chocolate with fork just before chocolate sets.

tips Florentines can be made a month ahead and stored, covered, in the refrigerator; they are also suitable to freeze. To melt chocolate, choose a heatproof bowl that just fits inside a small saucepan; add enough water to pan to come almost to the level of the bottom of the bowl, then bring water to a boil. Chop chocolate roughly, and place in bowl over the pan of boiling water. Remove pan from heat, and stir constantly until chocolate is melted.

Fruity white chocolate bars

preparation time **15 minutes** cooking time **45 minutes** makes about **16**

²/₃ cup (90g) slivered almonds
1¼ cups (210g) brazil nuts, coarsely chopped
1½ cups (135g) desiccated coconut
1 cup (150g) chopped dried apricots
1 cup (150g) dried currants
¼ cup (35g) plain flour
250g white chocolate, melted
½ cup (160g) apricot jam
½ cup (180g) honey
1 tablespoon icing sugar

1 Preheat oven to moderately slow. Lightly grease 19cm x 29cm rectangular slice pan; cover base with baking paper.
2 Combine nuts, coconut, fruit and flour in large bowl. Stir in combined hot chocolate, sieved jam and honey. Spread evenly into prepared pan; bake in moderately slow oven 45 minutes. Cool in pan before cutting into pieces.

tip These bars can be made a week ahead and kept, covered, in the refrigerator; bars can also be frozen for up to two months.

Chocolate chip cookies

preparation time **40 minutes** (plus refrigeration time)
cooking time **15 minutes** makes **40**

250g butter, softened
¾ cup (165g) white sugar
¾ cup (165g) firmly packed brown sugar
1 egg
2¼ cups (335g) plain flour
1 teaspoon bicarbonate of soda
300g dark cooking chocolate, chopped coarsely

1 Preheat oven to moderate.
2 Beat butter, sugars and egg in small bowl with electric mixer until light and fluffy. Transfer to large bowl.
3 Stir combined sifted flour and soda, in two batches, into egg mixture.

Stir in chocolate, cover; refrigerate 1 hour.

4 Roll level tablespoons of dough into balls; place on greased oven trays 3cm apart. Bake, uncovered, in moderate oven about 12 minutes. Cool

Tangy lemon squares

preparation time **15 minutes** cooking time **20 minutes** makes about **16**

125g butter
¼ cup (40g) icing sugar
1 ¼ cups (185g) plain flour
3 eggs
1 cup (220g) caster sugar
2 teaspoons grated lemon rind
½ cup (125ml) lemon juice

1 Preheat oven to moderate. Grease 23cm-square slab pan; line base and two opposite sides of pan with baking paper.

2 Beat butter and icing sugar in small bowl with electric mixer until smooth. Stir in 1 cup (150g) of the flour. Press mixture over base of prepared pan. Bake in moderate oven about 15 minutes or until browned lightly.

3 Place eggs, caster sugar, remaining flour, rind and juice in medium bowl; whisk until combined. Pour egg mixture over hot base. Bake in moderate oven about 20 minutes or until firm. Cool in pan on wire rack.

4 Lift slice from pan and cut into squares.

serving suggestion Dust squares with sifted icing sugar to serve.

tip The squares can be made three days ahead and kept, covered, in the refrigerator.

Snickers rocky road

preparation time **15 minutes** (plus refrigeration time)
cooking time **5 minutes** makes **54 squares**

4 x 60g snickers bars, chopped coarsely
1 cup (35g) rice bubbles
150g toasted marshmallows, chopped coarsely
1 cup (150g) roasted unsalted peanuts
400g milk eating chocolate, chopped coarsely
2 teaspoons vegetable oil

1 Grease 19cm x 29cm slice pan. Line base and two long sides with baking paper, extending paper 2cm above sides of pan.
2 Combine snickers, rice bubbles, marshmallows and nuts in large bowl. Stir chocolate and oil in small saucepan over low heat until smooth. Cool 5 minutes.
3 Pour chocolate mixture into snickers mixture; mix until well combined. Spoon rocky road mixture into prepared pan; refrigerate, covered, about 30 minutes or until set. Remove from pan, trim edges of mixture; cut into 3cm squares. Store, covered, in refrigerator.

Triple choc brownies

Preparation time **25 minutes** cooking time **35 minutes** makes **12**

125g cold butter, chopped
200g dark cooking chocolate, chopped
½ cup (110g) caster sugar
2 eggs, lightly beaten
1¼ cups (185g) plain flour
150g white eating chocolate, chopped
100g milk eating chocolate, chopped

1 Preheat oven to moderate. Grease deep 19cm square cake pan; line base and sides with baking paper.
2 Combine butter and dark chocolate in medium pan; stir over low heat until melted. Cool 10 minutes. Stir in sugar and egg, then sifted flour; mix in remaining chocolate. Spread mixture into prepared pan.
3 Bake in moderate oven about 35 minutes or until mixture is firm to touch. Cool in pan before cutting.

Fruit chews

preparation time **25 minutes** cooking time **45 minutes** makes about **18**

⅓ cup (75g) firmly packed brown sugar
90g butter
1¼ cups (185g) plain flour
1 egg yolk

Topping
2 eggs
1 cup (220g) firmly packed brown sugar
⅓ cup (50g) self-raising flour
½ cup (85g) raisins
¾ cup (120g) sultanas
1¼ cups (185g) roasted unsalted peanuts
1 cup (90g) desiccated coconut

1 Preheat oven to moderate. Grease 20cm x 30cm lamington pan; line base and two long sides with baking paper, extending 2cm above edge of pan.
2 Combine sugar and butter in medium saucepan; stir over medium heat until butter is melted. Stir in sifted flour and egg yolk. Press mixture over base of prepared pan. Bake in moderate oven about 10 minutes or until browned lightly; cool.
3 Make topping.
4 Spread topping over cold base; bake in moderate oven about 30 minutes or until browned lightly. Cool in pan before cutting into pieces.

Topping Beat eggs and sugar in small bowl with electric mixer until changed to lighter colour and thickened slightly; fold in sifted flour. Transfer mixture to large bowl; stir in remaining ingredients.

tip This recipe can be made up to a week ahead; store fruit chews in an airtight container.

DRINKS

Sugar syrup

preparation time **5 minutes**   cooking time **10 minutes**   makes **about 350ml**

Sugar syrup, often called gomme syrup, is used for sweetening drinks.

1 cup (220g) white sugar
1 cup (250ml) water

1 Place sugar and the water in small saucepan; stir over low heat, without boiling, until sugar dissolves.
2 Bring syrup to a boil, reduce heat; simmer, uncovered, without stirring, for 5 minutes. Remove from heat, cool.

tip   Store syrup in an airtight container in the refrigerator up to two months.

Long island iced tea

preparation time **10 minutes**   serves **1**

1 cup ice cubes
30ml vodka
30ml tequila
30ml bacardi
30ml gin
15ml cointreau
15ml fresh lemon juice
15ml sugar syrup (see recipe above)
30ml cola

1 Place ice in 300ml highball glass; add vodka, tequila, bacardi, gin and cointreau, one after the other.
2 Add juice and syrup, top with cola; stir.

serving suggestion   Serve with twist of lemon rind, mint leaves, swizzle stick and straw.

Cosmopolitan

preparation time **5 minutes** serves **1**

1 cup ice cubes
10ml citron vodka
20ml vodka
30ml cointreau
60ml cranberry juice
10ml fresh lime juice

1 Combine ingredients in cocktail shaker; shake vigorously.
2 Strain into chilled 150ml cocktail glass.

serving suggestion Serve with twist of lime rind.

Piña colada

preparation time **10 minutes** serves **1**

1 cup ice cubes
45ml bacardi
120ml bottled pineapple juice
30ml coconut cream
15ml malibu
15ml sugar syrup (see p362)

1 Combine ingredients in jug of blender; blend on high speed until smooth.
2 Pour into 400ml tulip-shaped glass.

Traditional daiquiri

preparation time **5 minutes** serves **1**

1 cup ice cubes
45ml bacardi
30ml fresh lime juice
15ml sugar syrup (see p362)

1 Combine ingredients in cocktail shaker; shake vigorously.
2 Strain into 150ml cocktail glass.

Dry martini

preparation time **5 minutes** serves **1**

45ml gin
15ml dry vermouth
1 cup ice cubes

1 Combine ingredients in cocktail shaker; shake vigorously.
2 Strain into chilled 90ml martini glass.

serving suggestion Serve topped with caperberry.

Classic tom collins

preparation time: **5 minutes** serves **1**

60ml gin
80ml lemon juice
2 teaspoons icing sugar
80ml soda water
¼ cup ice cubes

1 Place ingredients in chilled 340ml highball glass; stir to combine.

serving suggestion Serve topped with maraschino cherry.

Bellini

preparation time **5 minutes** serves **8**

2 medium peaches (300g), chopped coarsely
½ cup (125ml) peach schnapps
750ml chilled champagne
8 sugar cubes

1 Blend or process peach and schnapps until smooth. Combine peach mixture with champagne in large jug.
2 Place one sugar cube in each of eight champagne glasses; top with bellini mixture.

Pimm's with lemonade

preparation time **10 minutes** serves **6**

Ice cubes
1 ¼ cups (300ml) pimm's
150g strawberries, sliced
¼ cup firmly packed fresh mint leaves
100g piece telegraph cucumber, sliced
1 litre lemonade or dry ginger ale, chilled

1 Combine ice, pimm's, strawberries, mint and cucumber in large jug; slowly add lemonade.
2 Add a little more ice, if necessary; serve immediately

tips Strawberries and cucumber can be sliced several hours ahead. This recipe is best made just before serving.

Cucumber, celery, apple and spinach juice

preparation time **10 minutes** (plus refrigeration time) makes **1 litre**

1 telegraph cucumber (400g), chopped coarsely
2 trimmed celery stalks (200g), chopped coarsely
2 large apples (400g), cored, chopped coarsely
50g baby spinach leaves, stems removed
1 cup (250ml) water
⅓ cup firmly packed fresh mint leaves

1 Blend or process ingredients, in batches, until pureed; strain through coarse sieve into large jug.
2 Refrigerate, covered, until cold.

Lime and mint spritzer

preparation time **5 minutes** cooking time **5 minutes** serves **8**

½ cup sugar syrup (see p362)
1 cup (250ml) lime juice
1.25 litres (5 cups) chilled sparkling mineral water
¼ cup coarsely chopped fresh mint

1 Combine syrup in large jug with juice, mineral water and mint.
2 Serve immediately, with ice.

Tomato, carrot and red capsicum juice

preparation time **10 minutes** (plus refrigeration time) makes **1 litre**

1 medium red capsicum (250g), chopped coarsely
4 medium tomatoes (300g), chopped coarsely
2 medium carrots (240g), chopped coarsely
⅓ cup firmly packed fresh flat-leaf parsley leaves
1 cup (250ml) water
Dash tabasco

1 Blend or process ingredients, in batches, until pureed; strain through coarse sieve into large jug.
2 Stir in tabasco; refrigerate, covered, until cold.

Mixed berry smoothie

preparation time **5 minutes** makes **1 litre**

250ml frozen low-fat strawberry yogurt, softened slightly
1 ⅓ cups (200g) frozen mixed berries
3 cups (750ml) milk

1 Blend or process ingredients, in batches, until smooth. Serve immediately.

Banana passionfruit soy smoothie

preparation time **10 minutes** (plus refrigeration time) makes **1 litre**

You need about six passionfruit for this recipe.

½ cup (125ml) passionfruit pulp
2 cups (500ml) soy milk
2 medium ripe bananas (400g), chopped coarsely

1 Strain pulp through sieve into small bowl; reserve liquid and seeds.
2 Blend or process passionfruit liquid, milk and banana, in batches, until smooth. Pour smoothie into large jug; stir in reserved seeds.
3 Refrigerate, covered, until cold.

Grapefruit and blood orange juice

preparation time **5 minutes** serves **1**

2 small blood oranges (360g)
1 small grapefruit (350g)

1 Juice oranges and grapefruit on citrus squeezer; pour into glass.

Cardamom and chamomile tea

Preparation time **5 minutes** cooking time **10 minutes** makes **1 litre**

2 tablespoons loose-leafed chamomile tea
4 cardamom pods, bruised
1 litre (4 cups) water

1 Combine ingredients in small saucepan. Bring to a boil then reduce heat; simmer, uncovered, 5 minutes. Cool 5 minutes; strain.

Spiced iced coffee milkshake

preparation time **10 minutes** makes **1 litre**

¼ cup (20g) ground espresso coffee
¾ cup (180ml) boiling water
2 cardamom pods, bruised
¼ teaspoon ground cinnamon
1 tablespoon brown sugar
3 scoops (375ml) vanilla ice-cream
2½ cups (625ml) milk

1 Place coffee then the boiling water in coffee plunger; stand 2 minutes before plunging. Pour coffee into small heatproof bowl with cardamom, cinnamon and sugar. Stir to dissolve sugar; cool 10 minutes.
2 Strain coffee mixture through fine sieve into blender or processor; process with ice-cream and milk until smooth. Serve immediately.

Pineapple orange frappé

preparation time **10 minutes** makes **1 litre**

1 medium pineapple (1.25kg), chopped coarsely
½ cup (125ml) orange juice
3 cups crushed ice
1 tablespoon finely grated orange rind

1 Blend or process pineapple and juice, in batches, until smooth.
2 Pour into large jug with crushed ice and rind; stir to combine then serve.

Strawberry and papaya juice

preparation time **5 minutes** serves **1**

4 strawberries (80g)
80g papaya
½ cup (125ml) water

1 Blend or process ingredients until smooth; pour into glass.

Strawberry, honey and soy smoothie

preparation time **5 minutes** serves **1**

6 strawberries (120g)
½ cup (125ml) soy milk
1 teaspoon honey

1 Blend or process ingredients until smooth; pour into glass.

Apple and melon lassie

preparation time **5 minutes** serves **4**

700g honeydew melon, chopped coarsely
2 cups (500ml) clear apple juice
500g yogurt
2 cups crushed ice
½ cup firmly packed fresh mint leaves
4cm piece fresh ginger (20g), grated
1 cup (250ml) water

1 Blend or process ingredients, in batches, until almost smooth.
2 Combine batches in large jug. Serve immediately.

GLOSSARY

ALLSPICE Also known as pimento or Jamaican pepper, allspice tastes like a combination of nutmeg, cumin, clove and cinnamon. Available from most supermarkets and specialty spice stores.

ALMONDS

Blanched Brown skins removed.

Meal Also known as ground almonds; nuts are powdered to a coarse flour-like texture, for use in baking or as a thickening agent

Slivered Small pieces cut lengthways.

ANCHOVY FILLETS Salty, strong-flavoured small fish; most commonly available canned. Used in salads, vegetable dishes, pasta and on pizza.

ANISEED Also called anise or sweet cumin. Dried, they have a strong licorice flavour. Available whole and as ground seeds.

APRICOTS Used in sweet and savoury dishes; have a velvety, golden-orange skin and aromatic sweet flesh. Also dried.

ARROWROOT A starch made from the rhizome of a Central American plant, used mostly for thickening. Cornflour can be used but will not give as clear a glaze.

ASPARAGUS These fragile shoots are a member of the lily family; cook with care to avoid damaging the tips.

AVOCADO A mild-flavoured fruit with soft, buttery flesh. Best eaten raw, when ripe. Test for ripeness by gently pressing the stem end; it should feel tender or give slightly.

BACARDI Colourless white rum distilled from sugar cane; a product of Puerto Rico.

BACON RASHERS Also known as bacon slices; from cured and smoked pork side.

BASIL An aromatic herb; the most commonly used is sweet basil.

BEANS

Black Also called turtle beans, black beans; a common ingredient in Caribbean and Latin American dishes. Available from health food stores and gourmet food outlets.

Black-eyed Also known as black-eyed peas, are the dried seed of a variant of the snake or yard bean.

Borlotti Also called roman beans; can be eaten fresh or dried. Borlotti can also substitute for pinto beans because of the similarity in appearance – both are pale pink or beige with darker red spots.

Broad Also known as fava or windsor; are available dried, fresh, canned and frozen. Fresh and frozen, they are best peeled twice (discard the outer long green pod and beige-green tough inner shell).

Cannellini Small white bean similar in appearance and flavour to great northern and navy or haricot beans. Sometimes sold as butter beans.

Green Sometimes called french or string beans; are consumed pod and all.

Salted black Also called chinese black beans; are fermented and salted soy beans available in cans and jars. Used most often in Asian cooking; chop before, or mash during, cooking to release flavour. Available from Asian food stores.

Sprouts Also known as bean shoots, are tender new growths of assorted beans and seeds. The most common are mung bean, soy bean, alfalfa and snow pea sprouts.

BEETROOT Also known as beets or red beets; firm, round root vegetable.

BICARBONATE OF SODA Also known as baking soda.

BOK CHOY Also called bak choy or chinese chard; has a fresh, mild mustard taste. One of the most commonly used Asian greens, its stems and leaves are stir-fried, braised or stirred through soup. Available from supermarkets and greengrocers.

BREADCRUMBS

Packaged Fine-textured, crunchy, purchased, white breadcrumbs.

Stale One- or two-day-old pieces of bread, grated, blended or processed into crumbs.

BRIOCHE Rich French yeast-risen bread made with butter and eggs. Available from pâtisseries or specialty bread shops.

BROCCOLINI A cross between broccoli and chinese kale; is milder and sweeter than broccoli. Each long stem is topped by a loose floret that looks like broccoli, and is completely edible. Available from some supermarkets and greengrocers.

BURGHUL Also known as bulgur wheat; hulled steamed wheat kernels, once dried are crushed into various size grains.

BUTTER Use salted or unsalted (sweet) butter; 125g is equal to 1 stick butter.

CAJUN SEASONING A packaged blend of assorted herbs and spices which can include paprika, basil, onion, fennel, thyme, cayenne and tarragon.

CAPERS The grey-green buds of a warm climate shrub; sold either dried and salted or pickled in vinegar brine.

CAPSICUM Also called bell pepper; available red, green, yellow or orange or purplish black. Seeds and membranes should be discarded before use.

CARDAMOM Native to India and used in its cuisine; belonging to the ginger family, it attains a sweet yet spicy flavour. Available in pod, seed or ground form from most supermarkets and spice stores.

CARAWAY SEEDS A member of the parsley family, caraway seeds have a nutty, anise-like flavour. Available from most supermarkets and spice stores.

CHEESE

Bocconcini Fresh, walnut-sized baby mozzarella; a delicate, semi-soft, white cheese traditionally made in Italy from buffalo milk. Spoils rapidly so must be refrigerated, in brine, for 1-2 days at most.

Fetta Greek in origin; a crumbly goat- or sheep-milk cheese with a sharp salty taste.

Gorgonzola A creamy Italian blue cheese with a mild, sweet taste. Available from some supermarkets and delicatessens.

Gruyere A firm, cow-milk Swiss cheese with small holes and a nutty, slightly salty flavour. Emmental or appenzeller can be used as a substitute. Available from some supermarkets and delicatessens.

Haloumi A firm, cream-coloured sheep-milk cheese matured in brine; has a minty, salty fetta flavour. Available from Middle Eastern food stores and supermarkets.

Mozzarella soft, spun-curd cheese; traditionally made from water buffalo milk. It has a low melting point and wonderfully elastic texture when heated and is used to add texture rather than flavour.

Parmesan Also known as parmigiano; is a hard, grainy, cow-milk cheese. The curd is salted in brine for a month, then aged for up to two years in humid conditions.

Pecorino The generic Italian name for sheep-milk cheese. A hard, white to pale yellow cheese, matured for 8-12 months. If unavailable, use parmesan.

Pizza cheese A commercial blend of varying proportions of processed grated mozzarella, cheddar and parmesan.

Ricotta Soft white cow-milk cheese, roughly translated as 'cooked again'; made from whey, a by-product of other cheese making, to which fresh milk and acid are added. Ricotta is a sweet, moist cheese with a fat content of around 8.5% and a slightly grainy texture.

CHERMOULLA A Moroccan blend of fresh herbs, spices and condiments, chermoulla is traditionally used for preserving or seasoning meat and fish.

CHERVIL While this aromatic feathery green herb tastes somewhat like a blend of fennel and celery, it's a member of the carrot family. Leaves are traditionally used; roots are also edible. Available both fresh and dried but has the best flavour when fresh. Chervil goes well with cream and eggs, white fish and chicken.

CHICKPEAS Also known as hummus, garbanzos or channa; an irregularly round, sandy-coloured legume.

CHILLI

Dried flakes Deep-red, dehydrated chilli slices and whole seeds.

Green Generally unripened thai chillies but sometimes different varieties that are ripe when green, such as habanero, poblano or serrano chillies.

Thai red Small, hot and red in colour.

CHINESE CABBAGE Also known as peking cabbage, wong bok or petsai. Elongated in shape with pale green, crinkly leaves. Can be shredded or chopped and eaten raw or braised, steamed or stir-fried. Available from supermarkets and greengrocers.

CHINESE COOKING WINE A clear distillation of fermented rice, water and salt; 29.5% alcohol by volume. Used for marinades and as a sauce ingredient. Available from most Asian food stores.

CHIVES Related to the onion and leek; has a subtle onion flavour.

CHOCOLATE

Compound For dipping and coating.

Dark cooking We used premium quality dark cooking chocolate rather than compound.

Dark eating Made of cocoa liquor, cocoa butter and sugar.

CHOCOLATE HAZELNUT SPREAD Also known as Nutella.

CHORIZO A sausage originally from Spain; made of coarsely ground pork and highly seasoned with garlic and chillies. Available from most delicatessens.

CHOY SUM also known as pakaukeio or flowering cabbage, choy sum is a member of the bok choy family. Its long stems, pale green leaves and yellow flowers, is eaten, stems and all, steamed or sitr-fried.

CINNAMON STICK Dried inner bark of the shoots of the cinnamon tree.

COCOA POWDER Dried, unsweetened, roasted then ground cocoa beans.

COCONUT

Cream Is obtained commercially from the first pressing of the coconut flesh, without the addition of water; the second pressing (less rich) is sold as milk. Available in cans and cartons at supermarkets.

Desiccated Unsweetened, concentrated, dried finely shredded coconut flesh.

Flaked Dried flaked coconut flesh.

Milk Diluted liquid from the second pressing from the white flesh of a mature coconut, not the juice inside (coconut water). Available in cans and cartons.

COINTREAU Citrus-flavoured liqueur.

CORIANDER Also called cilantro or chinese parsley; bright-green-leafed herb with a pungent flavour. Often stirred into or sprinkled over a dish just before serving. Also available ground.

CORNFLOUR Also called cornstarch; used as a thickening agent in cooking.

COUSCOUS A fine, grain-like cereal product, originally from North Africa, made from semolina. Couscous can be used in salads, as a base for stews or as a dessert mixed with sugar, nuts and dried fruit. Available from most supermarkets and Middle Eastern food stores.

CREAM We used fresh pouring cream (or pure cream). It has no additives, and contains a minimum fat content of 35%.

Thickened A whipping cream that contains a thickener. Has a minimum fat content of 35%.

CREAM CHEESE Commonly known as Philadelphia or Philly cheese. A soft, cow-milk cheese with a fat content of at least 33%. Available from supermarkets.

CREME FRAICHE A French variation of sour cream; is a mildly acidic, high fat, slightly nutty tasting thick cream. Crème fraîche can be used interchangeably with sour cream in some recipes; the former can also be whipped like cream and does not split or curdle when boiled. Available from most supermarkets and delicatessens.

CUCUMBER, LEBANESE Short, slender and thin-skinned; this variety is also known as the European or burpless cucumber.

CUMIN Also known as zeera or comino; is the dried seed of a plant having a spicy, nutty flavour. Available in seed form or dried and ground, from supermarkets.

CURRY POWDER A blend of ground spices; can consist of some of the following in varying proportions: dried chilli, cinnamon, cumin, coriander, fennel, fenugreek, mace, cardamom and turmeric. Available in mild or hot varieties.

CUSTARD POWDER Instant mixture used to make pouring custard; similar to North American instant pudding mixes.

DILL Green-coloured herb with feathery leaves and tiny green-yellow flowers. Commonly used in fish and egg dishes or finely chopped in salads.

EGGPLANT Also known as aubergine.

EGGS Some recipes in this book call for raw or barely cooked eggs; exercise caution if there is a salmonella problem in your area.

FENNEL Also called finocchio or bulb fennel; also the name of the dried licorice-flavoured seeds. Eaten raw, braised, fried, roasted or stewed, it is mildly sweet and has a subtle licorice-like flavour. Fronds and top shoots are usually discarded and the bulb trimmed at the base. A large fennel bulb can be as big as a grapefruit, while baby fennel can be slightly flat and weigh as little as 100g.

FIG Small, soft, pear-shaped fruit with a sweet pulpy flesh full of tiny edible seeds. Also available dried.

FIRM WHITE FISH Means non-oily fish. This category includes bream, flathead, whiting, snapper, jewfish and ling. Redfish also comes into this category.

FIVE-SPICE POWDER A fragrant ground mixture of cassia, clove, star anise, sichuan pepper and fennel seeds, five-spice, also known as chinese five-spice, can be used as a seasoning for stir-fries or as a rub for meats. Available from most supermarkets, Asian food stores or specialty spice stores.

FLOUR

Besan A fine, powdery flour made from dried ground chickpeas. Available from Asian and health food stores.

Plain An all-purpose wheat flour.

Self-raising Plain flour sifted with baking powder in the proportion of 1 cup flour to 2 teaspoons baking powder.

FRESH HERBS We have specified when to use fresh or dried (not ground) herbs in the proportion of 1:4; use 1 teaspoon dried herbs instead of 4 teaspoons (1 tablespoon) chopped fresh herbs.

FRIED SHALLOTS Sprinkled over just-cooked food or served as a condiment, they provide a crunchy finish to a salad, stir-fry or curry. Once opened, store for months in a tightly sealed glass jar. Available from Asian food stores.

GALANGAL Also known as ka, galangal is a rhizome with a hot ginger-citrusy flavour; used similarly to ginger. Fresh ginger can be usen instead but the flavour will not be the same. Available from some greengrocers and Asian food stores.

GARAM MASALA A blend of spices, originating in Northern India; consists of cardamom, cinnamon, coriander, cloves, fennel and cumin, in varying proportions, roasted and ground together. Available from some supermarkets, Indian food stores and specialty spice stores.

GELATINE We used powdered gelatine; also available in sheets called leaf gelatine.

GHEE A clarified butter with the milk solids removed. Can be heated to a high temperature without burning, so is good for deep-frying. Available from Middle Eastern and Indian food stores.

GINGER

Fresh Also known as green or root ginger; is the thick gnarled root of a tropical plant. Can be kept peeled, covered with dry sherry in a jar and refrigerated, or frozen in an airtight container.

Ground Also called powdered ginger; used as a flavouring in cakes, pies and puddings but not instead of fresh ginger.

GLUCOSE SYRUP Also called liquid glucose, is made from wheat starch; used in jam and confectionery. Available from health food stores and supermarkets.

GOLDEN SYRUP A by-product of refined sugarcane; pure maple syrup or honey can be substituted.

GRAPEFRUIT So named because they grow in clusters; is the largest citrus fruit. A pink-fleshed version is also available.

HAZELNUT Also known as filberts; plump, grape-size, rich, sweet nut with a brown inedible skin. Remove skin by rubbing heated nuts together in a tea towel.

Meal Also known as ground hazelnuts.

HUMMUS A Middle Eastern salad or dip made from softened dried chickpeas, garlic, lemon juice and tahini (sesame seed paste); can be purchased, ready-made, from most delicatessens and supermarkets.

HORSERADISH A plant grown for its pungent, spicy roots; they are generally grated and used as a condiment, particularly with roast beef or fish, or in sauces. Is also available bottled or dried.

KAFFIR LIME LEAVES Sold fresh, dried or frozen; used as a flavouring throughout Asia. Dried leaves are less potent so double the amount if you substitute them for fresh leaves. Available from most greengrocers and Asian food stores.

KALAMATA OLIVES Purplish-black Greek olives cured in vinegar and sometimes preserved in olive oil.

KUMARA Polynesian name of orange sweet potato often confused with yam.

LAMB

Backstrap The larger fillet from a row of loin chops or cutlets.

Fillet The smaller piece of meat from a row of loin chops or cutlets.

French-trimmed shanks Also called drumsticks or Frenched shanks; all the gristle and narrow end of the bone is discarded and remaining meat trimmed.

LAVASH A soft, thin, flat, unleavened bread of Mediterranean origin; can be used for wraps or cut into triangles, toasted and used as a dipper. Available from most supermarkets.

LEEK A member of the onion family, with a mild flavour. Its thick white stem must be washed thoroughly before use; separate its layers and rinse any dirt. Can be boiled, steamed or braised.

LEMON GRASS A tall, clumping, sharp-edged aromatic tropical grass that smells and tastes of lemon. Generally only the stem end of the plant is used in cooking. It is sold fresh in most supermarkets, greengrocers and Asian food stores.

LENTILS Dried pulses often identified by and named after their colour (red, brown, yellow). Also known as dhal.

Puy Originally from the French region of the same name; a small, dark-green, fast-cooking lentil with a delicate flavour.

LETTUCE

Butter Have small, round, loosely formed heads with soft, buttery-textured leaves ranging from pale green on the outer leaves to pale yellow-green on the inner leaves. Has a sweet flavour.

Cos Also known as romaine lettuce; is the traditional Caesar salad lettuce.

Curly endive Also known as frisée. A curly-leafed green vegetable with a prickly texture and bitter taste; mainly used in salads. Available from most greengrocers.

Iceberg A heavy, firm round lettuce with tightly packed leaves and crisp texture.

Mesclun A salad mix of young lettuce and other green leaves, including baby spinach leaves, mizuna and curly endive.

Mizuna Often in mesclun; is a wispy, green salad leaf from Japan. Available from most supermarkets and greengrocers.

MALIBU Coconut-flavoured rum.

MAPLE SYRUP A thin syrup distilled from the sap of the maple tree. Maple-flavoured syrup is not an adequate substitute for the real thing.

MARSALA A sweet fortified wine.

MASCARPONE A cultured cream product made in much the same way as yogurt; whitish to creamy yellow in colour, with a soft, creamy texture. Available from most supermarkets and delicatessens.

MILK

Buttermilk Sold alongside other milk products; is commercially made similarly to yogurt. It is low in fat and is a good substitute for cream or sour cream; good in baking and in salad dressings.

Evaporated Unsweetened canned milk from which water has been extracted by evaporation. Also available skim with a fat content of 0.3%.

Sweetened condensed From which 60% of the water has been removed; the remaining milk is sweetened with sugar.

MIRIN A Japanese champagne-coloured cooking wine made of glutinous rice and alcohol expressly for cooking; not to be confused with sake. Available from some supermarkets and Asian food stores.

MIXED SPICE A blend of ground spices usually cinnamon, allspice, cloves and nutmeg. Available from supermarkets and specialty spice stores.

MUSHROOMS

Button Sometimes called champignons, are the youngest variety, and usually the smallest. The body of this mushroom is firm and tightly closed against the stem, with none of the gill-like 'veil' exposed.

Cup Slightly bigger and darker than the button, with its veil (or velum) just starting to open; are among the most versatile; great in soups, stir-fries and sauces.

Flat Large, flat mushrooms with a rich earthy flavour and meaty texture; ideal for filling and barbecuing as a meal on its own rather than just another ingredient.

Shiitake Available both fresh and dried. Before use: when fresh, shiitake need to have their woody stems removed; when dried, they must be soaked in water.

Swiss brown Also known as cremini or Roman mushrooms, are light to dark brown mushrooms with full-bodied flavour and hold their shape during cooking. Button or cups can be substituted.

MUSTARD

Dijon Is a pale-yellow to brown French mustard often flavoured with white wine.

Wholegrain Also known as seeded mustard, is a coarse-grain mustard made from black and yellow mustard seeds and dijon-style mustard.

NOODLES

Hokkien Also called stir-fry noodles; are fresh wheat noodles resembling thick, yellow-brown spaghetti needing no pre-cooking before being used.

Rice noodles Chewy and pure white; do not need pre-cooking before use.

Soba Also known as buckwheat noodles, are made from various proportions of buckwheat flour. Usually available dried, but can be purchased fresh.

NUTMEG Its aromatic, full-bodied flavour goes well with pumpkin, kumara, cheese sauces, and sweet spicy cakes. Available ground or whole, from most supermarkets and specialty spice stores.

OIL

Olive Made from ripened olives. Extra virgin and virgin are the best; extra light or light refers to the taste not fat levels.

Peanut Pressed from ground peanuts; most commonly used oil in Asian cooking because of its high smoke point (capacity to handle high heat without burning).

Sesame Made from roasted, crushed, white sesame seeds; a flavouring rather than a cooking medium.

Spray We used a cholesterol-free cooking-oil spray made from canola oil.

Vegetable Any number of oils sourced from plants rather than animal fats.

ONION

Green Also known as scallion or, incorrectly, shallot; an immature onion picked before the bulb has formed, having a long, bright-green edible stalk.

Red Also known as spanish onion; a sweet-flavoured, large, purple-red onion.

Spring Crisp, narrow green-leafed tops and a round sweet white bulb larger than green onions.

PANCETTA Unsmoked bacon; pork belly cured in salt and spices, rolled into a sausage shape and dried for weeks. Available from supermarkets and delicatessens.

PAPRIKA Ground, dried red capsicum (bell pepper). Available sweet and hot from supermarkets and specialty spice stores.

PARSLEY, FLAT-LEAFED Also known as continental parsley or Italian parsley.

PASTA

Gnocchi Italian 'dumplings' made of potatoes, semolina or flour.

Orecchiette Translates as 'little ears', a shape this short pasta resembles. If not available, use any small pasta you like.

Penne Translated literally as 'quills'; ridged macaroni cut diagonally into short lengths.

Tagliatelle Long, flat strips of durum wheat pasta, slightly narrower and thinner than fettuccine.

Tortellini Circles of fresh pasta filled with meat or cheese, then folded into little hats.

PASTE

Green curry The hottest traditional paste; great in chicken and vegetable curries. Also good added to stir-fries and noodle dishes.

Laksa A bottled paste containing lemon grass, chillies, onions, galangal, shrimp paste and turmeric; used to make the classic soup laksa. Available from some supermarkets and Asian food stores.

Panang curry A complex, sweet and milder variation of red curry paste; good with seafood.

Red curry The most popular curry paste; a hot blend of different flavours that complements pork, duck and seafood, also works well in marinades and sauces.

Shrimp A strong-scented, almost solid preserved paste made of salted dried shrimp. Available from Asian food stores.

PECANS Native to the United States and now grown locally; golden-brown, buttery and rich. Good in savoury and sweet dishes; especially good in salads.

PEPITAS Dried pumpkin seeds.

PINE NUTS Not in fact a nut but a small, cream-coloured pine cone kernel. Used commonly in pesto and salads. Available from supermarkets and nut stores.

PISTACHIOS Pale green, delicately flavoured nut inside hard off-white shells. To peel, soak shelled nuts in boiling water 5 minutes; drain, pat dry with absorbent paper. Rub skins with cloth to peel.

PITTA BREAD Round, dinner-plate sized Lebanese bread eaten on its own; torn and used as a dipper; or filled with a combination of meats and salad and rolled into a substantial sandwich.

POLENTA A flour-like cereal made from dried corn (maize) sold ground in several different textures and available at most supermarkets. Can be eaten soft and creamy, or chilled and grilled.

POPPY SEEDS Small, dried, bluish-grey seeds of the poppy plant; have a crunchy texture and a nutty flavour. Available whole or ground in most supermarkets.

POTATOES

Desiree Oval, smooth and pink-skinned with waxy yellow flesh; good in salads, boiled and roasted.

Kipfler A small, yellow-skinned, finger-shaped potato with a nutty flavour; great baked and in salads. Available all year from most greengrocers.

New Also called chats or baby potatoes; an early harvest potato with very thin skin. Good unpeeled steamed, eaten hot or cold in salads.

Pontiac Large, round, red-skinned with deep eyes, white flesh; good grated, boiled and baked.

Russet burbank Also known as Idaho; russet in colour, fabulous baked.

Sebago White skin, oval; good fried, mashed and baked.

PRAWNS Also called shrimp. Peel and devein: remove the head by holding it in one hand and twisting the body with the other; peel the legs and shell from the body, but leave the tail intact, if you like, for decorative purposes. Remove and discard the centre vein from the back using a small sharp knife or your fingers.

PROSCIUTTO Salted, air-cured and aged; usually eaten uncooked. Available from some supermarkets and delicatessens.

READY-ROLLED PASTRY Packaged sheets of frozen puff and shortcrust pastry. Available from supermarkets.

RHUBARB Classified as a vegetable, is eaten as a fruit and so considered as one. Leaves must be removed before cooking as they contain traces of poision; the edible pink-red stalks are chopped and cooked.

RICE

Arborio Commonly used for making risotto; is a round-grain rice well-suited to absorbing large amounts of liquid. Available from most supermarkets.

Basmati From Hindu meaning 'fragrant'. This fine, long-grain, highly aromatic rice has a light, fluffy texture with a nutlike flavour. Available from most supermarkets and Indian food stores.

Brown Natural whole grain.

Jasmine Also sold as Thai fragrant rice due to its sweet aroma. Available from supermarkets and Asian food stores.

Rolled Flattened rice grain rolled into flakes; similar in appearance to rolled oats.

White Is hulled and polished, can be short- or long-grained.

ROCKET Also called arugula; a pepper-tasting green leaf used similarly to baby spinach leaves, in salads or in cooking.

SAFFRON One of the most expensive spices in the world. Available from supermarkets and specialty spice stores.

SAMBAL OELEK A spicy Indonesian condiment made from chillies, shrimp paste, sugar and salt. Available from supermarkets and Asian food stores.

SAUCE

Char sui Also called chinese barbecue sauce; paste-like, dark-red-brown in colour that's sweet and spicy. Available from supermarkets and Asian food stores.

Fish Also called nam pla or nuoc nam; is made from pulverised salted fermented fish (often anchovies). Has a pungent smell and strong taste, so use sparingly. Available from supermarkets and Asian food stores.

Hoisin A thick, sweet chinese barbecue sauce made from salted fermented soy beans, onions and garlic; can be used as a marinade or a baste, or as a flavouring for stir-fried, braised or roasted foods. Available from supermarkets and Asian food stores.

Kecap manis An Indonesian sweet, thick soy sauce made with palm sugar, used in marinades, dips, sauces and dressings, as well as a table condiment. Available from supermarkets and Asian food stores.

Oyster Made from oysters and their brine, cooked with salt and soy sauce then thickened; available from most supermarkets and Asian food stores.

Plum A thick, sweet and sour dipping sauce made from plums, vinegar, sugar, chillies and spices.

Soy Made from fermented soy beans. Several variations are available in most supermarkets and Asian food stores.

Sweet chilli The comparatively mild, thin sauce made from red chillies, sugar, garlic and vinegar; often used as a condiment.

Tabasco Brand name of extremely fiery sauce made from vinegar, hot red peppers and salt.

Teriyaki Usually made from soy sauce, mirin, sugar, ginger and other spices.

Tomato Also called ketchup.

Worcestershire A thin, dark-brown spicy sauce used as a seasoning for meat, gravies and cocktails and as a condiment.

SEMOLINA Made from crushed durum wheat hearts, ground to a very fine flour; is used for making pasta and breads. Available from supermarkets.

SESAME SEEDS Black and white are the most common; a good source of calcium. To toast, spread seeds evenly on oven tray, toast briefly in moderate (180°C/160°C fan-forced) oven.

SHALLOTS Also called French shallots, golden shallots or eschalots; small, elongated, brown-skinned member of the onion family. Grows in tight clusters similar to garlic.

SILVERBEET Also known as swiss chard; has fleshy white stalks and large, dark green leaves. Prepared like spinach.

SNOW PEAS Also called mange tout ('eat all'). Available from supermarkets and greengrocers.

SOUR CREAM Thick, smooth and slightly acidic cream; adds richness to soups and stews, also dolloped on potatoes and soups.

SPATCHCOCK Also called poussin; a small chicken, no more than six weeks old, weighing a maximum of 500g.

SPINACH Also known as english spinach and, incorrectly, silverbeet. Its tender green leaves are good uncooked in salads or added to soups, stir-fries and stews just before serving.

SPLIT PEAS Also known as field peas; green or yellow pulse grown especially for drying, split in half along a centre seam. Used in soups, stews and, occasionally, spiced and cooked on their own.

SPONGE FINGERS Also called savoiardi sponge finger biscuits; Italian-style crisp fingers made from sponge-cake mixture.

STAR ANISE The dried, star-shaped seed pod can be used whole as a flavouring and the seeds used alone as a spice; both can be used ground. Available from supermarkets and Asian food stores.

STOCK Available in cans or tetra packs. Stock cubes or powder can be used. As a guide, 1 teaspoon of stock powder or 1 small crumbled stock cube mixed with 1 cup (250ml) water will give a fairly strong stock. Be aware of the salt and fat content of stock cubes, powders and prepared stocks.

SUGAR

Brown A very soft, fine granulated sugar retaining molasses for its characteristic colour and flavour.

Caster Also known as superfine or finely granulated table sugar.

Icing Also called confectioners' sugar or powdered sugar. Granulated sugar crushed together with a small amount of cornflour.

Palm Also called nam tan pip or jaggery; made from the sap of the sugar palm tree. Light brown to black; sold in rock-hard cakes from some supermarkets and Asian food stores. If unavailable, use brown sugar.

Raw Natural brown granulated sugar.

TAMARIND The product of a native tropical African tree. Dried tamarind is reconstituted in a hot liquid which gives a sweet-sour, astringent taste to food.

TACO SEASONING MIX A packaged seasoning meant to duplicate the Mexican sauce made from oregano, cumin, chillies and other spices.

TOFU Also called bean curd, tofu is an off-white, custard-like product made from the milk of crushed soy beans. Available fresh as soft or firm. Silken tofu refers to the method by which it is made – it is strained through silk. Available from supermarkets and Asian food stores.

TOMATOES

Canned Peeled tomatoes in natural juice. Available whole, crushed and diced.

Cherry Also known as Tiny Tim or Tom Thumb tomatoes; are small and round.

Egg Also called plum or roma; are smallish, oval-shaped used in Italian cooking or salads.

Grape Baby egg tomatoes.

Paste Triple-concentrated tomato puree used to flavour soups, stews and sauces.

Dried Semi-dried partially dried tomato pieces in olive oil; softer and juicier than sun-dried. We used **sun-dried** tomatoes packaged in oil, unless stated otherwise.

TORTILLA Pronounced tor-tee-yah; are made either of wheat flour or ground corn meal. Available from supermarkets.

TURKISH BREAD Also known as pide; comes in long (about 45cm) flat loaves as well as individual rounds. Available from most supermarkets and bakeries.

TURMERIC A member of the ginger family; dried and ground, this rich yellow powder is used in most Asian cuisines. Intensely pungent in taste but not hot. Available from supermarkets and Asian food stores.

VANILLA BEAN Dried long, thin pod from a tropical golden orchid. The black seeds inside the bean are used to impart a vanilla flavour in baking and desserts.

VIETNAMESE MINT Not a mint at all, but a pungent, peppery narrow-leafed member of the buckwheat family. Available from most greengrocers.

VINEGAR

Apple cider Made from fermented apples.

Balsamic Originally from Modena, Italy, there are now many balsamic vinegars on the market ranging in pungency and quality depending on how, and how long, they have been aged.

Rice Also called seasoned rice vinegar; a colourless vinegar made from fermented rice, flavoured with sugar and salt.

White Made from spirit of cane sugar.

WALNUTS A rich, buttery and flavourful nut. Should be stored in the refrigerator because of its high oil content.

WASABI An Asian horseradish used to make the pungent, green-coloured paste traditionally served with Japanese raw fish dishes. Available as a powder or paste, from supermarkets and Asian food stores.

YEAST Allow 2 teaspoons (7g) dried granulated yeast to each 15g fresh yeast.

YOGURT We used plain, unflavoured yogurt, unless stated otherwise.

ZUCCHINI Also known as courgette.

INDEX

tex-mex spare ribs with grilled corn salsa,
197
thai banquet, 319–21
thai chicken noodle stir-fry, 225
thai chicken salad, 286
thai fish burgers, 207
three-bean salad, 43
tiramisu trifle, 339
toast
    cinnamon, with caramelised apples, 22
    french, with berry compote, 6
tofu
    cauliflower, pea and fried tofu curry,
    176
    chinese cabbage and tofu stir-fry, 145
    larb, 136
    sweet chilli tofu stir-fry, 131
    vietnamese beef, chicken and tofu
    soup, 31
tom collins, classic, 364
tomato
    baked fish with tomatoes and olives,
    204
    beef, tomato and pea pies, 212
    chicken, tomato and leek casserole, 268
    chilli tomato chicken, 261
    creamy tomato pesto tortellini, 84
    egg, tomato and mayonnaise sandwich,
    61
    fresh tomato and chilli pasta, 287
    fresh tomato and herb sauce, 149
    fresh tomato soup, 30
    gnocchi with burnt butter and, 73
    gnocchi with spinach, pine nuts and,
    266
    ham, cheese and tomato melt, 302
    orecchiette with ham, artichokes and
    sun-dried tomatoes, 80
    salad, 133
    slow-roasted lamb shanks with tomato
    and olives, 314
    tomato and tortellini salad, 90
    tomato, carrot and red capsicum juice,
    366
    tomato, fetta and spinach galettes,
    289
    tomato pesto tortellini, 288
    tomato, spinach and cheese muffin, 14
    tuna, bean and tomato salad, 70

tomato salsa
    cajun chicken with, 230
    penne with tuna and, 284
tomato sauce
    fish cutlets in, 275
toppings
    baked potatoes, 126
    pasta, 100–1
    pizza, 348
    potato, 215
tortellini
    cheese and spinach, 82
    creamy tomato pesto, 84
    tomato and tortellini salad, 90
    tomato pesto, 288
tortillas
    pork and corn salsa tortilla wraps,
    280
    spanish, 23
traditional daiquiri, 363
traditional pesto, 101
traditional tapenade, 100
trifle, tiramisu, 339
tuna
    crunchy-topped tuna pasta, 86
    pasta bake, 290
    penne with tomato salsa and, 284
    shells, capers, olives and green beans,
    with, 294
    tuna and avocado muffin, 14
    tuna and fetta turnovers, 55
    tuna and sweet corn sandwich, 60
    tuna, bean and tomato salad, 70
    tuna pasta salad, 46
    tuna salad on focaccia, 302
tunisian spicy nut pilaf, 109
turkey baguette, 302
turkish bread, haloumi salad on, 148
turkish herbed lamb pizza, 52
turnovers, tuna and fetta, 55
tuscan bean soup, 38
tuscan white bean salad, 147
tzatziki
    dip, 304
    lamb fillets with greek salad and,
    279
    lamb patties with beetroot and,
    216

CONVERSION CHART

These conversions are approximate only, but the difference between an exact and the approximate conversion of various liquid and dry measures is minimal and will not affect your cooking results.

Measuring equipment
The difference between one country's measuring cups and another's is, at most, within a 2 or 3 teaspoon variance. (For the record, one Australian metric measuring cup holds approximately 250ml.) The most accurate way of measuring dry ingredients is to weigh them. For liquids, use a clear glass or plastic jug with metric markings.

Note: NZ, Canada, the US and the UK all use 15ml tablespoons. Australian tablespoons measure 20ml. All cup and spoon measurements are level.

How to measure
When using graduated measuring cups, shake dry ingredients loosely into the appropriate cup. Do not tap the cup on a bench or tightly pack the ingredients unless directed to do so. Level the top of measuring cups and measuring spoons with a knife. When measuring liquids, place a clear glass or plastic jug with metric markings on a flat surface to check accuracy at eye level.

Dry measures

metric	imperial
15g	½oz
30g	1oz
60g	2oz
90g	3oz
125g	4oz (¼lb)
155g	5oz
185g	6oz
220g	7oz
250g	8oz (½lb)
280g	9oz
315g	10oz
345g	11oz
375g	12oz (¾lb)
410g	13oz
440g	14oz
470g	15oz
500g	16oz (1lb)
750g	24oz (1½lb)
1kg	32oz (2lb)

We use large eggs with an average weight of 60g.

Liquid measures

metric	imperial
30ml	1 fluid oz
60ml	2 fluid oz
100ml	3 fluid oz
125ml	4 fluid oz
150ml	5 fluid oz (¼ pint/1 gill)
190ml	6 fluid oz
250ml (1 cup)	8 fluid oz
300ml	10 fluid oz (½ pint)
500ml	16 fluid oz
600ml	20 fluid oz (1 pint)
1000ml (1 litre)	1¾ pints

Helpful measures

metric	imperial
3mm	⅛in
6mm	¼in
1cm	½in
2cm	¾in
2.5cm	1in
6cm	2½in
8cm	3in
20cm	8in
23cm	9in
25cm	10in
30cm	12in (1ft)

Oven temperatures
These oven temperatures, for conventional ovens, are only a guide. For fan-forced ovens, check the manufacturer's manual.

	°C (Celsius)	°F (Fahrenheit)	Gas Mark
Very slow	120	250	½
Slow	150	275-300	1-2
Moderately slow	170	325	3
Moderate	180	350-375	4-5
Moderately hot	200	400	6
Hot	220	425-450	7-8
Very hot	240	475	9